Diversification in
modern language teaching

How do modern language pupils respond to languages other than French? What are the organisational implications of diversification?

As the effects of European integration become more widely felt, the effective teaching of modern languages is moving towards the centre of the educational agenda and more and more schools are considering starting pupils on a first foreign language other than French – a development encouraged by the National Curriculum Orders in Modern Languages.

Diversification in modern language teaching gives language teachers and heads of department the evidence upon which to decide if diversification is right for them. It presents findings from a longitudinal study, the Oxford Project on Diversification of First Foreign Language Teaching (OXPROD), which looked both at pupils' learning experiences and at the organisational questions affecting schools in which the policy was implemented. Throughout it argues first that there is nothing in the nature of German or Spanish that makes these languages unsuitable as first foreign languages for the whole ability range and second that the decision on whether to diversify first foreign language provision must be a purely educational one, based on pupil motivation and accessibility as well as on particular local strengths among staff and parents.

David Phillips is lecturer in educational studies and tutor in German at the Department of Educational Studies of the University of Oxford and and Fellow of St Edmund Hall. He has written widely on the theory and practice of modern language teaching and on comparative and historical topics in education.
Caroline Filmer-Sankey, an experienced teacher of modern languages in comprehensive schools, is currently research officer for the Oxford Project on Diversification of First Foreign Language Teaching (OXPROD).

Diversification in modern language teaching

Choice and the National Curriculum

David Phillips and
Caroline Filmer-Sankey

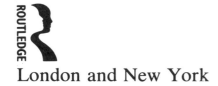

London and New York

First published 1993
by Routledge
11 New Fetter Lane, London EC4P 4EE

Simultaneously published in the USA and Canada
by Routledge
29 West 35th Street, New York, NY 10001

© 1993 David Phillips and Caroline Filmer-Sankey

Typeset in 10/12pt Times by
J&L Composition Ltd, Filey, North Yorkshire
Printed in Great Britain by
Mackays of Chatham plc, Chatham, Kent

British Library Cataloguing-in-Publication Data
A catalogue record for this book is available from the British Library

ISBN 0–415–07200–X
     0–415–07201–8 (pbk.)

Library of Congress Cataloging-in-Publication Data
Phillips, David, 1944 Dec. 15–
   Diversification in modern language teaching: choice and the
national curriculum/David Phillips and Caroline Filmer-Sankey.
      p.   cm.
   Includes bibliographical references (p.   ).
   ISBN 0–415–07200–X. — ISBN 0–415–07201–8 (pbk.)
   1. Languages, Modern—Study and teaching (Secondary)—Great
Britain. I. Filmer-Sankey, Caroline, 1958– . II. Title.
PB38.G5P47   1993
418'.0071'2—dc20   92–15265
                                                        CIP

Contents

List of figures

List of tables

Acknowledgements

A study of this kind depends on the co-operation of a large number of people, too numerous for most of them to be named individually.

Sarah Cox drafted a preliminary document during the earliest stages of planning for the project, following wide consultation over a three-month period. The project as it emerged owes much to her original ideas. We have been loyally assisted throughout by a steering committee chaired by Professor John Woodhouse and by an advisory committee which helped with the drafting and piloting of research instruments. We have benefited greatly from discussions with members of these committees, and from research advice and much practical assistance provided by John Backhouse, Keith Postlethwaite and Peter Dickson. Michael Buckby generously allowed us to adapt a language aptitude test developed by him in connection with a project on graded tests at the University of York; Peter Green similarly allowed us to make use of his well-known language aptitude test.

Headteachers, heads of department and subject teachers in our project schools and other associated schools have given freely of their time, responding to our various requests and ensuring the smooth running of the work in schools. Local authority advisers have provided us with much useful information about diversification in their localities, and representatives of those LEAs in receipt of a special Education Support Grant for diversification have been particularly helpful to us.

We had the good fortune to work with Jill Slater, Georgina Clark, Hazel Geatches, Kate Harrison and Karen Chidwick who for various periods acted as research assistants to the project, helping with the processing and analysis of data and with the drafting of reports. We are indebted to Georgina Clark for her analysis and description of policy documents and LEA provision incorporated into parts of Chapter 2 and Chapter 6 and to Karen Chidwick, who oversaw the production of the final manuscript of this book, provided general research assistance, and prepared the bibliography and index. Josefina Bello, who was a research student at Oxford for much of the period covered by the project, undertook valuable research into the history of Spanish teaching and helped us generally with our investigation of Spanish. Suzy Roessler similarly assisted us while researching pupils' abilities in listening comprehension in French, German and Spanish. Much of their work has been incorporated into this present study and is acknowledged separately as appropriate. In addition we had admirable secretarial support from Susie Martin and Marie-Noëlle May.

The Leverhulme Trust provided the project's main funding, which allowed us to undertake a costly longitudinal study; the Trust has been a generous and supportive body throughout our work. In addition we have received a special grant for staffing from the General Board of the University of Oxford and funds from the Goethe-Institut, the Spanish Cultural Institute and the Italian Institute. Funds provided by the three institutes allowed participating schools to purchase teaching materials in German, Spanish and Italian so that they could bring provision up to the level existing for French. We are particularly indebted to Ute Grauerholz, Isidro López de la Nieta, Anna-Maria Lelli and Angela Vegliante for their ready help. Permission was kindly granted by the Controller of Her Majesty's Stationery Office to reproduce Figures 6.1 and 6.2 in the text.

We are most grateful to all of the above and to many others who have helped over several years to make our investigation into the teaching and learning of first foreign languages a pleasurable and profitable experience. On the few occasions when we encountered hostility it came from predictable sources.

What success the project has enjoyed is due largely to the support and hard work of the many linguists with whom it has been a delight to be in contact. The shortcomings in what follows are attributable to the authors alone.

David Phillips
Caroline Filmer-Sankey
Oxford, November 1991

Introduction

This book is concerned with the teaching of 'languages other than French' in British secondary schools. This term (often reduced by an infelicitous shorthand to LOTF) has usually been taken to cover German, Italian, Russian and Spanish, as the most commonly taught modern foreign languages after French, though it must now include other European languages, as well as the languages – normally called 'community languages' – of Britain's ethnic minorities.

There has been much endeavour over many decades to secure the position of such languages on the school curriculum, whether as first or second foreign languages, but it was mainly with attempts during the 1980s to formulate and implement a policy on what is now termed 'diversification' of first foreign language (FL1) teaching that serious advances were made. It is now possible to speak of diversification as government policy, despite the fact that no specific mention of it is made in the Education Reform Act of 1988. In a document from Her Majesty's Inspectorate (HMI) of 1987, paragraphs 64 and 65 refer specifically to the issue of which languages should be taught up to age sixteen:

> 65. The majority of pupils currently learn French as their first foreign language. The reasons for this relate to tradition and the supply of teachers rather than to any intrinsic advantages possessed by French. Although German, Spanish and, occasionally, Italian and Russian are offered as second foreign languages, the number of pupils taking them is small and even fewer continue to study them after the age of 16. As far as the educational value of learning a foreign language is concerned, it is unimportant which language is studied. Nationally, however, there is a need for people fluent in a range of languages, particularly those of our European trading partners. Although some languages important in business, science and diplomacy are more appropriately learned in further or higher education, greater diversification in schools is desirable. Languages other than French could be introduced more frequently as first foreign languages, either on their own or as alternatives to French.

66.   A start could be made in this direction in that there is already a pool of teachers with good qualifications in languages (notably German and Spanish) which they are not at present teaching at all or on any scale. For many teachers, an in-service training programme would be needed to revive dormant language skills. It is important that LEAs should have a policy for the provision of languages other than French: this might lead to the concentration of teachers of these languages in a smaller number of schools to make teaching of them not only practicable but cost-effective. In the meantime, where they have appropriately qualified staff, schools themselves may be able to take some initiatives, for example by changing the first foreign language, or possibly, in large schools, by dividing the new entry into two 'populations' and offering one of two first foreign languages to each.[1]

These two paragraphs provided a clear statement of intended policy, identified the key issues, and suggested some courses of action. In the following year the Department of Education and Science (DES) produced a statement of policy on modern languages, following the circulation and discussion of two previous draft documents on similar lines.[2] *Modern Languages in the School Curriculum* has eleven paragraphs on the question of diversification. It records the fact that about 8 per cent of secondary schools were offering German as first or alternative first foreign language, the comparable figure for Spanish being 1.5 per cent – 'provision of other languages as a first foreign language is virtually non-existent'. And the document goes on in paragraph 32 to make an unequivocal statement on diversification:

This position is not satisfactory. **LEAs and schools should ensure that a reasonable proportion of their pupils of all abilities study a language other than French as their first foreign language.** Although it would be impossible to specify an ideal mix of language provision in schools, the current situation is clearly inappropriate to the needs of a modern trading nation. In trading terms alone, a number of studies suggest that German and French are equally in demand by exporting companies; and that there is also a strong need for Italian and Spanish. A capability in German or Spanish is useful not only to firms operating in Western Europe but also to those with markets in Eastern Europe and Latin America respectively. On commercial and cultural grounds, priority should be given to the main languages of the European community. [Original emphasis.][3]

We shall return in Chapter 2 to the implications of this particular statement. Suffice it at this stage to note its significance as a clear indication of the 'official' position *vis-à-vis* the need to implement forms of diversification. Later the final report of the National Curriculum Modern Foreign Languages Working Group[4] reaffirmed the commitment to diversification:

We hope that the inclusion of a modern foreign language as a foundation subject in the National Curriculum will be accompanied by a strengthening of languages other than French. . . . If diversification is properly planned and resourced centrally as well as locally as part of an integrated school policy, it is likely to have important consequences for the availability of second foreign languages in schools (paragraph 16.5).

By 1988, then, a position had been reached where it was possible to talk in terms of a stated policy on languages other than French in the curriculum. At the same time, however, considerable fears were being expressed about the position of *second* foreign languages. In an Oxford-based study published in 1983[5] one of the present authors had considered in detail the many problems surrounding the second foreign language (FL2) in the curriculum of comprehensive schools. The future at that time looked bleak enough – a Schools Council report had just appeared with the ominous title *The Second Foreign Language in Secondary Schools: A question of survival*[6] – and it was felt by many that, while a strong case could still be made to secure the position of the second foreign language, the battle for languages other than French generally might be better fought on the *first* foreign language front. We decided to follow the Oxford study with a further investigation, this time focusing on the possibilities for diversification of FL1 provision.

We took as the starting point of our investigation a hypothesis drawn from another Schools Council report – the product of a committee chaired by Colin Hadley – whose principal conclusion was:

There is nothing in the nature of a language other than French or in its teaching context that makes it either more or less feasible than French as first foreign language in a secondary school; there is nothing intrinsically associated with the language or its teaching that makes it likely to be either more or less successful than French if introduced as first language.[7]

The hypothesis we formulated for the Oxford project was:

There is nothing in the nature of German and Spanish as subjects in the school curriculum that makes those languages unsuitable as first foreign languages for the whole ability range.

And this hypothesis was incorporated into a diagram which guided the design of the 'Oxford Project on Diversification of First Foreign Language Teaching' (OXPROD) (Figure 1.1). There is here no specific mention of French (i.e. in terms of its being less suitable as FL1 than German or Spanish, for example), and this was deliberate, since at no stage in the investigation did we intend to champion German and Spanish at the expense of French. Our aim throughout was to conduct an objective enquiry into matters affecting decisions as to which modern foreign

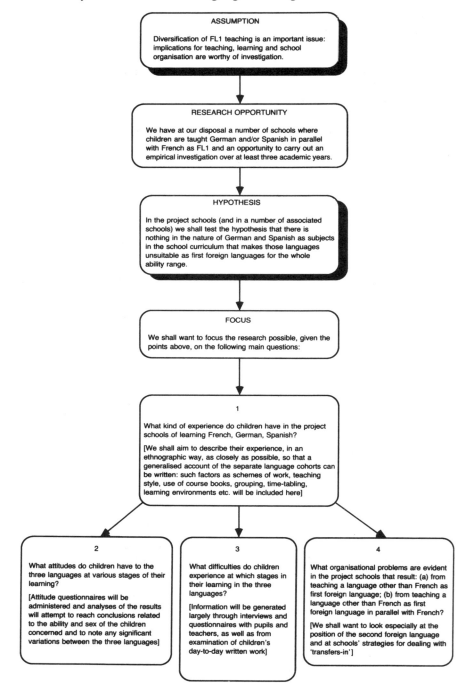

Figure 1.1 Research design

language(s) to provide on the curriculum of secondary schools for eleven-year-old beginners of both sexes and all abilities. Our principal questions were to be:

1 What attitudes do children have to French, German and Spanish at various stages of their learning?
2 What difficulties do children experience in French, German and Spanish at which stages of their learning? and
3 What organisational problems result from teaching a language other than French as first foreign language?

It is the outcome of this research,[8] combining as it does an ethnographic investigation of a number of schools having experience of diversification with an account of developments in England and Wales, that forms the core of this present study. We begin with an historical account of the various developments since the early years of the century which have led to the present policy position. The question of the dominance of French on the language curriculum in British schools is addressed, together with the arguments for the teaching of alternative languages as they have evolved historically.

Chapter 2 considers more recent policy developments. Since the mid-1970s there has been a stream of official publications on the school curriculum, and modern foreign languages have figured prominently in them. The chapter describes and analyses the debate about provision in modern languages as it has developed in those documents and in the discussions that have followed their publication.

The third chapter provides an overview and evaluation of what research to date is specific to the provision of various first foreign languages. It shows how the Oxford project aims to complement such research and to provide insights into problems of diversified provision which are essentially new, as a result of the project's longitudinal nature and the detailed information collected on the pupils and teachers involved in the survey. In addition to such practical concerns as staffing and timetabling, the chapter highlights the main educational issues – such as those of pupil motivation and language difficulty – to be considered by schools when decisions are made about foreign language provision.

Chapter 4 describes the design of the project and the schools and pupils involved in it. Chapters 5 and 6 are largely concerned with the project's results, the focus being on pupils' experience of learning the three languages with which we are principally concerned and on the organisational problems which are manifest when languages other than French are offered as first foreign languages. Among other things they suggest ways in which parental opposition might be countered, consider the problems involved in coping with pupils who transfer to 'diversified' schools, and suggest ways in which languages other than French can be included in the curriculum. The concluding chapter summarises the main findings and offers a checklist of advice on future developments.

NOTES

1 Department of Education and Science (DES), *Modern Foreign Languages to 16* (= Curriculum Matters 8), London, HMSO, 1987, pp. 29–30.
2 DES/Welsh Office, *Modern Languages in the School Curriculum: A statement of policy*, London, HMSO, 1988; the previous documents were: *Foreign Languages in the School Curriculum: A Consultative Paper*, London, HMSO, 1983, and *Foreign Languages in the School Curriculum: A draft statement of policy*, London, 1986.
3 DES/Welsh Office, op. cit., 1988, pp. 8–9.
4 DES/Welsh Office, *Modern Foreign Languages for Ages 11 to 16* (Proposals of the Secretary of State for Education and Science and the Secretary of State for Wales), London, HMSO, October 1990.
5 David Phillips and Veronica Stencel, *The Second Foreign Language: Past development, current trends and future prospects*, London, Hodder & Stoughton, 1983.
6 Schools Council Modern Languages Committee, *The Second Foreign Language in Secondary Schools: A question of survival* (Series: Occasional Bulletins from the Subject Committees), London, 1982.
7 Hadley, C.G., *Languages other than French in the Secondary School: An exploratory study of other languages as first or equal first foreign languages*, London, Schools Council, 1981.
8 OXPROD has generated a number of publications describing the work undertaken from 1987 to 1992. We list them chronologically:

   (1) David Phillips, 'Diversification of FL1 teaching: a new research project', *Modern Languages*, Vol. 68, No. 1, 1987, pp. 29–31.
   (2) David Phillips, 'OXPROD – An Oxford research project on diversification of first foreign language teaching', *British Journal of Language Teaching*, Vol. 25, No. 1, 1987, pp. 50–1.
   (3) OXPROD Newsletter No. 1, July 1987, University of Oxford Department of Educational Studies.
   (4) David Phillips, 'A language of "unusual simplicity and facility": Spanish as first foreign language', *Vida Hispánica*, Vol. 37, No. 2, 1988, pp. 11–12.
   (5) OXPROD Newsletter No. 2, February 1988, University of Oxford Department of Educational Studies.
   (6) OXPROD Newsletter No. 3, October 1988, University of Oxford Department of Educational Studies.
   (7) Caroline Filmer-Sankey, 'Diversification: The OXPROD project', in: Coloquio 40: *Proceedings of the Colloquium on the Teaching of Spanish, December 1987*, Association of Teachers of Spanish and Portuguese, 1988.
   (8) David Phillips and Georgina Clark, *Attitudes Towards Diversification: Results of a survey of teacher opinion*, OXPROD Occasional Paper 1, Oxford, University of Oxford Department of Educational Studies, 1988.
   (9) Josefina Bello, 'Spanish as a first foreign language in British schools: past development and present practice', unpublished Special Diploma dissertation, University of Oxford, 1988.
   (10) Josefina Bello, *Spanish as First Foreign Language in Schools: Past and present perspectives*, OXPROD Occasional Paper 2, Oxford, University of Oxford Department of Educational Studies, 1989.
   (11) David Phillips and Caroline Filmer-Sankey, '*Vive la différence?* Some problems in investigating diversification of first foreign language provision in schools', *British Educational Research Journal*, Vol. 15, No. 3, 1989, pp. 317–29.

(12) Suzy Roessler, 'Listening comprehension in three first foreign languages: A study of beginners in two secondary schools', unpublished M.Litt. thesis, University of Oxford, 1989.
(13) Caroline Filmer-Sankey, *A Study of First-year Pupils' Attitudes towards French, German and Spanish*, OXPROD Occasional Paper 3, Oxford, University of Oxford Department of Educational Studies, 1989.
(14) David Phillips and Hazel Geatches, *Diversification and 'Transfers-in'*, OXPROD Occasional Paper 4, Oxford, University of Oxford Department of Educational Studies, 1989.
(15) David Phillips (ed.), *Which Language? Diversification and the National Curriculum*, London, Hodder & Stoughton, 1989.
(16) David Phillips, 'Diversification: Current developments and future outlook', *Language Learning Journal*, Vol. 1, No. 1, 1990, pp. 18–21.
(17) Josefina Bello, 'The teaching of Spanish in secondary schools: 1900–1950', unpublished M.Litt. thesis, University of Oxford, 1990.
(18) Caroline Filmer-Sankey, *A Study of Second-year Pupils' Attitudes towards French, German and Spanish*, OXPROD Occasional Paper 5, Oxford, University of Oxford Department of Educational Studies, 1991.
(19) Caroline Filmer-Sankey, 'Attitudes towards first foreign languages in the early stages of secondary school: an investigation into French, German and Spanish', unpublished M.Litt. thesis, University of Oxford, 1991.
(20) J.R. Woodhouse, 'OXPROD: *Il progetto Oxford per la diversificazione delle lingue straniere*', in I. Baldelli and B.M. Da Rif (eds), *Lingua e Letteratura Italiana nel Mondo Oggi II*, Firenze, Leo S. Olschki, 1991.
(21) David Phillips and Karen Chidwick, *In Defence of the Second Foreign Language*, OXPROD Occasional Paper 6, Oxford, University of Oxford Department of Educational Studies, 1992.

1 Historical development

INTRODUCTION

Throughout the century there have been consistent calls for the more widespread teaching of 'languages other than French'. These have ranged from the impassioned pleas of individuals desperately concerned about the future for 'their' language, through the reasoned arguments of professional organisations, to official reports and statements of various kinds.

French had been introduced into the curriculum of schools without question as the natural choice of modern foreign language. The acceptability of the very notion of teaching *modern* languages had of course been much disputed, and the subject was for long accorded low status, its inferior position symbolised by the fact that it was so often taught either by inexperienced native speakers or by teachers with little command of the language who approached it in the same way as they would Latin or Greek. The choice of French, however, was understandable: 'French is by far the most important language in the history of modern civilisation' was how the influential Leathes Committee viewed the language's justification for inclusion in the curriculum,[1] and it is clear that – quite apart from the fact of the geographical proximity of France – the acknowledged importance of French culture and the acceptance that knowledge of the language through which it was expressed was considered to be an essential feature of the educated person's intellectual attainments assured its pre-eminent standing.

This dominance of French in the curriculum of British schools has always presented linguists with a fundamental moral dilemma. The position of French has had to be challenged, but only by scrupulous avoidance of the chauvinism so easily espoused by those defending a cause, however justified it might be. It is indeed in the very nature of their discipline for linguists to be concerned to defend the study of the language of one of the world's richest cultures; to attack it would be quite contrary to those humanistic principles they have traditionally held so dear. And yet the embittered Germanist or Hispanist, Italianist or Russophile (even this consciously alphabetical listing could be taken to betray a latent prejudice), frustrated by decades of lack of progress in the study of any of those languages in schools, can quickly succumb to the temptation to launch assaults or make unreasonable comparisons.

It is easy to demonstrate how this might be done. In the early stages of learning any foreign language it is clearly advisable not to present learners with difficulties that are likely to result in lack of immediate success. It is often asserted that some languages present fewer problems in those early stages than others, German being frequently quoted as an example of a language in which quick initial success can be guaranteed. And so it would be possible to contrast the content of some notional first lessons in French with that of similar lessons in German and to demonstrate the greater accessibility of German, at least for English-speakers. We might take, for example, utterances like these:

> *Voici Marie-Claude qui arrive!*
> *Qu'est-ce que c'est, Charles?*
> *Tu peux me donner le livre?*
> *Viens ici, s'il te plaît!*

and contrast them with their German 'equivalents':

> *Hier kommt Maria!*
> *Was ist das, Karl?*
> *Kannst du mir das Buch geben?*
> *Komm hierher, bitte!*

It would then be demonstrable from such a contrast that French poses problems in phonology, morphology, syntax and lexis which do not appear to be present in German. An eleven-year-old beginner of average intelligence, it might be argued, would not even be able to identify the proper noun in *Voici Marie-Claude qui arrive!* on first hearing the phrase. From this it might be postulated that French is a 'difficult' or 'inaccessible' language for English-speaking learners.

Such a postulation would of course be based on selective use of evidence. In the example quoted careful use has been made of cognate or easily recognisable forms in German, and these contrast starkly with what appear to be problematic equivalents in French. The comprehensibility of the particular utterances chosen could in any case be enhanced through the means by which they would be introduced by the teacher: mime, gesture, emphasis, and the use of visual aids would all contribute to learners' initial comprehension. We might instead have chosen examples in French which demonstrate far fewer obstacles:

> *De quelle couleur est la fleur?*
> *Passe-moi le crayon!*
> *Antoine passe les vacances en France*

and these could then be contrasted with apparently more difficult German equivalents:

Welche Farbe hat die Blume?
Überreichst du mir den Bleistift?
Anton verbringt die Ferien in Frankreich

Arguments about the relative difficulties of pronunciation in the two languages, and about the relationship between the spoken and the written language in each case, would rest on much surer ground.

Allison Peers, a prolific writer in defence of the teaching of Spanish, was prone, despite his insistence that he had 'no inborn Hispanic prejudices',[2] to making comparisons which operated to the considerable detriment of French:

> A pupil who has learned in babyhood to say 'What's that?' will be impatient with a language which seems to say: 'What is it that it is that that?' (*Qu'est-ce que c'est que cela?*) and much more drawn to one which says *¿Qué es eso?*[3]

In making this particular point Peers is illustrating his view that one of the 'intrinsic qualities' of any modern foreign language widely taught in schools should be that it is 'an easy language in its early stages'. A second essential quality for Peers is that such a language should be 'as nearly as possible phonetic'; in this regard, he believes, 'like German, Spanish is vastly superior to French'. The third quality he identifies is that a widely taught language should be able to help learners to go on to learn other languages for themselves, that is – to use Eric Hawkins's term – it should be able to serve as an 'apprenticeship' language.[4] Peers concludes:

> Intrinsically and educationally . . . Spanish is a better bargain for the average school-child than French, while on the third count it is at least an equally good one.[5]

It would be quite unjust to impute any degree of linguistic chauvinism to Allison Peers, but he was, understandably, so concerned in his influential book to make the case for 'his' language that he slipped easily into the assumption that Spanish has the supreme claim to be included on the school curriculum. French comes off very badly by comparison.

The fact is, of course, that *no* foreign language has an unchallengeable claim to be taught above any other in British schools, whatever assertions might be made in its favour. One of the problems which must be faced in the context of policy for foreign language provision is indeed precisely to sort out the assertions from the demonstrable truths. It must be logically the case that the English-speaking learner of average ability will find language A 'easier' or more 'accessible' than language B, and that language B will in the same way have greater claims than language C – but to identify languages A, B and C and prove the case is quite another matter, and one that has not often been addressed even by the more knowledgeable of those arguing against the dominance of French. We shall return to the question of language difficulty in Chapter 3 below; next, however, we must consider the historical development of the arguments for the teaching of languages other than French.

SOME EARLY DEVELOPMENTS AND THE UTILITARIAN DILEMMA

In 1912 the Board of Education had issued its Circular No. 797 on Modern Languages, in which the position of German was described as especially precarious: it was 'completely disappearing from the curriculum of schools in which it formerly found a place'. The Circular is particularly notable, however, for its clear statement questioning the assumption that French should be the language studied by those pupils who would learn only one language.[6] By 1918 a committee appointed by the Board had produced a major report on modern foreign languages in the school curriculum. The influential Leathes Committee, far from attacking the position of French, reasserted the claims of that language for inclusion in the curriculum – for historical, cultural and literary reasons and also because of its utilitarian advantages:

> Even for practical purposes the great majority of our witnesses give French the first place. Not only is French the language of diplomatic intercourse, but in countries where English has not established itself French is found most commonly useful as an intermediary between any two persons of different nationality.[7]

But the Committee went beyond these not unfamiliar defences and asserted that French offered considerable advantages of a broader educative kind:

> Our careless articulation may be corrected by the precise and studied utterance of the French; our modes of written expression might gain much from study of the perspicuous phrasing, logical construction, and harmonious proportions of their prose. From every point of view French is, for us above all, the most important of living tongues; it has, and it should retain, the first place in our schools and Universities.[8]

For the Leathes Committee, then, there was no doubt that French should retain its paramount position. But even before 1918 considerable efforts had been made to promote the notion of teaching languages other than French more widely. The Board of Education memorandum of 1912[9] had stated that

> There are . . . strong utilitarian reasons why an opportunity should be given for the learning of Italian and Spanish in select schools and districts having a considerable trade with countries in which those languages are spoken, and the Board would favourably consider any proposal for the introduction of either language into the curriculum.

Josefina Bello[10] has documented the early arguments for an increase in the teaching of Spanish, and it is clear that utilitarian (particularly commercial) considerations dominated in a way that had not generally applied to the teaching of French. Such arguments ignored those claims for the teaching of modern foreign languages which were essentially *educational* in nature (fully documented for the early years of the century by Harry Radford[11]), and they tended to diminish the status of the languages in whose defence they were applied. Bello reminds us that the Modern Language Association had been founded in 1892 with its main stated objective being

> To obtain for modern languages the status in the educational curricula of the country to which their *intrinsic value, as instruments of mental discipline and culture*, entitles them apart from their acknowledged commercial and utilitarian importance [present writers' emphasis].[12]

Modern languages had of course to compete with the classics, whose position in the curriculum of schools remained unquestioned. Supporters of the classical languages feared, however, that an increase in 'modern studies' would begin to undermine that hitherto secure position. The Final Honour School of Medieval and Modern Languages was established in Oxford by a statute of 1903, following discussions which had been frustrated in one way or another since 1724, so great had been the resistance to the study of non-classical languages. A leading figure in the Oxford debate about the introduction of the new Honour School described the problem in basic terms:[13]

> The real question at issue is whether the modern European languages and literatures are worthy of being treated as a serious subject of University study: of a study, that is, as thorough, and as well organised as the study of Greek and Latin languages is at present.

Cambridge had first examined modern languages in 1886, and the new subject had been dismissively dubbed the 'courier tripos'; a one-time Professor of Modern History at Oxford records in his memoirs an equally cynical view of the new developments:[14]

> Mademoiselle Lefèvre can get 'distinction' for Colloquial French, and Signorina Rossi for Colloquial Italian. . . . I have heard it said that this is the honour school for intending schoolmistresses . . .

In view of this kind of reaction from the universities, it was of great importance, as the Modern Language Association had recognised, to present a proper case in *educational* terms for the inclusion of modern languages in the curriculum. The common defence of modern language study in terms of practical application actually created a tension which, as Bello has argued,[15] has operated in particular to the considerable disadvantage of Spanish, dubbed an 'easy' language because of its promotion as a *langue véhiculaire* in commerce. Once French had become so established as the 'natural' first language for British schools, however, it was understandable that arguments in favour of other languages, principally German and Spanish, tended to have a utilitarian focus. Towards the end of 1918 – to take one school case study unearthed by Bello – the Headmaster of Plymouth School announced at a speech day that Spanish had been added to the curriculum as an alternative to Greek or German; he 'did not think German would be of practical use after the war for commercial or personal intercourse'. The *Western Morning News* reported the Headmaster's speech and went on to discuss the question of what languages schools should teach. It argued that it would be important for reasons of potential trade advantage to continue to be able to communicate in neutral markets with some eighty million German speakers in Central Europe, concluding that

> though on many grounds we favour the inclusion of Spanish and Italian in our school curricula, yet on commercial, even more than . . . military grounds . . . it is necessary that German should be retained.[16]

Over a quarter of a century later Allison Peers was lamenting the fact that as a consequence of its perceived practical value, Spanish had been labelled a 'commercial' subject, *tout court*: '"Commercial" Spanish . . . is spoken of as if it were the main end of our teaching, to which we are applying a superficial coating of regard for culture'.[17] And a few years after the publication of *Spanish – Now*, the Incorporated Association of Assistant Masters (IAAM) was pointing out that emphasis on the commercial value of learning a language can seriously misfire if jobs in which it might be used are not forthcoming. Such was the case with Spanish, the IAAM argued, since even before the Civil War 'the jobs promised were non-existent' and what is more 'the cultural value of the subject had been overlooked in the eagerness to master the conventions and abbreviations of Spanish correspondence'.[18]

Peers worked throughout his professional life to dispel the image of Spanish as little else than 'useful', and Hispanists owe much to his endeavours to make the more substantive educational case which would defend the language and its culture in terms applicable equally to French and to the classical languages. The tension between utilitarian and broader educational/cultural defences of individual languages and of modern languages in general has persisted right up to the present; it is evident in the depth of feeling at the turn of the century recalled in Radford's graphic phrase describing the anti-utilitarian argument: 'modern languages must no longer be treated dismissively as simply a utilitarian workshop for mediocre minds'.[19]

OFFICIAL REPORTS AND DOCUMENTS, 1918–43

The report of the Leathes Committee constituted the first major inquiry of the century into modern language teaching. As we have seen, it had much to say on the matter of the most appropriate foreign languages for British pupils to learn. The subject recurs in subsequent Board of Education documents of various dates. Thus in 1929 a pamphlet of the Board addressed itself entirely to the position of German in grant-aided secondary schools, asserting that if 'in a given school . . . only one foreign language is studied, it is not a self-evident proposition that that language should necessarily be French', and speaking of the 'unhealthy uniformity' characterising the action of school authorities in determining which language(s) should be taught. The pamphlet is particularly notable for its introduction of the notion that foreign language provision should be *planned* on a local basis:

> The fact that one school omits German from its Curriculum is *per se* a reason why a neighbouring School should make provision for that language. It is only by mutual consultation and agreement among School Authorities that the Secondary Schools of a given area can do their part in contributing, severally and collectively, to the national system.[20]

In 1930 the Board published the results of an inquiry into the position of foreign languages in 'modern' schools.[21] Of the 512 such schools in which a foreign language was being taught in 1929, only eight were offering any German, and ten some Spanish; this provision was felt to be 'absurdly out of relation to the true needs of the situation', as far as the relative importance of the main European languages for commerce and industry was concerned. While recognising the value of French – 'the great majority of the schools must, for the present, offer French or nothing' – the pamphlet makes the case for German and Spanish. German is seen as particularly accessible to eleven-year-old beginners; Spanish, 'a simple, direct language', is 'well suited to pupils who do not look forward to a university course' – a view, we may think, not designed to endear the arguments in favour of the language to many policy-makers. The Inspectors who produced the report 'agreed that the standard attained in German and Spanish was higher than that achieved in French' and they attributed this in part to 'the greater educational suitability of these languages for this type of school'. The virtual monopoly of French was seen to be neither in the interest of the schools nor the country.

The year 1930 also saw the publication of a report on modern languages from the Committee on Education for Salesmanship.[22] On the question of modern languages studied in England and Wales the Committee had this to say:

> In the Secondary Schools the popularity of French is still very marked, though not so marked as it is in the Modern Schools. In 1925–26, out of some 1,250 grant aided schools, 872 provided only French as a modern language, 327 provided French and German, 31 French and

Spanish, and 26 French, German and Spanish. Another test of the comparative popularity of languages will be found in the results of the examination for the Secondary School Certificate . . . which show that in July, 1928, 54,273 students offered French, 3,837 German, and 719 Spanish. There is a widespread feeling that this proportion cannot be justified, though the cultural value of French is generally recognised. The subject . . . is very much in the minds of modern language teachers throughout the country.[23]

Among the points for consideration raised by the report were the questions: 'What is the relative importance to this country of the various languages from the cultural and practical standpoints? How should their respective claims be balanced, and, in particular, what provision should be made for instruction in Spanish?' The singling out of Spanish for special mention is notable. So too, and particularly in the context of modern foreign languages and *salesmanship*, is the insistence that the cultural dimension be taken into account; indeed, the report, which includes case studies of language teaching in Denmark, Germany, Holland, Sweden and Switzerland, makes the point that the higher status accorded to the study of foreign languages in those countries was due to an appreciation of their 'intrinsic importance'. Languages were 'regarded not only as having high practical value, but also as effective instruments of education in the broadest sense'.

In 1938 the Consultative Committee on Secondary Education published a report 'with special reference to grammar schools and technical high schools'.[24] The Spens Report, as it has come to be known, urged that all pupils should have the opportunity to learn at least one language other than their own; at the same time, however, it argued that those showing no aptitude for language study should be allowed to abandon it. The Committee saw the main cultural value of language learning as consisting in greater linguistic understanding and competence in the mother tongue, but it pointed out too that the 'enlargement of sympathy and interest' was of equal importance. As to which language to teach, the Committee felt that this should be left to the schools, 'but if the first language is to be a modern one, the claims of other languages [than French] are at least as cogent'. The second language, the Committee argued, should be started 'about a year after taking up the first', and a strong case was made for the teaching of an ancient language at this stage.

The Norwood Committee, set up by R.A. Butler in 1941 to investigate the secondary school curriculum and examinations, recognised that there are utilitarian reasons for studying modern languages, though it warned commerce and industry that schools 'cannot bring [pupils] to the state of proficiency required for business purposes',[25] and pointed out that if Spanish were more widely taught but pupils failed to find suitable posts in which the language might be used, its status would be unfavourably affected; the same would apply to Portuguese, Russian or Italian. It was careful in fact to sound a warning against a too utilitarian emphasis. Courses in foreign languages should be 'worthwhile, exacting and dignified':

> There may be a danger of syllabuses of work being adopted which offer superficial attractions but lack solid basis, which though encouraging and improving oral work may encourage glibness on trivial themes and the reading of texts lacking in scholarliness and dignity.[26]

The Norwood Report had much to say on the range of languages offered in schools, and on the dominance of French:

> The position occupied by French needs no lengthy explanation; the historical relation of France and England, the connexion of French and English cultures and their common origins – these in themselves account for the special place which the French language has maintained in English education. In addition, teachers trained in the French language have themselves trained their pupils to teach French and a routine of French teaching has been set up.[27]

Allison Peers reported shortly after the appearance of the Norwood Report that the most common response he would get when asking headteachers why French dominated the curriculum in their schools was 'just tradition',[28] the kind of self-perpetuating tradition that the report describes. The report continues:

> The question is whether as a nation and as individuals the British people can afford, on grounds cultural, international and economic, to neglect the language of nations whose achievements are great in varied fields and with whom it must come into contact in the spheres of international relations and commercial dealings; knowledge and understanding of these actions is of no less importance for ultimate ends than knowledge of our nearest neighbour.[29]

The Norwood Report clearly came out in favour of French and German, but it had a lot to say about Spanish, and quoted some of the arguments put to the Committee at some length.[30] Spanish is given a special place in the Committee's two recommendations on the languages to be taught:

> (*i*) French and German might be alternative more often than is the practice in schools; in particular German should be taken by Science pupils.
> (*ii*) Spanish should become a chief language in some schools and particularly in areas where commerce has special ties with Spanish-speaking countries; such schools would become known as producing pupils with knowledge of Spanish, and firms in other neighbourhoods would satisfy their needs from those schools.[31]

There was in all these Board of Education documents an intellectual, if not a political, will to encourage the teaching of languages other than French. German and Spanish were the languages most frequently mentioned, and the arguments in their favour hovered between utilitarian and broader educational/cultural defences. While it was clearly felt that a trading nation *needs* to produce people competent in a wider range of languages, there was nevertheless a strong feeling that French was an important, indeed vital, part of the curriculum of schools: especially at a time when it was hoped to provide a secondary education for all pupils, a knowledge of that language was regarded as *the* mark of such an education. With secondary education available to all, all pupils would, it was hoped, have an opportunity to learn a language, and that language might, for various groups, be a language other than French. The Norwood Report brought all the arguments together in the three adjectives 'cultural, international and economic'. Many of the arguments sound very familiar, since they have been reiterated so often in the 1980s; take, for example, the following:

> Under modern competitive conditions – when we have to go to the world to sell, instead of the world coming to us to buy – it is essential for the manufacturer at home and his representatives on the spot to study thoroughly and continuously the conditions of each foreign market with which trade is carried on; to get to understand the characteristics of the people of the country and their likes and dislikes; and to have a good grasp, not merely of trade conditions and regulations, but also of social and political factors.[32]

That statement appears in the 1930 report *Education for Salesmanship*; some sixty years later it would not appear out of place in a policy statement on modern languages.

THE POST-WAR PERIOD

In a pamphlet of 1946, D.H. Stott, a teacher at Watford Grammar School, addressed the question of the dominance of French:

> French enjoys its overwhelming preponderance, not so much because it is more useful, or easier, or more attractive, or more educative than German, but for reasons of social and educational prestige. A smattering of French has become the badge of a secondary education. . . . [T]o substitute another language would be regarded as almost as great a blasphemy as to displace cricket in favour of baseball.[33]

The 'New Education', with its avowed aim of 'secondary education for all', in fact gave encouragement to central schools to introduce French into their curricula, so that their pupils might be entered for the School Certificate. This further strengthened the position of French – a couple of decades later the introduction of 'Primary French' was to have the same effect – and set back the claims of other languages, whose defence again tended towards those utilitarian arguments which had not helped particularly in the past. Stott himself concluded that 'for those who will deal mainly with things and matter – the scientists and the technicians – I would choose German; for those who will have to deal with people I would choose French'.[34]

A report of the Incorporated Association of Assistant Masters (IAAM) of 1949 dealt with the question 'What modern languages shall we teach?' at some length. Its conclusions and suggestions are worth recording in full as a précis of contemporary thinking on the subject:

1 That many of the reasons leading to the general adoption of French as the first foreign language to be taught are still valid, above all for A and B pupils in Grammar Schools.

2 That opportunities for learning Spanish and German should be greatly increased, and that in some schools they might provide the first foreign language.

3 That Spanish should generally be the first foreign language for 'C' pupils, e.g. for many in Secondary Modern Schools.

4 That in Grammar Schools and in certain Technical Schools, where French is the first foreign language to be taught, it should be made possible for a second language to be taken up in the second or third years, and that this be preferably German or Spanish.

5 That, reciprocally, where German or Spanish are the first languages, it should be possible for any pupil to take up French at some stage.

6 That intensive Sixth-Form courses in French, German and Spanish should, where possible, be made available for Arts, Science and Commerce students if they have been prevented from studying any of these in the general school course.

7 That in exceptional cases Russian might be introduced in 'A' forms below the Sixth; otherwise this language should not be taught below the Sixth Form.

8 That Italian and Portuguese might find a place in Sixth Forms both in Arts and in Commerce courses, for pupils who have already specialised in French or Spanish.

9 That in large towns a differentiation of curricula be made between secondary schools so as to permit a wider choice of languages, either as first languages or in later stages.

10 That, where local circumstances and commercial considerations render it advisable, different parts of the county or different towns should specialise or provide extra facilities in certain languages, e.g. Swansea, Cardiff and Liverpool in Spanish, Hull and N.E. areas in Russian or Scandinavian languages.[35]

This statement – from one of the most influential organisations of the period and later to be extensively referred to in a Ministry of Education pamphlet of 1956 – raises a number of familiar issues: the position of French was secure; there should, however, be more teaching of German and Spanish; Spanish might be more suitable for less academic pupils; Russian would be best limited to the more able, and largely in the sixth form, where there should be more *ab initio* courses; efforts should be made to include other languages in the secondary school curriculum in particular circumstances; and, interestingly, there should be a *policy* of differentiation of language provision within localities. This latter point, approached in the Norwood Report, has only properly been addressed in the years following the 1988 *Statement of Policy* from the Department of Education and Science (DES). Of the other nine points, those relating to the position of Spanish and Russian are worthy of particular note. The suggestion to associate those languages with the less and more able pupils respectively was an unfortunate step, which was simply to make the task of arguing for their more widespread teaching that much more difficult.

The Ministry of Education (as it now was) returned to the question of foreign language choice in its Pamphlet No. 29 of 1956. In some fourteen pages devoted to the subject, the document argues that it is not in the national interest for foreign language studies to be concentrated largely on one nation. It acknowledges the freedom enjoyed by governing bodies and headteachers to determine the curricula of their schools, and reminds us that neither the Ministry nor any other 'official' body exercises pressure on schools to teach a particular language. The whole tenor of the pamphlet, however, demonstrates the Ministry's clear belief that languages other than French should be more widely taught.

The 1956 pamphlet rehearses the reasons why French was still dominating the curriculum. 'Recent wars' had affected the teaching of German, Spanish and Italian; relations with the Soviet Union, it is implied, were too difficult for much progress to be envisaged in Russian. But the main factor is seen to be the teacher's 'intimate knowledge' of the country and people of France, and pupils' actual or potential contact with young French people:

> It must be accepted that it is at present more practicable for both teachers and pupils to enter into personal relations with the French than with any other nation; for many pupils the heavier expense involved would rule out a visit to most other countries.[36]

The pamphlet points out too the difficulty of providing Spanish and Italian foreign language assistants in most areas. An arrangement to exchange assistants with the Soviet Union was not possible.

The 'claims' of French, German, Spanish, Italian and Russian (placed in that not uncommon order) are briefly described, at times with an idealistic enthusiasm that would belie much classroom experience; comments on the relative attractions of the literatures of those countries, for example, include the following: 'The high poetic and human quality combined with the fire and vigour of German drama . . . is often more keenly appreciated by English boys and girls than is French drama, with the possible exception of Racine'; 'the German *Volkslied* is ever a source of the keenest enjoyment to most English boys and girls'; 'one of the greatest qualities of Spanish literature is its spontaneous appeal to young people'. The question of language difficulty is also addressed, and the 'considerable difficulties' of French in the early stages of learning are recognised, while it is admitted that German pronunciation, intonation and vocabulary present fewer problems; Spanish has the advantage of the 'comparative simplicity of its pronunciation and syntax', but Russian 'presents difficulties for the average Englishman' and was not recommended for inclusion anywhere in the school curriculum by ninety-six out of 200 schools specifically asked for their views by the Ministry. The verdict on language difficulty is – not unreasonably – that 'no living languages are easy; it is merely that the difficulties of each are differently distributed'.

The Ministry of Education also provided in Pamphlet No. 29 an analysis of figures relating to provision in the various European languages. While it could be reported that examination entries in Spanish had virtually trebled between 1939 (School Certificate) and 1954 (GCE O level), the actual figures were so small that the proportional increase was insignificant. At advanced level, however, the number of candidates in French had more than doubled over the same period, and the other four languages had enjoyed an even greater increase in proportional terms. The figures for language entries are shown in Table 1.1.[37] The pattern of provision deducible from these figures is the familiar one of French domination, with German managing to hold its own and Spanish remaining in a weakish third place, while Italian and Russian battle for the almost insignificant fourth and fifth positions. It confirms Allison Peers's ironic formula: Modern Languages = French + German.

For schools the 1950s were principally a period of consolidation, during which the provisions of the 1944 Act were making themselves felt. Foreign language teaching was largely still the province of the independent and grammar schools, catering as they did for a minority of academically able pupils. Even in the grammar schools it was not always expected that *all* pupils would study a language. A *Memorandum on Modern Language Teaching* from the Assistant Mistresses' Association felt it necessary to present the case against the view that while all grammar school pupils should be given the chance to study a foreign language 'it is useless to compel those with no linguistic ability to continue . . . after the second or third year'.[38] There was, however, a general sense of complacency about foreign language provision and about methodology.[39] There was little anticipation of the expansion that would occur over the next decade or so, and the modern technology (principally the tape-recorder) was being introduced only slowly. Examination syllabuses remained 'traditional' in style, covering translation from and into the foreign language, formal

Table 1.1 Examination entries in Spanish, 1939 and 1954

| | School Certificate 1939 | | GCE O level 1954 | |
	Total	% of lang. entry	Total	% of lang. entry
French	75,078	83.3	97,806	82.7
German	10,630	11.8	13,863	11.7
Spanish	1,252	1.4	3,371	2.8
Italian	355	0.4	209	0.2
Russian	7		76	0.1
	Higher Certificate 1939		GCE A level 1954	
	Total	% of lang. entry	Total	% of lang. entry
French	4,700	80.6	10,342	72.4
German	873	15.0	2,540	17.8
Spanish	145	2.5	660	4.6
Italian	12	0.2	79	0.6
Russian			457	3.2

essay, dictation, and only a token oral test. Textbooks too remained rooted in a style associated with, and more appropriate to, the teaching of classical languages. This complacency was put to the test with the rapid changes of the 1960s.

THE 1960s

The 1960s saw some of the most significant developments in modern foreign language teaching since the days of the 'Great Reform'. Against the background of important advances in methodology – in particular the extension of 'audio-lingual' principles to a new 'audio-visual' approach – an experiment was started to introduce modern language teaching in the primary school. The language chosen was, of course, French, and that very choice, inevitable though it was ('since it would have been impossible to provide an adequate teaching force for the implementation of the experiment if any language other than French had been chosen'[40]), dealt a severe blow to the chance of other languages being taught extensively as first foreign languages in secondary schools. Despite the eventual sorry outcome of the Primary French experiment, it clearly made sense for children who had started the language before the age of eleven to continue with it in the first year of their secondary education. Hopes that a *second* foreign language might be introduced at age eleven for pupils with two or three years of French behind them, proved futile.

   The audio-visual course designed for use in primary schools was the Nuffield/Schools Council course *En Avant*.[41] Other 'state of the art' courses followed from the same source: *Vorwärts* for German, *Adelante* for Spanish, and *Vperyod!* for Russian. Each of the most commonly taught languages except Italian now had a modern course specifically designed to take account of the latest advances in methodology. Italian was conspicuous by its absence, and there is no doubt that its cause was harmed by the omission. The Spanish course was written with the slower learner in mind, as – later – would be the ILEA course *Claro*;[42] again, this association of Spanish with the less able pupil did little to help the general cause of the language.

The year 1962 had seen the publication of the Annan Committee's report on the teaching of Russian.[43] Pamphlet No. 29 reported in 1956 on a Ministry survey of the position of Russian which found that the language was being taught in only twenty-nine secondary schools, fifteen of which were in the independent sector. In addition courses were being run in twelve evening institutes and twelve 'commercial colleges'. Staffing was precarious: out of nineteen teachers interviewed only three had an honours degree in Russian; two were *émigrés* and no fewer than fourteen were self-taught. Only two of the nineteen were found to have spent time in the Soviet Union.[44]

The Annan Committee undertook its own investigation of provision in LEAs and in the independent sector. Of 342 schools circulated, 221 indicated that Russian 'appeared in the normal curriculum'; additionally, some 236 further education institutions appeared to be running regular courses.[45] There had been a notable increase in the number of schools introducing the language in 1958 and 1959 as a direct result of the 'sputnik shock', which had caused politicians in Britain and the United States to consider what curricular lessons might be learnt from the Soviet achievement.[46] Ironically, by 1958 the Joint Services Schools of Languages, which had run intensive Russian courses for those on National Service, were being wound up, and so an important supply of teachers abruptly ceased. The Annan Committee proposed that one-year intensive courses for at least forty seconded teachers be introduced without delay in order to help with the teacher supply problems which would otherwise impede the expansion in Russian teaching that the Committee recommended.

Two recommendations of the Annan Committee are worth singling out for their implicit support for the general notion of diversification. They are that

> Russian should become a normal subject in the curriculum of many schools, introduced as long as possible before pupils reach the sixth form;

and that

> some schools, both large and small, should experiment by making Russian the first or second foreign language.[47]

Such exhortations, as we have seen, have a long and depressingly unproductive history. Russian studies were to be dealt a severe blow in 1979 with the publication of the University Grants Committee's report recommending *inter alia* that 'all practicable steps should be taken to reduce overall the number of staff [at British universities] teaching Russian-based courses'.[48]

In 1961 the Central Advisory Council for Education had been asked by Sir David Eccles to report on the education of thirteen- to sixteen-year-olds of average and less than average ability. The result was *Half Our Future*, produced under the chairmanship of John Newsom and published in 1963. The Newsom Report recorded that most 'modern' schools provided no opportunity to learn a foreign language: about a third of the children in about half of the total number of such schools were learning French, and these were largely the ablest pupils. The report argues strongly, largely on educational grounds, that pupils of all abilities should be given a chance to study a foreign language; the less than average in particular would thereby gain increased self-respect and develop an improved general attitude to learning. The contact with a different people and culture which knowledge of another language facilitates is also seen as an important reason for extending foreign language teaching to a broader range of pupils. On the question of which language the pupils in question should learn, the report, while admitting that ensuring 'a succession of good teachers, whatever language is chosen', was the main problem, felt constrained to mention the difficulties French poses: 'It is not . . . the easiest in its early stages, and Spanish and Italian have been more successfully taught to the less able pupils in some schools'.[49]

The most significant developments in the 1960s centred around the rapid growth of comprehensive schools, following the 1964 Labour government's issuing of Circular 10/65 which required LEAs to submit plans for reorganisation. The changes that comprehensivisation implied had a serious effect on modern language teaching. There was rapid expansion: pupils – of all abilities – who previously would not have studied a foreign language now had a chance to do so, but at a time when teachers were having to adjust their teaching to the new methods necessary if the audio-visual courses were to be used properly. Modern language teachers had to adapt quickly to the needs of the slower learners they were not used to teaching. The two processes, expansion on the one hand and the development of a new methodology on the other, created tensions which resulted in much failure and frustration and some serious questioning of the value of modern language study at school level.

THE 1970s

The expansionist 1960s were followed by a decade which has often been seen as a crisis period for modern language teaching. The Primary French experiment was dealt the *coup de grâce* by the appearance of the 1974 NFER report, *Primary French in the Balance*.[50] Despite the welcome development of 'alternative' examination syllabuses at GCE O level and the greater opportunities offered to less gifted pupils by the CSE examination; despite, too, the exciting prospects of the early years of the 'graded test' movement, there was a widespread feeling that the promise of the 1960s was not being realised. Prime Minister Callaghan's Ruskin College speech of 1976 sparked off a debate which was to throw into question many complacent assumptions about the school curriculum and which unlocked the door to what Sir David Eccles had once called its 'secret garden'. Callaghan's speech was followed by a spate of DES and HMI documents on the curriculum, the most significant of which for modern language teaching was the 1977 HMI report, *Modern Languages in Comprehensive Schools*.[51] Before considering the HMI report, however, it is necessary to recall three now little-known documents that preceded it.

The Scottish Education Department had produced a pamphlet on alternative first foreign languages in 1971, and the Welsh Education Office a booklet on languages other than French in 1973.[52]

The Scottish document rehearses some of the arguments for diversification, mentioning better communications, increased travel abroad, growth in commercial and industrial links with the rest of Europe, and greater interest in European life: 'Whether or not Britain enters the Common Market, her comparative isolation from the countries of the European mainland is a thing of the past'. It focuses particularly on staffing problems, concluding that it was now desirable to extend the teaching of languages other than French and 'to institute practical measures to enable a supply of trained, qualified teachers to be made available'. An appendix covers administrative problems – staffing, consultation with parents (including the question of parental choice and difficulties associated with pupil transfer), and school organisation. This important publication anticipated much of the detailed debate that was to ensue from the mid-1980s onwards, and we shall return to consider the kind of questions it raises in Chapter 6 below.

The Welsh survey, produced by members of the Inspectorate, is a detailed study of provision in 121 schools. The report attaches due importance to staffing problems, and in particular to the obviously 'self-perpetuating' nature of French on the curriculum, previously described in the Norwood Report. It argues that while 'it may not be possible to establish a final, authoritative order of importance to the languages concerned, nor even to state with certainty that one language is of greater educational, cultural or commercial value than another', nevertheless 'it can no longer be claimed with conviction that French should, always, be the first modern language to be taught in the schools of Wales'. Detailed separate sections are devoted to German, Spanish, Russian and Italian, and the report concludes with a plea that, 'in default of any concerted national view as to what modern language provision should be', the introduction of languages other than French as first foreign languages should result from 'consultation between local authorities and schools, and involving others concerned with curriculum development and with modern language teaching'. Here, then, is a clear anticipation of the move towards *planning* local provision, rather than relying on the haphazard or *ad hoc* measures which characterise much of the traditional British approach to curriculum development.

Early in 1977 the Inspectorate produced a paper appraising 'problems in some key subjects': *Mathematics, Science and Modern Languages in Maintained Schools in England.* This forerunner of *Modern Languages in Comprehensive Schools*, in which the 'total impact' of changes since the Second World War, and especially since the late 1950s, is described as having led to a situation of 'growing concern' about the future, devotes a paragraph to languages other than French:

> The position of languages other than French . . . is frequently the source of adverse comment and, given Britain's present position in Europe and in the world, is perhaps hard to justify. While other countries can find good reasons for offering their pupils English as a first foreign language, we cannot so easily justify our preference for French. This has become a matter of concern now that the difficulty of satisfactorily maintaining other languages as a first or second foreign language in the comprehensive school has come to be appreciated. A significant modification in the balance of languages is only likely to occur if more schools can be persuaded to offer a language other than French as their first foreign language.[53]

The paragraph in question goes on to suggest that very large schools can offer different languages to different groups in the first year, while average or smaller size schools can offer only one. It also mentions the fact that some teachers of German, Spanish, Russian and Italian find that they have 'insufficient work' in their specialist languages, and have to teach French, even though they might not be qualified to do so. The document therefore covers some key issues in the diversification debate: the political dimension (preparing for Britain's role in a wider Europe), the difficulty of sustaining variety of foreign language provision in comprehensive schools, and organisational and staffing problems.

The Inspectorate had started its major study of modern language teaching in eighty-three comprehensive schools in 1975, 'at a time of rapidly growing concern about the future of language learning in our schools'[54] (a phrase which echoes the earlier HMI 'appraisal'). The HMI's report *Modern Languages in Comprehensive Schools* is generally gloomy in tone, finding much to criticise in the schools visited. One whole section is devoted to languages other than French. Primary French, comprehensive reorganisation, and two-tier school systems are mentioned as factors which might be said to have 'militated against the survival, let alone the expansion of other languages'. The schools surveyed provided an indication of the national situation. Approximate percentages of pupils learning

Table 1.2 Approximate percentages of pupils taking modern foreign language
courses in the sample schools (1975–6)

Year	I	II	III	IV	V
French	81	77	71	32	27
German	4	14	18	9	9
Spanish	5	5	5	3	3
Italian	0.5	0.5	0.5	0.5	0.1
Russian	Nil	Nil	0.1	0.1	0.1

particular languages in each of years 1–5 in the sample schools are shown
in Table 1.2.[55]

The report addresses itself to the patterns existing in the sample schools
for the introduction of languages other than French. While it finds of
course that such languages were for the most part begun as second or third
languages, it provides a useful account of the variety of provision found
when these languages were sole or joint first foreign languages:

> In 65 of the 66 schools visited which offered pupils their first intro-
> duction to modern language study, French figured on the first-year
> timetable. In the remaining school German was taught. In six schools
> French was parallel with another language in the first year, and in a
> seventh school with two other languages. With the exception of one
> school where Italian was taught, the language involved was German or
> Spanish. In the majority of schools the number of pupils taking each of
> the parallel languages was approximately the same. As might be
> expected, schools adopting this practice were large ones, the average
> first year intake for 1975–76 being 290. One school introduced French
> and Spanish as the first modern language in alternate years.[56]

In this brief account we find three patterns for first foreign language
diversification: a language other than French as sole foreign language; two
or more languages offered in parallel; and the so-called 'wave' model, with
two languages alternating in successive years. These patterns were to figure
prominently in the discussions about the practicalities of diversification
that would begin in earnest in the 1980s. While Dickson and Lee are
mistaken to assert that 'in 1977 HMI first introduced the idea of provision
based on a variety of first languages',[57] it is nonetheless true that the 1977
report marks the beginning of a serious reappraisal of modern language
policy and provision which was to continue throughout the next decade
and beyond. The report concludes its account of languages other than
French on a challenging note:

> The only fact to emerge clearly is that . . . no more than a small
> proportion of the age-group was entered for the first major public
> examination in a language other than French. Fewer than a third of
> the pupils concerned achieved a level which might be considered a

satisfactory base for advanced study. This is not a situation which should be viewed with complacency.[58]

The major policy developments of the 1980s, to which we shall come in Chapter 2, moved the debate away from complacency and towards a conviction based on serious commitment to change.

THE HISTORICAL LEGACY

This outline historical survey demonstrates the long tradition that has existed in Britain of rhetorical challenge to the position of French on the school curriculum and enthusiastic encouragement of alternative languages. In recent years political considerations consequent upon Britain's future role in Europe have played an important part in the formulation of government policy, but it is clear that this is not a new phenomenon: since the early years of the century, wider economic and cultural arguments have been consistently adduced by policy-makers at all levels when presenting the case for the teaching of languages other than French.

While the position of French has been challenged, and the difficulties the language presents – usually qualified by a phrase like 'at least in the early stages of learning' – have been outlined, care has usually been taken to present the case for the continued study of French language and literature, albeit in a context of wider opportunities to learn other languages. Various arguments have been used in favour of German, Spanish, Italian and Russian. As one official document puts it, 'it is possible to argue a case, on grounds cultural, geographical, commercial, scientific, or historical, for a dozen languages'. It continues:

> German is valuable for reading scientific documents; Spanish is the commercial language of South America; the learning of Russian enables one to read 'Anna Karenina' in the original; French is the diplomatic lingua franca of Europe.[59]

If there is one dominating argument over a long period during which the question of diversification has been addressed, it is that it clearly does not make sense for these 'other' languages to be so under-represented on the curriculum of schools in a country where the 'normal' first foreign language has gained its position of dominance through 'historical accident'.[60]

There is an immense feeling of frustration evident in much of the writing on the subject. While it has been recognised that control over curricular matters has traditionally rested with headteachers and their governors, there have been regular calls for some degree of co-ordinated planning of foreign language provision, on at least a local basis. By the end of the 1970s, however, very little progress had been made in this direction. The Oxford study of 1983 concluded that it was above all the development of local plans that was needed to ensure the survival of languages other than French on the curriculum.[61] At that time there was much talk too of the need for a national plan. By the end of the 1980s there was in place a national policy for foreign languages which included proper support for diversification. Chapter 2 will examine the processes that led to this significant breakthrough.

NOTES

1 *Modern Studies* (The Leathes Report), London, HMSO, 1918, reprinted 1928, p. 59.
2 E. Allison Peers, *Spanish – Now*, London, Methuen, 1944, p. vii.
3 Ibid., p. 6.
4 Eric Hawkins, *Modern Languages in the Curriculum*, Cambridge, Cambridge University Press, 1981, p. 77ff.
5 Peers, op. cit., p. 8.
6 Board of Education, *Modern Languages*, London, HMSO, 1912 (= Circular 797).
7 *Modern Studies*, p. 60.
8 Ibid.
9 Board of Education, *Memorandum on the Teaching of Modern Languages in Secondary Schools*, London, HMSO, 1912, p. 13.
10 Josefina Bello, 'The teaching of Spanish in secondary schools, 1900–1950', unpublished M.Litt. thesis, University of Oxford, 1990.
11 Harry Radford, 'Modern Languages and the curriculum in English secondary schools', in Ivor F. Goodson (ed.), *Social Histories of the Secondary Curriculum: Subjects for study*, London, Falmer Press, 1985, pp.203–37.
12 Bello, op.cit., p. 12.
13 Henry Nettleship, 'A brief statement of the case for the proposed Final Honour School of Modern Languages and Literature', 1887, p. 8; quoted in Sir Charles Firth, *Modern Languages at Oxford*, 1724–1929, London, Oxford University Press, 1929, p. 73.
14 Sir Charles Oman, *Memories of Victorian Oxford*, London, Methuen, 1941, p. 238.
15 Bello, op. cit., pp. 53–4.
16 2 November 1918.
17 Peers, op. cit., pp. 1–2.
18 The Incorporated Association of Assistant Masters (IAAM), *The Teaching of Modern Languages*, London, University of London Press, 1949, p. 35.
19 Radford, op. cit., p. 216.
20 Board of Education, *Position of German in Grant-aided Secondary Schools in England*, London, HMSO, 1929 (= Educational Pamphlets, No. 77), pp. 10 and 11.
21 Board of Education, *Foreign Languages in 'Modern' Schools*, London, HMSO, 1930 (= Educational Pamphlets, No. 82).
22 Second Interim Report of the Committee on Education for Salesmanship, *Modern Languages*, London, HMSO, 1930.
23 Ibid., p. 40.
24 Board of Education, *Report of the Consultative Committee on Secondary Education* (The Spens Report), London, HMSO, 1938.
25 Board of Education, *Curriculum and Examinations in Secondary Schools* (The Norwood Report), London, HMSO, 1943, p. 117.

26 Ibid., p. 119.
27 Ibid., p. 114.
28 Peers, op. cit., p. 79.
29 The Norwood Report, op. cit., p. 114.
30 The arguments made to the Committee are worth quoting more fully:

(*i*) As new secondary schools are founded, Spanish should be adopted as the first (or only) modern language in a great number of them. Education Authorities should be asked always to consider this.

(*ii*) In new post-primary (one-language) schools . . . and in any elementary schools in which modern language teaching may henceforth be started, Spanish should, except for special reasons, be the language studied, since the chief aim here is to advance the pupil as far as possible in a short space of time, and in its early stages children can make more rapid progress in Spanish than in French or German. For schools of this type a specially constructed and simplified course should be used.

(*iii*) In secondary schools, where two languages are aimed at, Spanish should be in a considerable number of cases the first language studied. In every large urban area there should be at least one school in which Spanish is the first language.

(*iv*) Pupils of high linguistic capacity should be encouraged by teachers to study Spanish, whether as a first language, or as a second. Schools with a large proportion of such pupils should be encouraged by the Inspectors of the Board of Education and by Local Authorities to adopt Spanish.

(*v*) Such schools as are able at any time to switch over to Spanish as a first language, or to introduce it as a second language, should be given every encouragement to do so.

(*vi*) A liaison bureau should be created as soon as possible between the schools on the one hand and the Chamber of Commerce and larger business houses on the other. At the present time there is little correlation of supply and demand.

The Norwood Report, op. cit., pp. 114–15.

31 Ibid., p. 117.
32 Committee on Education for Salesmanship, op. cit., p. 2.
33 D.H. Stott, *Language Teaching in the New Education*, London, University of London Press, 1946, p. 94.
34 Ibid., p. 100.
35 IAAM, op. cit., pp. 40–1.
36 Ministry of Education, *Modern Languages*, London, HMSO, 1956 (= Pamphlet No. 29), p. 10.
37 Ibid., p. 96.
38 Association of Assistant Mistresses in Secondary Schools, *Memorandum on Modern Language Teaching*, London, University of London Press, 1956, p. 13.
39 See David Phillips, 'From complacency to conviction: Thirty years of language teaching theory, practice and policy', in David Phillips (ed.), *Languages in Schools: From Complacency to Conviction*, London, Centre for Information on Language Teaching and Research (CILT), 1988, pp. 6–25.
40 Clare Burstall *et al.*, *Primary French in the Balance*, Windsor, National Foundation for Educational Research (NFER), 1974, p. 11.
41 Nuffield Foundation, Modern Language Materials: *En Avant*, E.J. Arnold; *Adelante*, Macmillan; *Vorwärts*, E.J. Arnold; *Vperyod!*, Macmillan/Lund Humphries, 1967–75.
42 ILEA Learning Materials Service, *¡Claro!*, Level 1, 1980, Level 2, 1981, London, Mary Glasgow Publications.

43 *Report on the Teaching of Russian* (The Annan Report), London, HMSO, 1962.
44 Pamphlet No. 29, op. cit., p. 8.
45 The Annan Report, op. cit., p. 1.
46 The reaction in the United States to the launching of the first sputnik is nicely encapsulated in the title of A.S. Trace's book *What Ivan Knows that Johnny Doesn't*, New York, Random House, 1961.
47 The Annan Report, op. cit., p. 29.
48 University Grants Committee, *Report on Russian and Russian Studies in British Universities*, London, December 1979.
49 Central Advisory Council for Education (England), *Half Our Future* (The Newsom Report), London, HMSO, 1963, p. 162.
50 Burstall *et al.*, op. cit.
51 Department of Education and Science (DES), *Modern Languages in Comprehensive Schools* (= HMI series: Matters for Discussion 3), London, HMSO, 1977.
52 Scottish Education Department (National Steering Committee for Modern Languages), *Alternatives to French as a First Foreign Language in Secondary Schools*, Edinburgh, HMSO, 1971; Welsh Office, *Modern Languages other than French in Secondary Schools* (= Welsh Education Survey No. 2), Cardiff, HMSO, 1973.
53 *Mathematics, Science and Modern Languages in Maintained Schools in England: An appraisal of problems in some key subjects by HM Inspectorate*, London, January 1977, p. 2.
54 DES, op. cit., 1977, p. 3.
55 Ibid., p. 31.
56 Ibid., p. 32.
57 Peter Dickson and Barbara Lee, *Diversification of Foreign Languages in Schools* (Evaluation of ESG Programme of Diversification of First Foreign Language), Slough, NFER, 1990, p. 1.
58 DES, op. cit., 1977, p. 34.
59 *Modern Languages other than French in Secondary Schools*, op.cit., p. 22.
60 Ibid., p. 5.
61 David Phillips and Veronica Stencel, *The Second Foreign Language: Past development, current trends and future prospects*, London, Hodder & Stoughton, 1983, particularly Chapter 7.

2 Recent policy developments

TOWARDS A NATIONAL POLICY

We have seen in Chapter 1 how over many decades there was considerable enthusiasm – and not only on the part of those with vested interests – for some expansion of provision in the teaching of languages other than French in secondary schools. That enthusiasm rarely translated itself into the kind of action that made any significant impact nationally, though there were important exceptions like the publication of the Nuffield courses in the 1960s. In 1983 an HMI survey of modern languages in Wales found, for example, that only some little progress could be reported in languages other than French since the subject was last addressed ten years earlier:

> French remains the first language in nearly all schools, taken by over 120,000 pupils. Over the same period, German has expanded and is at present taken by 17,000 pupils, as compared with 11,000 10 years ago. The number of pupils taking Spanish has modestly increased from 1,500 to over 2,000. Russian and Italian are each taken by about 300 pupils, which amounts to a doubling of numbers taking Italian, and a considerable reduction in numbers taking Russian.[1]

The survey saw advantages in extending the provision of languages other than French as FL1, but mentioned the need to plan such provision 'with area policies for modern languages within LEAs'[2] so that continuity of curriculum could be assured for pupils changing school. The notion of developing plans and policies, with a degree of consensus and co-ordination that had mostly been lacking in the past, was to inform much of the thinking about foreign language teaching throughout the 1980s. Some LEAs – Nottinghamshire was an early example[3] – had started producing guidelines on the teaching of foreign languages in their localities, and with the growing importance of the advisory service (despite uneven provision across authorities) such developments encouraged greater local co-ordination of thinking. The graded test movement, itself the product of local initiatives, further encouraged co-operation and the pulling-together of ideas within LEAs. In February 1983 the Modern Language

Association issued a policy statement suggesting that 'each LEA be asked to guarantee a variety of choice between languages in its area'.[4] And in the early 1980s there was much anticipation of a promised DES consultative document on language teaching which it was hoped would help to establish something approaching a national policy for England and Wales. The mood was ripe for such an initiative.

The Schools Council too addressed itself both to the question of languages other than French in the curriculum and to the precarious position of the second foreign language. We have already noted that in 1981 a working party chaired by Colin Hadley produced an 'exploratory study' of languages other than French as first or equal first foreign language.[5] The Hadley Report, to which we shall return in Chapter 3, reached some positive conclusions on the experiences of twenty-three schools selected for investigation. The second Schools Council report, published in the spring of 1982, was concerned with the 'survival' of the second foreign language, seen by then to be under increasing pressure.[6]

These two reports drew welcome attention to the question of diversified provision in modern languages. At the same time the curriculum in general was being subjected to closer scrutiny than ever before. The far-reaching debate initiated by Prime Minister Callaghan's famous Ruskin College speech of 1976 had led inexorably towards the formal establishment of a National Curriculum (*avec majuscule*) through the provisions of a radically new Education Act. As we have noted above, the way had been paved by a series of DES and HMI documents[7] rehearsing the arguments in favour of greater commonality in curricular provision. Of most relevance to the present discussion is a series of DES documents issued from 1983 onwards.

A precursor of these documents, however, dealing with the state of foreign language provision nationally, is the report of a schools survey undertaken by the Assessment of Performance Unit (APU) in the autumn of 1982 as preparation for its 1983 investigation of the performance of thirteen-year-olds in French, German and Spanish.[8] It is described as giving a 'snapshot' of school foreign language provision in England, Wales and Northern Ireland. Among its conclusions are figures suggesting that about 690,000 pupils in 5,800 schools were being taught French as FL1 (in England, Wales and Northern Ireland); some 40,000 pupils in 360 schools had German, while 5,000 pupils in sixty schools were being taught Spanish as FL1. These totals are then translated into percentages:

> The proportions of schools teaching French, German and Spanish as first languages in autumn 1982 are in the region of 98 per cent, 6 per cent and 1 per cent respectively, and of pupils learning French, German and Spanish around 87 per cent, 5 per cent and 0.6 per cent respectively.

The report describes patterns of curricular provision in the schools sampled and examines some of the factors which were seen to be determinants of change: school reorganisation, falling rolls, staffing (reduction, shortage, changes), policy decisions, timetabling problems, and various innovations and experiments. In Chapter 3 we look in detail at the findings of the 1983 APU survey of performance in French, German and Spanish (published in 1985) which eventually emerged.[9]

THE DES POLICY STATEMENT (1988)

In 1983 the first of a series of important DES policy documents was issued, the consultative paper *Foreign Languages in the School Curriculum*.[10] At the time that the DES was formulating a national policy for foreign language provision, the advent of 1992 had assumed a dominant position in the thinking of government planners, and the implications of the changes that the Single Market would bring for national resources in foreign language competence were beginning to loom large. Diversification of FL1 provision was by now seen as essential if the United Kingdom was not to remain out of step with the rest of Europe.

Almost five years separated the publication of the consultative paper from the issuing of the final policy document, *Modern Languages in the School Curriculum: A statement of policy*.[11] Over that period subtle but significant changes were introduced. We shall look particularly at the question of diversification as it affects first and second foreign languages, but that in turn is inextricably related to the wider policy issue of compulsory language learning for all pupils up to age sixteen and its attendant resource implications, particularly for staffing.

In its focus on 'secondary schools before 16' (paragraphs 26–29) the consultative paper left open the question of what proportion of pupils under the age of sixteen should study a modern language and for how long. At this point 'major issues of policy to be decided' included:

- the case for all pupils beginning to learn a foreign language at age 11;
- the possible postponement of the start of foreign language learning for some pupils to age 12, 13 or 14; and
- the means of identifying those, if any, for whom foreign language learning is not appropriate.

In a section headed 'Which languages?' it was recognised that:

> In any case the scope for diversification of provision is limited by the capacity of the existing teaching force, the cost incurred in utilising that capacity differently and the willingness of teachers, pupils, parents and LEAs to adapt.
>
> (paragraph 34)

In terms of costs, 'the economical use of teaching expertise' was deemed to be vital, since it was

> unrealistic to expect that new resources [would] be immediately available to the schools for the improvement of foreign language teaching

on the scale . . . of the 1960s or early 1970s so as to extend the scale of foreign language provision.

(paragraph 55)

The supply of teachers necessary to extend provision and take-up of modern languages, however, was not thought to be a problem. Paragraph 56 opens with the confident statement: 'The supply of foreign language teachers has improved and it seems likely that most of the comparatively few vacancies arising in schools will readily be filled'. Drawing on figures from the Secondary School Staffing Survey of 1977, paragraph 57 adds: 'The evidence . . . suggests that there may be a reserve of teachers able to provide teaching in a wider range of languages than is now the case'. Paragraph 58 suggests that some teachers without a formal qualification in a foreign language 'nevertheless know it sufficiently well to make a valuable contribution to teaching it, especially in oral and conversational work'.

The consultative paper thus clearly ignored a warning of 'grave difficulties' in staffing modern languages made by the Education, Science and Arts Committee in 1981. It acknowledges, however, that because of limitations on financial resources 'it is likely that the pattern of provision, particularly the diversification of the languages taught, can be developed only gradually' (paragraph 55). But it raises questions about potential reserves of talent in the teaching force,[12] about qualifications (and by implication training and retraining) that were later to be addressed specifically in relation to policy on diversification.

In June 1986 a developed version of the consultative document appeared: *Foreign Languages in the School Curriculum: A draft statement of policy*.[13] This publication set the learning of languages firmly in the context of national requirements:

Compared with many trading nations, ours has a damagingly small proportion of people who understand and speak a foreign language. Although our prosperity depends on trade overseas, many companies attempting to export conduct all their business in English. This is possible in markets such as North America and the Commonwealth, but nearly 60 per cent of our exports now go to Western Europe. And even in those non-English speaking countries where the English language has currency, complete reliance on it narrows opportunities in business and other respects.

(paragraph 3)

The three main thrusts of the draft policy statement were:

- that more pupils should study foreign languages throughout compulsory education and beyond;
- that more pupils should have opportunities to study languages other than French; and

– that standards of communication in foreign languages should be improved among pupils of all abilities.

The main target for action was to secure an increase in the take-up of first foreign languages in years four and five, especially among boys. This would entail that 'LEAs and schools should take steps to make a foreign language one of the compulsory elements of the 14–16 curriculum for those pupils who can benefit from it'. In addition, it was proposed that schools should make a second language available as an optional subject in years four and five, possibly from year two or three if curriculum time could be made available from that allocated to all language studies. It was further acknowledged in paragraph 30 that 'policies for widening provision [might] also call for one-off spending in relation to planning, teacher training and the acquisition of materials'.

Many schools, it was recognised, offered German, Spanish or Italian as FL2s, but the number of pupils who took them was small. To increase the uptake of languages other than French it was proposed that some larger schools offering only French as FL1 should consider offering two FL1s and that smaller schools might break altogether with the tradition of French and offer some other language in its place, with French as FL2. It was acknowledged that this might mean that pupils changing schools would not be able to depend on continuity of language study, but paragraph 38 of the document suggests that 'if enough schools offer a range of languages and if LEAs and schools are ready to respond positively to pupils' needs, adverse effects should be minimised'. On the subject of diversification, paragraph 43 concludes:

> The need for diversification is pressing. However, constraints on resources will, to some extent, affect how quickly it can be brought about. The costs of preparing schools and teachers to offer a different or alternative first foreign language will present the education service with difficult decisions about priorities. However, a short term redirection of existing resources, together with careful planning, would enable authorities to tap a resource which is at present wasted. The result nationally would be a richer and more motivating experience for young people and a curriculum better suited to the country's needs.

Much of the rest of the draft policy statement focuses on the desire to improve standards in modern languages, its arguments resting on results of the APU surveys of 1983 and 1984.[14] Paragraph 71 concludes:

> We recognise that some – but by no means all – of the necessary developments will require extra resources, and that the pace of change will depend on the rate at which those resources can be made available. We believe however that much can be done in present circumstances through a recognition of the importance of foreign languages and a determination to make a start on reshaping provision.

The draft policy statement thus acknowledged that in order to implement changes investment of both time and money would be necessary. The pace at which diversification could be introduced would depend upon resource constraints. The goal of a language for all remained a goal and not anything approaching a statutory requirement. A second foreign language was to be offered, possibly from year two or three, and it was recognised that widening the provision of language teaching would call for additional spending in relation to planning, the training of teachers, and the acquisition of new materials.

In 1987 some indication of the extra cost in teaching and material resources necessary to achieve the goal of 'a language for all' was given in an HMI survey with the ludicrous title *An inquiry into practice in 22 comprehensive schools where a foreign language forms part of the curriculum for all or almost all pupils up to age 16.*[15] This document, which we shall call *The 22 Schools*, looked at provision in those schools in which a modern language already formed part of the common curriculum of pupils aged eleven to sixteen. Resourcing French as a compulsory subject to age sixteen was not felt to be an insurmountable problem. In terms of teaching periods, to increase the take-up of foreign languages from the then national average of 42 per cent to the average of 97 per cent in the survey schools, a further 31.8 teacher periods was felt to be necessary – the equivalent of 0.99 of a teacher. However, this was calculated on the basis that 'pupils in the sample schools are taught in larger, more economical groups'.

The findings reported in *The 22 Schools* also had important implications for the teaching of languages other than French. In order to include a language, usually French, as part of the common curriculum, an average 80 per cent of curriculum time was used in delivering the common core, compared with an average of 60 per cent in matched schools which did not include a compulsory language element for all pupils up to age sixteen. This meant that only 20 per cent of time remained available for optional subjects, including a second foreign language. This reduced time available for options in the schools surveyed was noted to have a marked effect on the take-up of FL2s – only 10.1 per cent compared with 13.6 per cent in the matched schools. The likelihood was, therefore, that in schools with the common core extended to include French, 'the second language faces much more competition and the proportion of pupils taking it is likely to be reduced'.

This clearly lent some urgency to the introduction of diversification of FL1 provision if a language were to become part of the common curriculum nationally. Paragraph 120 of *The 22 Schools* includes the statement:

> The most critical aspect of curriculum policy is the relationship between the first and the second foreign languages. Even if more pupils take a

second foreign language in the second or third year, the evidence of the inquiry suggests that it is unlikely to increase the take-up of that language in the fourth year. The major factor affecting the second foreign language in the fourth year would appear to be the proportion of time given to the core curriculum; the more extensive the core, the lower the take-up is likely to be for a second foreign language, all other factors being equal. If the number of pupils taking languages other than French is to be maintained, let alone increased, then the most likely way forward would seem to be to offer these languages more frequently as first or equal first languages.

The report thus had important implications for the government's definitive policy position in *Modern Languages in the School Curriculum: A statement of policy*, issued in February 1988.

By the time that the government was ready to release *Modern Languages in the School Curriculum*, the Education Reform Bill[16] introducing the proposals for a new National Curriculum had been read in Parliament. The policy statement made it clear that: 'The Government's proposals for the national curriculum are that a modern foreign language should be a foundation subject studied by all pupils throughout compulsory schooling'. In anticipation of the passing of the Education Reform Act,[17] paragraph 20 stressed that:

LEAs and schools should take steps now to make continuation of a modern foreign language one of the compulsory elements of the 14–16 curriculum for the great majority of pupils.

On the question of diversification, addressed in paragraphs 30–40, it was made clear, as we have noted in the Introduction, that:

LEAs and schools should ensure that a reasonable proportion of their pupils of all abilities should study a language other than French as their first foreign language. . . . On commercial and cultural grounds, priority should be given to the main languages of the European Community.

(paragraph 32)

As in the draft policy statement, it was again suggested that in order to implement this, larger schools should offer two alternative foreign languages, while smaller schools might offer a language other than French as FL1, retaining French as a second language option. In spite of the fact that twenty months had elapsed between the publication of the draft policy statement and its final version, their wording is virtually identical. There are, however, a limited number of significant shifts of emphasis from one policy statement to the next, influenced, as we have suggested, by the HMI findings in *The 22 Schools*.

As we have seen, *The 22 Schools* had suggested that a language could be made compulsory for all or almost all pupils up to age sixteen without undue stress on resources. This affected policy development in three ways. First, whereas the draft statement focuses on *more pupils* studying a language, the 1988 policy statement talks instead in terms of *the vast majority* of pupils. Second, the draft still refers to the possibility of pupils studying a language for the first three years of secondary education, while the final document makes it clear that pupils are to continue language study throughout the period of compulsory secondary schooling. Third, and perhaps most importantly for schools and LEAs called upon to implement these more demanding policy changes, the draft statement had recognised that widening provision – even to the more limited extent it had proposed – called for 'one-off spending in relation to planning, teacher training and the acquisition of materials', a statement tellingly omitted from the equivalent paragraph of the final document.

There were also significant changes with regard to the provision for FL2s. Whereas the draft statement still retained the notion of introducing a second foreign language for some pupils from years two or three, the final version maintains that this would be 'inconsistent with the central aim of achieving a broad and balanced curriculum in those years', a sinister statement which was to have serious implications for the already precarious situation of the second foreign language.

On the issue of diversification, while the draft statement had simply referred to the dominance of French in secondary schools as 'inappropriate to the needs of a modern trading nation', the final document makes it plain that 'this position is not satisfactory'. Furthermore, while the draft suggested that 'some larger schools . . . should consider offering two first foreign languages', the final statement urges that 'in order to secure diversification, larger schools should . . . offer two alternative first foreign languages', the omission of the words 'some' and 'consider' lending much greater weight to the government's support for diversification of FL1 provision. Once again, however, reference to the costs of implementing this policy was cut. Whereas the draft statement acknowledged that 'the costs of preparing schools and teachers to offer a different or alternative first foreign language will present the education service with difficult decisions about priorities', this sentence appears in the final version with the words 'the costs of' omitted, thus significantly altering its import. Finally, the opening statement of the concluding paragraph of the document was amended from the draft form

> We recognise that some – but by no means all – of the necessary developments will require extra resources, and that the pace of change will depend on the rate at which these extra resources can be made available

to

> We expect that the resources currently devoted to local policies for modern foreign language teaching will be directed in support of the policies outlined in this statement.

The policy statement of February 1988 was thus considerably more demanding of schools and LEAs than the preceding draft, while at the same time indicating that all necessary changes had to be made within existing resources.

POLICY AND DIVERSIFICATION

The development of a national policy for modern languages, despite the government's failure to provide proper extra resources to implement it, was in the main at least welcomed as an indication of seriousness of intent. Cynics would point out, however, that political considerations were the real motivating factor behind the posturing: no government of an EC country, contemplating the Single Market of 1992 and cognizant of Community policy statements anticipating a time when *all* pupils would be learning *two* foreign languages, could fail to declare itself in favour of all pupils learning *one* foreign language throughout the period of compulsory schooling. Nor could such a government ignore the advantages of proposing that more than just one of its partners' languages should be taught in its schools. It was, indeed, expected by the Community that 'at least one of the languages taught [in Member States] should be an official language of the European Communities'.[18] Such a political dimension in policy making would become more clearly manifest in the aftermath of the passing of the Education Reform Act in 1988.

In the year before the appearance of the DES statement of policy, Her Majesty's Inspectorate had produced an addition to its 'Curriculum Matters' series, the report on *Modern Foreign Languages to 16*.[19] It has of course become increasingly difficult to separate HMI from the DES. The supposedly independent Inspectorate has been too closely involved in policy-making processes for there to remain much of a distinction between views expressed in DES documents and those in HMI reports on similar subjects. We would not expect, therefore, that there would be any divergence of views between their respective statements on modern languages.

Modern Foreign Languages to 16, as we have noted in the Introduction, constituted a clear statement of intent *vis-à-vis* diversification policy. Paragraphs 64 and 65 emphasise the need for a wider range of languages to be taught ('particularly those of our European trading partners'), declare that there is an untapped pool of teachers able to teach languages other than French (especially German and Spanish), and call on LEAs to develop policies on diversification.

Paragraphs 67 and 68 deal with the second foreign language, and it is here that great damage was done. The Inspectorate – and we may surmise that the Staff Inspector for modern languages of the time was chiefly responsible – came out in favour of the second foreign language being delayed until year four, thus contemplating its removal altogether from the lower school curriculum. Many linguists had been arguing that the second foreign language was already at a considerable disadvantage as a result of its not being introduced in most schools until year three. A start in year two would have been greatly preferable if something approaching parity with the first foreign language were to be reached.

This consideration became increasingly important with the introduction of the new General Certificate of Secondary Education (GCSE) syllabuses, which demanded the kind of preparation not generally possible in a short course. Though this latter point was conceded in the HMI's document – 'two years is a short time in which to achieve [the standard required] without recourse to narrow objectives and restricting methods' – the main argument for the recommended delayed FL2 start had to do with the cornerstone of DES policy, the National Curriculum. At a time when policy was developing inexorably towards the notion of commonality of curricular provision in maintained schools, the problems always created by the introduction of a second foreign language in years two or three could no longer be easily tolerated; the task was to preserve 'balance' in the curriculum:

> While the intention of most schools is to provide a common curriculum over the first three years, the inclusion of a second foreign language, by whatever ingenious arrangements, distorts the balance of that curriculum, and not only for those pupils who elect to take a second language. The most desirable solution seems therefore to be to offer the second foreign language from the beginning of the fourth year when option choices are made.

This effective demotion of the second foreign language was welcome news to many headteachers and their timetablers who had grappled for years with the very real problems involved in accommodating a second foreign language in the lower school curriculum, and it was a considerable setback for languages other than French in those schools without diversified FL1 provision. That such a recommendation should have originated with the Inspectorate is the more deplorable since its members were in a better position than most to appreciate the very good arguments in favour of an early start to the second foreign language, even for those pupils with proven ability in the language begun in year one. A senior member of the Inspectorate later publicly regretted the recommendation and its effects.[20]

The recommendation and its justification were reiterated in *Modern Languages in the School Curriculum: A statement of policy* in the following year, the policy position finding expression in paragraph 22:

> **A second foreign language should . . . be offered wherever possible for able and committed pupils.** But after careful consideration of the timing of the introduction of a second foreign language we have concluded that the practice of offering a second language from year 2 or 3 is

inconsistent with the central aim of achieving a broad and balanced curriculum in those years. **So schools should make available second foreign languages as an optional subject from year 4.** [Original emphasis]

The succession of DES and HMI documents we have described paved the way for decisions at government level about the modern language component of the National Curriculum. Though the Bill of 1987 and the Education Reform Act of 1988 devoted no space to the detail of what compulsory foreign language study from eleven to sixteen would actually entail, they sparked off a chain of developments that would form the framework for modern language provision in maintained schools in the 1990s. We shall consider those developments in some detail, but first it is necessary to describe an important government initiative that was to do much to highlight the issue of diversification and to encourage LEAs to develop policies that would enable it to become a reality.

THE 'ESG AUTHORITIES'

The need to develop clear policies for diversification at both local and national levels was given additional impetus in 1988, when a government-funded pilot project on diversification was begun. Its task was to examine the feasibility of introducing languages other than French as first foreign languages in a number of LEAs. This project, together with some very valuable work on in-service training (INSET) being undertaken at the same time by Michael Calvert at the University of York,[21] helped to raise the profile of languages other than French against the background of the most important policy developments ever for modern languages generally.

In a draft Circular of 30 July 1987, bids for a share of an Education Support Grant (ESG) were invited from 'LEAs in which high standards of foreign language teaching have been achieved and where a measure of diversification in first foreign languages provision already exists or where there is a firm commitment to the principle of diversification'.[22] A total of forty-three LEAs submitted applications, and ten were selected to participate in the scheme: Avon, Birmingham, Bolton, Buckinghamshire, Croydon, Essex, Hampshire, Havering, Lancashire and Staffordshire. They provided between them not only a wide geographical spread but also a considerable variety of provision. Some authorities, such as Hampshire, had over 100 secondary schools, while others, like Bolton and Havering, had fewer than twenty. In some LEAs there were middle schools with secondary transfer at 13+, and in others selective systems were still operating.

For the first year of the pilot scheme, £30,000 was allocated to each LEA to fund the appointment of diversification co-ordinators, who would identify schools within their authority in a position to diversify their foreign language provision. Criteria for selection of the schools varied from authority to authority, but included the spread of languages and geographical location within the LEA, different diversification models, the qualifications of the staff and the commitment of the schools to diversification. In the two very small authorities no selection criteria were needed, since all as yet undiversified schools could be included. The brief of the co-ordinators was to assist the schools in planning and preparing for diversification, to investigate teacher shortages in languages other than French and to identify teachers not teaching languages in which they were qualified, to organise appropriate INSET courses, and to disseminate information to interested parties. Thus it was planned to address a number of policy issues (planning, staffing, training) which had been identified over a number of years of debate.

In the second year of the scheme (1989–90), £50,000 was allocated to each participating LEA to cover the cost of resources and INSET in the schools concerned. Funding for the third year (for diversification schemes in other LEAs) was deferred until 1991–2.

Work in the ESG authorities was conducted at considerable pace, and it attracted much attention locally and nationally. The specially appointed co-ordinators met regularly, made their plans for development available through the Centre for Information on Language Teaching and Research (CILT),[23] spoke at local, regional and national conferences on diversification, and generally created an awareness of the need for diversification and an enthusiasm for change.

As we shall see, the work in the ten ESG authorites was evaluated both by the NFER[24] and in a brief report from Her Majesty's Inspectors.[25] As that work was continuing, policy developments at national level were proceeding apace.

THE EDUCATION REFORM ACT AND ITS AFTERMATH

The Education Reform Act (ERA) includes a modern foreign language for all pupils aged eleven to sixteen among the 'foundation' subjects of the National Curriculum. The text makes no specific reference to diversification; it provides, however, for the Secretary of State to issue an Order specifying which languages might be taught as the National Curriculum language:

> the other foundation subjects are – . . .
> (b) in relation to the third and fourth key stages,[26] a modern foreign language specified in an order of the Secretary of State.

And in an Order issued in May 1989 the two 'schedules' of languages which would fulfil the requirements of Section 3(2)(b) of the Act were published.[27] A DES Circular[28] listed the criteria by which the languages which would now qualify as a foundation subject had been selected:

> The first modern language studied should

(*a*) extend the pupil's linguistic knowledge, skills and understanding;
(*b*) lay a foundation for learning any subsequent languages;
(*c*) widen the pupil's cultural horizons and promote international understanding; and
(*d*) be of practical value in future employment, for trading purposes, or in adult life more generally.

It would be invidious to speculate about which languages would *not* fit these particular criteria; Swedish (with nine million speakers) or Polish (with thirty-five million), to name but two European languages which come to mind, would surely not be ineligible.

The first schedule consisted of the eight 'working languages' of the EC: Danish, Dutch, French, German, Modern Greek, Italian, Portuguese and Spanish. The second was a mixture of eleven non-EC languages, including various community languages widely spoken in the UK: Arabic, Bengali, Chinese (Cantonese or Mandarin), Gujerati, Modern Hebrew, Hindi, Japanese, Panjabi, Russian, Turkish and Urdu. Schools were required to offer at least one language from the first schedule as the first foreign language; they would be able to offer in addition any language from the second schedule, and that language could be chosen by pupils as their 'National Curriculum language', *provided that* an EC language was also on offer.

The two schedules, creating as they did the impression of a classification into first- and second-class languages, proved highly controversial. Those involved with 'community' languages were outraged that the languages for whose place on the curriculum they had long been fighting were not accorded parity with European languages; Russian teachers were offended by the assumption that a language like Danish appeared to be more important than the mother tongue of some 150 million people. The schedules were of course again determined by a political consideration: the government could not allow an EC language to be perceived as less important than a non-EC language, nor could it ignore the Community's expectation that at least one of the languages taught should be an 'official' EC language. Later developments removed the division while still granting precedence to the languages of Britain's European partners.

As with the other National Curriculum subjects, a working group was set up to advise on attainment targets and programmes of study, and to address various other issues. Among matters which were specifically requested[29] to be covered in the group's initial advice were:

– any grounds for changing the lists of modern foreign languages which may, in accordance with the Order made under Section 3(2)(b) of the Education Reform Act, be offered to pupils as the National Curriculum language;
– circumstances in which it may be inappropriate for a pupil to study the same language throughout the five years of key stages 3 and 4.

The working group's *Initial Advice*[30] appeared in 1990 and devoted considerable space to the schedules. The group recognised that the format decided upon reflected 'the central position of the EC languages in terms of their value in commerce and employment, particularly with the advent of the Single Market in 1992 and the UK's obligations to its Community partners', but it expressed its concern about the 'hierarchy of languages' implied by the schedules. It therefore recommended that the Order be revised so that the languages included would appear on a single list; the working group concluded, however, that 'each pupil must be offered the opportunity of choosing to study a working language of the EC to meet the National Curriculum modern foreign language requirements'. There was therefore no *de facto* change in the requirements of the Order: the group's recommendation was simply a device to avoid the distinctions created by the original schedules.

The Working Group's final report, submitted in July 1990 and published in October of that year,[31] confirmed the recommendation of the Initial Advice. In May 1991 the National Curriculum Council (NCC) in turn published its report[32] on the statutory consultation which had taken place following the publication of the Working Group's document (which itself of course constituted the *de facto* proposals of the Secretary of State). Some 80 per cent of the 294 responses the NCC had received on the matter of the Section 3 Order had proved to be in favour of the suggested revision, and so the Council in turn recommended that the Order be revised accordingly.

In July 1991 the Secretary of State issued a draft Order for modern foreign languages in the National Curriculum.[33] That Order limited itself to attainment targets and programmes of study, but in a written answer to a Parliamentary Question on the day of its publication, Kenneth Clarke indicated his acceptance of the NCC's recommendation on the Section 3 Order and his intention to issue a new Order in November 1991.[34] Thus a compromise was reached which mitigated the offence caused by the two schedules but left the position of precedence for EC languages in effect unchanged.

The Secretary of State had used the occasion of the annual North of England Conference in January 1991 to make a major speech including an announcement of some importance for modern foreign languages:

> I agree with NCC that all pupils must study technology and a modern foreign language at key stage 4. However, I do not consider that all should be required to study these subjects to GCSE or equivalent qualifications. Many pupils will of course do so but, for others, shorter courses in these subjects should also be available.[35]

He went on to instance combined subjects ('business studies with French') and to suggest that certification might be provided for such courses by the vocational examining bodies.

There had been much discussion of teacher shortages in modern languages, variously estimated around a figure of some 2,000. Without an increased teaching force of approximately that order it was reckoned that the National Curriculum could not be delivered. The Working Group's final report, using government projections, had put the figure at 1,750, but it quoted estimates of 3,000 by the National Association of Head Teachers and the Association for Language Learning. Hawkins and Lawrence had sounded the alarm about the complacency of the DES in the 'acute problem' that schools would have with staffing, in two articles published in the summer of 1988 in which they also quote a figure of 3,000 as the number of extra teachers required to cope with the increased teaching in the fourth and fifth years.[36] A report from the NFER[37] had addressed itself to unused knowledge of foreign languages among the teaching force and to updating and retraining needs. By the autumn of 1988 the DES was undertaking a trawl of initial teacher training (ITT) institutions to identify what expertise they could provide in languages other than French and what INSET they could offer to upgrade 'rusty language skills for serving teachers'.[38] In March 1990 the DES had extended the ITT bursary scheme to include modern foreign languages.[39]

A cynical view of the Secretary of State's announcement, given the obvious potential staffing problems, might postulate that a *lessening* of the requirement for key stage 4 (pupils aged fourteen to sixteen) would help to ensure that *all* pupils in the age group concerned would be receiving some sort of foreign language teaching, though not quite of the kind originally envisaged, nor of the kind common in other EC countries. It is frankly unlikely that his decision would have been made on purely educational grounds, which would have implied an admission that some children would not be able to cope with the National Curriculum requirements. The suggestion that some of those children *not* working towards GCSE (and therefore presumably not deemed *able* to do so) might instead be following a course in 'business studies with French' is, to echo a phrase, pie in the sky.

What was not clear from the Secretary of State's statement was the extent to which his use of the term 'shorter courses' might imply the possibility of schools offering pupils the opportunity to study two or more languages *in succession*, a potentially attractive option under the umbrella of diversification for those pupils who have demonstrably reached a 'ceiling' (for whatever reason) in a language started at age eleven. The Education Reform Act's mention of 'a modern foreign language' as a foundation subject had been quickly interpreted by HMI to mean *one* language, and this has indeed been the DES assumption. Clarke's pronouncement, while clearly watering down the National Curriculum expectations for key stage 4, seemed to open the way for various alternative models.

We have noted above the work on diversification proceeding in the ten

'ESG authorities'. The NFER had been involved in evaluating that work, and so too had the Inspectorate. In September 1991 HMI issued a report on a survey, undertaken in the spring and summer of 1990, of thirty-one schools in the authorities in question.[40]

On the positive side HMI reported a significant increase of those learning German, with 'modest' increases for Spanish and Italian; positive teacher and pupil responses to diversification; a higher quality of work in 'diversified' languages than in French for pupils in the early stages of learning and evidence of effective in-service training. Negative factors included 'a poorer overall match between teachers' qualifications and the languages taught' and by implication a below-standard command of the target language in the use of the teachers; lack of attention to an appropriate ratio of teaching groups to take into account teacher qualifications; an inadequate time allocation when time available is simply divided between two languages; and problems in areas with middle schools introducing a change of language at age twelve.

The document, though encouraging about diversification, is a typically anodyne HMI report; broad generalisations sit alongside fussy attention to the detail of display and blackout.

TOWARDS THE NEW CENTURY

We concluded our account of the historical development of thinking about diversification with the important HMI report of 1977, *Modern Languages in Comprehensive Schools*.[41] That report, as we have seen, marked the end of a long period of complacency about modern language provision in schools and the beginning of a serious debate about standards and the rethinking that would be necessary to create improvement. The succeeding decade saw the development of a proper national policy for foreign language teaching and the formal securing of the subject in the now accepted notion of a compulsory curriculum.

The Schools Council and the APU had produced studies addressing major issues (languages other than French, second foreign languages, performance in the most widely taught languages) and moving the debate inexorably towards the formulation of some kind of policy framework within which the many problems might be solved. The combined forces of the DES and HMI enabled a national policy position to be agreed over a relatively short period in the late 1980s, and the 1988 Act saw the long-expressed hope that foreign language study might one day be compulsory for all 11–16 year olds become a potential reality.

The issue of diversification had achieved a secure place in the discussions, and had at last become a cornerstone of government policy. The Education Reform Act, though making no specific reference to the subject, allowed the Secretary of State to take steps to formalise the expectation that many more schools would be offering their pupils the chance to study a 'diversified' language as their National Curriculum language. Through the device of making (limited) funds available to LEAs through an Education Support Grant, the DES was able to promote the cause of diversification in a way that attracted considerable national attention.

Thus the way was set for a potential expansion, throughout the 1990s and into the twenty-first century, of the teaching of languages other than French in a way that enthusiasts like Allison Peers had argued for so convincingly. But a policy only provides the framework for delivery: in the following chapters we shall look in detail at research findings on diversification and at the practical problems which affect its implementation.

NOTES

1 Welsh Office, *A Survey of Modern Languages in the Secondary Schools of Wales* (= Education Survey 11), Cardiff, HMSO, 1983, p. 12.
2 Ibid., p. 14.
3 *Guidelines for the Teaching of Modern Languages: A document for discussion*, Nottinghamshire County Council, October 1978. Cf. also, among other similar documents, *A Working Party Report on Modern Language Teaching in Oxfordshire: Some notes of guidance for language departments*, Oxfordshire County Council, September 1980.
4 See: David Phillips and Veronica Stencel, *The Second Foreign Language: Past development, current trends and future prospects*, London, Hodder & Stoughton, 1983, p. 109.
5 C.G. Hadley, *Languages other than French in the Secondary School: An exploratory study of other languages as first or equal first foreign languages*, London, Schools Council, 1981.
6 Schools Council, *The Second Foreign Language in Secondary Schools: A question of survival* (Series: Occasional Bulletins from the Subject Committees), London, 1982.
7 Culminating in: Department of Education and Science (DES)/Welsh Office (WO), *The National Curriculum 5–16: A consultation document*, London, July 1987.
8 Assessment of Performance Unit (APU), *Foreign Language Provision*, Occasional Paper 2, London, DES, June 1983.
9 APU, *Foreign Language Performance in Schools: Report on 1983 survey of French, German and Spanish*, London, DES, 1985.
10 DES/WO, *Foreign Languages in the School Curriculum: A consultative paper*, London, 1983.
11 DES/WO, *Modern Languages in the School Curriculum: A statement of policy*, London, HMSO, 1988.
12 In a small-scale study of the position of second foreign languages in Oxfordshire schools undertaken in 1980, it was found that in some 71 per cent of the schools sampled there were teachers able to teach a language other than French who were not doing so; they included no fewer than four teachers of Russian in one school! (Veronica Stencel and David Phillips, *Second Foreign Languages: An investigation into organisation, teaching methods and pupils' attitudes in Oxfordshire schools*, Oxford, University of Oxford Department of Educational Studies, 1982.)

13 DES, *Foreign Languages in the School Curriculum: A draft statement of policy*, London, June 1986.

14 The 1984 survey, concerned only with French, is: APU, *Foreign Language Performance in Schools. Report on 1984 survey of French*, London, DES, 1986.

15 DES, 1987 (inquiry carried out during the autumn term of 1985).

16 *Education Reform Bill*, London, HMSO, November 1987.

17 *Education Reform Act*, London, HMSO, 1988, Ch. 40.

18 'Conclusions of the Council and the Minutes of education meeting within the Council, Luxembourg, 4 June 1984, on the teaching of foreign languages', paragraph 4; in 'The teaching of languages in the European Community', *Eurydice*, 1988.

19 DES, *Modern Foreign Languages to 16* (= Curriculum Matters 8), London, HMSO, 1987.

20 Michael Salter, speaking at the 1990 ALL conference in Exeter, as reported in the press: '"I think we were wrong," he told the conference. "With hindsight, I think it should start earlier"', *TES*, 30 March 1990.

21 See particularly: Michael Calvert, 'INSET and Diversification', in David Phillips (ed.), *Which Language? Diversification and the National Curriculum*, London, Hodder & Stoughton, 1989; Michael Calvert, *Towards Diversification*, York, Language Teaching Centre, University of York, 1989.

22 Extracts from the Draft Circular are provided in an appendix to Peter Dickson and Barbara Lee: Diversification of foreign languages in schools: The ESG Pilot Programme, Slough, NFER, 1990, p. 58.

23 Materials from the ESG authorities were made available through the Centre for Information on Language Teaching and Research (CILT) in January and March/April 1989 (documentation headed 'Diversification of first foreign language: Education [*sic*] Support Grant pilot project', London, CILT.

24 National Foundation for Educational Research (NFER), *Diversification of First Foreign Language in Schools* (Interim Report on the NFER Evaluation of the ESG Pilot Programme) Slough, n.d.; Peter Dickson and Barbara Lee, *Evaluation of ESG Programme of Diversification of First Foreign Language* (Project Report), Slough 1990; this latter pre-publication version of the evaluation was subsequently issued as: Peter Dickson and Barbara Lee, *Diversification of Foreign Languages in Schools: The ESG pilot programme*, Slough, August 1990.

25 DES, *Diversification of the First Foreign Language in a Sample of Secondary Schools* (spring and summer terms 1990; a report by HMI), London 1991.

26 In other words, pupils aged 11–16.

27 The Order was laid before Parliament on 19 May. A draft Order (which did not include Modern Hebrew) had been issued by the DES on 3 March 1989.

28 DES, *The Education Reform Act 1988: Modern Foreign Languages in the National Curriculum*, Circular No. 9/89, 19 May 1989.

29 DES, 'National Curriculum Modern Foreign Languages Working Group: Terms of reference', issued with *DES News*, 261/89, 15 August 1989.

30 DES, *National Curriculum Modern Foreign Languages Working Group: Initial advice*, London, 1990.

31 DES, *Modern Foreign Languages for Ages 11 to 16* (Proposals of the Secretary of State for Education and Science and the Secretary of State for Wales), London, HMSO, October 1990.

32 National Curriculum Council (NCC), *Modern Foreign Languages in the National Curriculum* (a report to the Secretary of State for Education and Science on the statutory consultation for attainment targets and programmes of study in modern foreign languages), London, 1991.

33 DES, *National Curriculum: Draft order for modern foreign languages*, London, 11 July 1991

34 *DES News* 229/91, 11 July 1991.

35 *DES News* 2/91, 4 January 1991, contains the full text of the speech.

36 Eric Hawkins and Gordon Lawrence, 'Modern language teachers – an endangered species', *Education*, 24 June 1988, pp. 537–8; 'Survival course for language teachers', *Education*, 1 July 1988, pp. 10–11. The shortage of modern language teachers was also discussed by Ted Wragg ('Foreign policies', *TES*, 18 March 1988) and later by Bob Powell ('Foreign language teacher supply: Continuity, opportunity and quality control', *Language Learning Journal*, Vol. 1, No. 1, March 1990).

37 Felicity Rees, *Languages for a Change: Diversifying foreign language provision in schools*, Windsor, NFER-Nelson, 1989.

38 DES, Teacher Training Circular letter 8/88: 'Increasing teachers of modern languages', October 1988.

39 *DES News*, 84/90: 'More funds for teacher training bursary scheme', 12 March 1990.

40 DES, *Diversification of the First Modern Foreign Language in a Sample of Secondary Schools*, A report by HMI, London, 1991.

41 DES, *Modern Languages in Comprehensive Schools* (= HMI series: Matters for Discussion 3), London, HMSO, 1977.

3 Previous research on languages other than French

INTRODUCTION

So far we have described the development of policy towards diversification in its historical context, citing evidence from various government and professional sources and the writings of individuals who have played a prominent part in carrying the debate forward, or at least keeping it alive. Much of such documentation is subjective in nature, based sometimes on assertion and at other times on reasoned argument, using where possible statistical information and such objective evidence as can be collected through direct personal experience or planned observation.

But from the mid-1960s a body of respectable research evidence began to become available, based on work in the UK, that would make a useful contribution to the diversification debate. In the past, major research projects on modern languages in schools had tended to concentrate largely on the psychology of language acquisition, on how children learn, rather than on such matters as relative attainment, or teacher/pupil attitude, or the identification of organisational problems within schools. Reports like *Primary French in the Balance*[1] of 1974 and *The Language Laboratory in School*[2] of 1975 heralded a new era of empirical research in modern languages which looked at actual classroom experience and developed instruments to measure such phenomena as attitude or aptitude or attainment.

In this chapter we shall be concerned with research in modern languages which has a direct bearing on diversification, examining first the studies which have focused on the organisational issues arising when languages other than French are on offer as FL1s, such as questions of staffing and timetabling, and then considering work which has investigated the key factors influencing pupils' experience of learning various languages and schools' views on the educational benefits of diversifying language provision. The aim of the chapter is to show how previous research provides a framework and background for the Oxford Project on Diversification of First Foreign Language Teaching (OXPROD), which forms the core of this book.

RESEARCH ON ORGANISATIONAL ISSUES

One of the first research studies to focus exclusively on the practical concerns related to the provision of languages other than French as FL1s was that carried out by the Schools Council from 1979 to 1980, to which reference has been made in the Introduction.[3] The aim of the report which emerged (known as the Hadley Report) was to provide schools and LEAs with information on problems encountered when languages other than French were introduced as FL1s, which would enable them to make better-informed decisions about their language provision. A questionnaire was sent to a total of seventy-nine schools where languages other than French had been established as sole or equal FL1s for a number of years. The questionnaire was designed to investigate staffing, patterns of organisation, time allocation, options systems, numbers of boys and girls learning languages, the position of the FL2 and the schools' reasons for adopting a language other than French as FL1. From the larger sample some twenty-three schools were selected for more detailed study. These varied in size, geographical position and age span, and included mixed and single-sex schools teaching German, Spanish, Italian and Russian in a variety of patterns. Returns from the questionnaire provided insights into the advantages of teaching languages other than French and the problems in introducing them. However, it was found, encouragingly, that many of the organisational problems raised in 'diversified' schools (such as the prevalence of double periods on the timetable, insufficient frequency of contact with pupils, setting difficulties and unsympathetic options systems) were exactly those mentioned by schools where French was the FL1. In fact, in schools where languages were well organised and the teachers committed, languages other than French flourished as much as French. The working party's conclusions, headed by the confident statement that 'There is nothing in the nature of a language other than French or in its teaching context that makes it either more or less feasible than French as first foreign language in a secondary school',[4] suggested that the introduction of diversified language provision would be unproblematic from an organisational viewpoint. The study did not, however, attempt to look at linguistic advantages to the learner of the languages in question, or indeed at the experience of the pupils learning them. This would be the focus of further research studies in the 1980s, which will be discussed later in this chapter.

On the question of staffing, the Hadley Committee found that participating schools had encountered no greater problems in finding teachers of languages other than French. In fact, schools with languages other than French as FL1s were found to attract a better field of candidates for vacancies than those where these languages were FL2s. It was recognised, however, that staffing would become a problem if provision of languages other than French were to expand rapidly.

Indeed, with increasing calls for the expansion of the teaching of languages other than French in various policy documents of the 1980s, described in Chapter 2, the issue of staffing was to become central in research into the feasibility of diversification of FL1 teaching. In 1987, for example, a research project entitled 'Languages other than French: teaching qualification and experience', which was reported by Rees in *Languages for a Change*,[5] was started by the NFER. Its aims were to provide information on the language qualifications and skills of the pool of teachers with expertise in languages other than French identified by the DES in their draft statement of policy,[6] and to assess their current situation and retraining needs. The four key areas of concern in the project were teachers' qualifications, their past and present teaching experience, the degree to which they had maintained their language skills, and their views on retraining. The sample of teachers included those who held any advanced qualifications in a language other than French and were either not teaching that language at all or teaching it only to a low level.

From September 1987 to August 1988 a total of 488 teachers completed questionnaires, and a further twenty-five teachers took part in follow-up interviews. Results from the survey revealed that there was a small number of qualified teachers whose language skills were sufficient to be able to teach German, Spanish, Italian or Russian without substantial retraining, but that a large number would need a period of intensive language work, ideally in the foreign country, to restore their confidence and fluency in the language in which they were qualified. Furthermore, some teachers with unexploited expertise would not be available to teach a language other than French, either because they were in senior management, or approaching retirement, or simply because they were unwilling to change. The report gave a more realistic picture of the numbers of teachers who might be redeployed to teach languages other than French and concluded that while there was some scope to expand provision of such languages by diversifying FL1 provision, many teachers would need substantial retraining. This, it was stressed, would entail good preparation and long-term planning at school, local and national level if existing human resources were to be utilised effectively.

The question of staffing for languages other than French was also investigated at a local level alongside other organisational problems within the government-funded pilot project on diversification of FL1 teaching, described in Chapter 2. The work in the ten LEAs selected for participation in the scheme was evaluated by the NFER in a twelve-month period overlapping the first two years of the pilot project and summarised in a report published in 1990.[7] The aims of the project were to assist the pilot schemes, to support local monitoring and evaluation, to help disseminate information about implementation of the schemes, and to guide the formulation of LEA and national policy when diversification was implemented more widely.

The evaluation was conducted in three phases. First, the co-ordinators' factual reports held at CILT on the preparatory work in the LEAs were consulted and each of the co-ordinators was interviewed. Then the reports submitted by the co-ordinators to the DES were reviewed and visits were made to a sample of fifteen schools selected from five of the LEAs in order to interview headteachers, heads of department and teachers involved in the scheme. Finally, a return visit was made to each of the ten LEAs to interview the co-ordinators and language advisers, and a round table discussion of the issues was held with the co-ordinators at the NFER. The findings of the evaluation, drawn from the opinions and experience both of those interviewed within the schools and of the co-ordinators and LEA advisers, were summarised in terms of recruitment and training, planning and organisation in schools, and implications for LEAs and national policy. These matters will be considered in more detail in Chapter 6.

In the second year of the pilot project the work in the ten LEAs was also the subject of an HMI study conducted to evaluate the impact of the introduction of diversification on teaching and learning. HMI's observations, published as a report entitled *Diversification of the First Foreign Language in a Sample of Secondary Schools*,[8] derive mainly from visits to some thirty-one schools in the pilot authorities and two schools in other authorities in the spring and summer terms of 1990, but also from schools visited by HMI for other reasons that year.

The report is based on observation of lessons and discussions with pupils and teachers, and it focuses, among other things, on the quality of work in French and 'diversified' languages, curricular planning, pupils' views, organisational patterns, staffing and resources. HMI's findings revealed diversification to be stimulating for teachers and popular with pupils, headteachers and parents. It was also felt that the quality of work in languages other than French was significantly higher than in French, though this was attributed to the experience, enthusiasm and good teaching methods of the staff involved in teaching these languages rather than factors related to the individual languages. Unfortunately, the report gives very little indication as to how the study was carried out or how the quality of work or pupils' experience of language learning was assessed, and it provides therefore no real evidence on the educational benefits of diversified language provision. It does, however, consider in its recommendations some of the organisational issues associated with a policy of diversified provision which will be discussed in Chapter 6.

The research described above is concerned with the practicalities of introducing languages other than French as FL1s, and clearly such concerns play a vital role in discussions on the feasibility of diversification at both school and national level. Other studies, however, have taken a different slant, in examining the advantages to the *pupil* in learning languages other than French. Empirical work in schools has focused in particular on issues such as language aptitude, pupils' attainment in different languages, and their attitudes towards language learning. Before research in these areas is examined, however, we shall consider briefly the question of language difficulty, which inevitably contributes to the debate as to which languages should be taught as FL1s across the ability range.

LANGUAGE DIFFICULTY

A body of analytical work exists on the linguistic factors in different languages which make them 'easy' or 'difficult' to learn,[9] but very little of the writing on the subject or of the views on the difficulty of various languages is based on research with foreign language learners. For example, a subjective but nonetheless useful impression of the relative difficulty of the five languages most commonly taught in British schools was presented by C.V. James in a paper of 1978 in which he estimated the 'linguistic distance' from English of French, German, Spanish, Italian and Russian.[10] In James's view the language most *distant* from English would also be the most *difficult* for the English-speaking learner, and his calculations, which took into account the phonology, grammar, lexis, orthography and spelling of the five languages, placed Italian closest to English and Russian the most distant.

Eric Hawkins points out, on the other hand, that degree of distance cannot always be equated with degree of difficulty: while problems with the pronunciation of the foreign language might arise because the sounds which learners are expected to produce are very unlike the sounds in their own language, a marked contrast between languages, for example, on a grammatical level, might actually facilitate learning.[11] Hawkins, who refers to the problems caused by linguistic distance as 'inter-language interference', defines a second source of error, 'intra-language interference', or the internal contradictions within languages (such as 'illogical gender' in German or inconsistent spelling in English) which will be a source of confusion for the learner.[12]

With these two distinct kinds of error in mind it is possible to pinpoint areas in different languages which might pose problems for the learner. The case system in German, and pronunciation and spelling (i.e. the relationship between the spoken and the written language) in French, for example, are potential areas of difficulty which will be familiar to anyone who has taught these languages. It is impossible, however, to view linguistic difficulty in isolation from the many other factors on which the difficulty of a language depends. These include a variety of factors in the language learning environment, such as the size and composition of the teaching group, the length, timing and frequency of the lessons, and availability of resources, as well as more fundamental factors such as the teacher's relationship with the class, teaching method and style. Vitally important too are factors related to the learner: the native language of the learner and its similarity to English, for example, will determine the extent of 'inter-language' interference which the learner has to overcome. In addition to this, previous experience of learning a language may well influence learners' perceptions of it. Finally, the learner's general ability and language learning aptitude will, of course, determine how easy or difficult the language is found to be. These complex and numerous factors help to explain the fact that empirical classroom studies of pupils' learning have not attempted to compare different languages in terms of their linguistic difficulty, though there have been studies in *comparative linguistics* which have touched on questions of complexity.

LANGUAGE APTITUDE

Language aptitude testing[13] impinges on our consideration of which languages pupils might learn in two respects: a measure of aptitude could give a *general* indication of how pupils might perform in language classes, and therefore could be used for *selection* purposes (particularly for FL2 teaching) or to identify pupils who have *not* been selected by other means (such as performance in FL1), and it could provide an indication of *language-specific* ability. In addition, consideration might be given to the question of ability in *specific areas* of language learning (listening comprehension, reading, etc.).

Ann Miller has described the difficulties involved in devising tests of 'generalisable' aptitude, as contrasted with aptitude in the various skills which make up 'ability' in a particular language. Since 'general' linguistic aptitude is so complex a concept, most aptitude tests limit themselves to testing quite *specific* aspects of language aptitude. A test developed in Oxford in the early 1980s, for example, was specific to German and concentrated in its final version on memory and listening ability, i.e. the aspects which emerged as the best predictors of ability during piloting of the test.

The most widely used test in the UK is that devised by Peter Green in the mid-1970s, generally known as the 'York Aptitude Test'. This test, administered to grammar-school pupils, was originally devised to provide controls in experiments on language teaching method and to create uniformly mixed-ability teaching groups for an investigation of the effectiveness of the language laboratory. It uses Swedish, and requires pupils to manipulate various simple grammatical forms in that language: it is therefore rooted in a language learning tradition which could be said to have been overtaken by approaches centred on 'communicative' methodology, in which strict grammatical accuracy is not such an important indicator of competence as it previously was. It remains, however, the best means available to test the aptitude of first-year beginners, and is the one chosen for use in OXPROD's project schools.

PUPIL ATTAINMENT

Another way to assess the easiness or difficulty of various languages might be to examine and compare the attainment of pupils across languages, but owing to the many variables already described which influence pupils' experience of foreign languages (such as the learner's ability, the language learning environment and teaching styles), information on pupils' attainment can only be viewed as a superficial means of gauging the relative accessibility of languages.

While research has been undertaken on pupils' achievement in languages, very little work exists which examines the question of pupil attainment across a number of languages. For example, the major NFER survey of pupils' levels of achievement and their attitudes towards language learning in primary and secondary schools carried out in the 1960s and 1970s, was focused exclusively on French.[14] Similarly, much of the APU's work in the 1980s on foreign language performance centred on the attainment of secondary school pupils in French only.[15]

The exception to this was an APU survey of 1983 which aimed to provide information on levels of attainment of pupils across the whole ability range in French, German and Spanish.[16] Schools were selected for participation in the study on the basis of information on FL1 provision gathered in the autumn of 1982 by the Monitoring Services Unit at the NFER.[17] All in all, 469 schools took part (283 with French, 151 with German and 35 with Spanish as FL1), with a total of 4,989 pupils learning French, 4,300 learning German and 2,901 learning Spanish. The pupils in the sample all had their thirteenth birthday in the school year 1982–3, were approaching their second year of learning French, German or Spanish as FL1 at secondary school, and were currently studying the language for at least seventy-five minutes per week. Their attainment was tested discretely in the four language learning skills of listening, speaking, reading and writing and in eighteen topic areas such as 'family', 'pastimes', 'holidays' and 'food and drink'.

The results of the survey provided a wealth of information on the topics and tasks with which pupils could cope in each language, but the APU found that

> the main characteristics of pupils' performance do not substantially differ from one language to another. The topics and tasks in which pupils are most successful are the same for each language, and the distribution of performances on particular kinds of tasks follows a similar pattern.[18]

The only instance where it was felt that there was a difference between languages in the level of pupils' achievement was in the case of the listening skill where pupils achieved higher scores in German than in French or Spanish, suggesting that English-speaking pupils find the German phonological system more accessible. This was supported by the finding that pupils whose first language was not English achieved significantly lower scores for the listening skill in German than English-speaking pupils.[19] As will be seen in Chapter 5, OXPROD's findings on the attitudes of pupils towards French, German and Spanish also suggest that pupils perceive German (and Spanish to a lesser extent) to be phonologically easier than French in the early stages.

The APU did not claim, however, to be able to make direct comparisons between pupils' attainment in French, German and Spanish. There were a number of reasons for this. First, there were differences in the composition of the three language populations: for example, although the pupils in the sample were all studying French, German and Spanish as FL1s, those learning German and Spanish were fewer, were concentrated in a smaller number of schools, and, in contrast to the French learners, were not evenly distributed across the country; a higher proportion of French learners than of German or Spanish learners had more than three years' experience of the language because they had started it at primary school; furthermore, owing to the large numbers of pupils in the sample it was not possible to gather comprehensive information on important variables such as pupil ability, the course books used and teaching styles, so that comparability of the three language populations could be assessed.

Second, it was impossible to gauge the effect of the complex interactions of the many background variables on pupils' attainment. These included school variables such as catchment area, sex of pupils and size of school, pupil/teacher ratio and pupil grouping for foreign languages, and pupil variables such as sex and age of pupils, mother tongue, starting age, other foreign languages studied, lesson and homework time, group size and experience of the foreign country.

Third, apart from the near impossibility of designing tests of equal difficulty in the three languages,[20] the format of the tests was not identical across the languages and none of the pupils took all the tests.

In addition to this the effect of pupils' attitudes on their performance was not examined, although a subsample of pupils completed an attitude questionnaire, to which we shall return. The relationship between attitudes and attainment was examined in the 1984 and 1985 surveys but these focused solely on French learners.[21]

PUPIL ATTITUDES TOWARDS LANGUAGE LEARNING

As has been seen, it is difficult to draw conclusions on the suitability of various languages as FL1s on the basis of criteria such as language difficulty and pupil attainment – though these are important contributory factors to pupils' experience of language learning – because the little research that exists on these subjects has not enabled true comparisons between languages to be made. Pupils' attitudes prior to language study and their motivation to learn languages during the learning process, on the other hand, represent a way in which pupils' experience of learning different languages and their progress with them might be compared.

A large body of work exists in the area of attitudes towards language learning, but many of the research studies carried out in the last thirty years have focused on pupils' attitudes towards French only, or to languages in general, rather than on the differences between pupils' attitudes towards various languages. Nonetheless, they provide important insights into the nature of pupil attitudes and their effect on language learning, which can contribute to the design of a comparative study.

In the 1960s and 1970s two major research projects were carried out on the subject of attitudes towards language learning.[22] The first of these was a twelve-year series of studies in North America conducted by Gardner and Lambert to investigate the role of attitudes, primarily with learners of French in various settings.[23] Gardner and Lambert distinguished between two different kinds of motivation, 'integrative' and 'instrumental', and argued that motivation to learn a language is 'integrative' if students are motivated by a sincere interest in the language and culture of another community, and 'instrumental' if they see a utilitarian value in it. In addition to this they found that ability and attitude influenced achievement, but that the two factors were independent of each other.

The second research study which contributed at this stage to the understanding of attitudes towards language learning was the longitudinal survey of pupils' achievement in French and their attitudes towards language learning, conducted at the NFER from 1964 to 1974 under the direction of Burstall.[24] The aims of the study as far as attitudes are concerned were to investigate the long-term development of pupils' attitudes towards foreign language learning and to investigate their relationship with levels of achievement in French. As in the work of Gardner and Lambert, the project identified two elements of motivation, 'integrative' and 'instrumental', but found that it was difficult to distinguish between the two. In addition to this, it was found that levels of achievement and pupils' attitudes were positively related: good attitudes promoted achievement in French which not only fostered positive attitudes but also promoted further success in the language.

In addition to the factors of 'integrative' and 'instrumental' motivation, other writers have stressed the importance of certain personality factors such as extroversion, empathy and self-confidence as influential in pupils' experience of language learning.[25]

Further research into various aspects of secondary school pupils' attitudes towards language learning has been carried out more recently by Buckby,[26] Powell and Batters,[27] Pritchard,[28] and the APU.[29]

Buckby's work, financed by the Schools Council, aimed to monitor the effects of graded objectives and tests on the attitudes of pupils learning French. Attitude questionnaires were administered in 1978 to over a thousand 13+ pupils learning French in Leeds and North Yorkshire. The questionnaire covered a number of attitudinal areas: the utility of French, general positive and negative attitudes, attitudes towards classroom experience, and parental attitudes. The aim was to investigate whether 13+ pupils following graded objectives courses showed significantly more positive attitudes towards French than those continuing to study French in whatever ways were normal in the schools concerned, and it was found that this was indeed the case. In addition to this, girls showed markedly more positive attitudes towards French than boys.[30] These findings were very much in line with those of Burstall, who reported girls to be consistently more highly motivated in languages,[31] and with later work carried out by the APU which revealed girls to be more positive in all aspects of their work.[32]

Work focused specifically on gender differences in foreign language learning was carried out in the mid-1980s by Powell. As part of a number of studies aimed at monitoring curriculum development and pupil attitudes towards foreign languages, an attitude survey was carried out with 953 twelve-year-old pupils in six mixed comprehensive schools at the beginning of the pupils' second year of French or German. The schools were all in south-west England and operated various systems of language provision. The areas of attitude examined, which had been defined by Morris in an earlier small-scale survey of pupils' attitudes towards French at 13+,[33] were views on the importance of languages, ethnocentricity, self-image, and attitudes to writing and oral work in the foreign language. Much of the analysis was focused on differences between the attitudes of girls and boys and, as in previous research studies, it was found that girls generally held more positive attitudes than boys. These findings corroborated the results from earlier work carried out by Powell and Littlewood with pupils at the options stage,[34] where it was found that the attitudes of girls were significantly more conducive to success in the subject and that girls were more likely to view languages as a necessary subject for many of the jobs they wished to do on leaving school.

Pritchard's work on differences between boys' and girls' attitudes, on the other hand, does incorporate a comparative element, in that it is focused on pupils learning French as FL1 and German as FL2.[35] In a small-scale study with 250 pupils in three Northern-Irish grammar schools Pritchard administered attitude questionnaires to investigate pupils' interest in languages, the relative difficulty of French and German, the usefulness of languages, and languages and gender. Quoting the research of Phillips and Stencel on the FL2,[36] she hypothesised that German might appeal more to boys because of its association in pupils' minds with 'masculine' images of war and harshness, reinforced by the nature of the language itself, and that boys would find German less difficult than French. Pritchard's study revealed that, despite the more masculine image of German, boys generally thought it was less interesting, more difficult and less useful to them than French.[37] From this research, however, it is difficult to make direct comparisons between pupil attitudes towards the languages because, as Pritchard herself admits, the two languages had not been studied for the same length of time.[38]

Research on a larger scale, examining the area of attitude across a number of languages, has been carried out by the APU. Within the framework of their large-scale survey of foreign language performance carried out in 1983,[39] they investigated and compared thirteen-year-old pupils' attitudes to learning French, German and Spanish within a sample of approximately 2,400 pupils. The aim was to examine how much pupils enjoyed the languages, how easy or difficult they found them, how useful they perceived them to be and whether they were keen to have contact with members of the foreign language community. In addition to this, pupils' attitudes to language learning activities in class were examined.

The general conclusions of the 1983 survey were very positive: more pupils thought that the foreign language was useful, enjoyable and not difficult and wanted contact with the foreign community than not, girls were generally more positive than boys, and those who had visited the foreign country were more positive in their attitudes than those who had not.[40] At the same time, it was found that pupils perceived Spanish to be most useful on the whole, and that the highest proportion of pupils finding the foreign language easy and enjoyable and wishing for contact with the foreign country was among pupils learning German.[41] As described earlier in this chapter, it was not possible in the 1983 survey to make *direct* comparisons between the three languages, but the APU's findings are of considerable interest, nonetheless, in the study of pupils' attitudes towards different FL1s.

SUMMARY

An examination of previous research on languages other than French, and, in particular, that which is directly concerned with the provision of FL1s, enables the many issues which contribute to the diversification debate to be identified, and suggested to us areas which a small-scale longitudinal study such as OXPROD might investigate further. Research studies of the 1970s and 1980s highlighted the practical problems associated with a policy of diversification, which OXPROD would be able to examine over a number of years, and empirical work with foreign-language learners revealed the many complex factors which would need to be considered in a study which aimed to compare learners' experience of different languages. Some of these factors, such as pupils' attitudes and their perceptions of the difficulty of the languages they were learning, form the focus of OXPROD's research; others, such as the sex of the pupils, their ability and language aptitude and their attainment, become variables according to which OXPROD's findings can be analysed and compared. In the next chapter the project's research design is described in detail.

NOTES

1 Clare Burstall *et al.*, *Primary French in the Balance*, Windsor, National Foundation for Educational Research (NFER), 1974.
2 Peter S. Green (ed.), *The Language Laboratory in School: Performance and prediction*, Edinburgh, Oliver & Boyd, 1975.
3 C.G. Hadley, *Languages other than French in the Secondary School: An exploratory study of other languages as first or equal first foreign languages*, London, Schools Council, 1981.
4 Ibid., p. 49.
5 Felicity Rees, *Languages for a Change: Diversifying foreign language provision in schools*, Windsor, NFER-Nelson, 1989.
6 Department of Education and Science (DES)/Welsh Office (WO), *Foreign Languages in the School Curriculum: A draft statement of policy*, DES/WO, 1986, p. 13.
7 Peter Dickson and Barbara Lee, *Diversification of Foreign Languages in Schools: The ESG pilot programme*, Slough, NFER, 1990.
8 DES, *Diversification of the First Foreign Language in a Sample of Secondary Schools*, spring and summer terms 1990; a report by HMI, London, 1991.
9 See, for example: Karl Breul, *The Teaching of Modern Foreign Languages and the Training of Teachers*, fourth edition, Cambridge, Cambridge University Press, 1913; Eric Hawkins, *Modern Languages in the Curriculum*, revised edition, Cambridge, Cambridge University Press, 1987; Anne E. Keene, 'German as joint or sole first foreign language in the secondary school', unpublished M.Sc. dissertation, University of Oxford, 1984; Josefina Bello, *Spanish as First Foreign Language in Schools: Past and present perspectives*, OXPROD Occasional Paper 2, Oxford, University of Oxford Department of Educational Studies, 1989; Caroline Filmer-Sankey, 'The basis of choice', in David Phillips (ed.), *Which Language? Diversification and the National Curriculum*, London, Hodder & Stoughton, 1989.
10 C.V. James, 'Foreign languages in the school curriculum', *Foreign Languages in Education*, NCLE Papers and Reports 1, 1978, London, Centre for Information on Language Teaching and Research (CILT), 1979.
11 Hawkins, op. cit, p. 82.
12 Ibid., p. 78.
13 This section draws on David Phillips and Caroline Filmer-Sankey: '*Vive la différence*? Some problems in investigating diversification of first foreign language provision in schools', *British Educational Research Journal*, Vol. 15, No. 3, 1989. See also: Ann Miller, *Report on the Pretesting of a Language Aptitude Test*, BP Modern Languages Project Occasional Paper 1, Oxford, University of Oxford Department of Educational Studies, 1980, and *The Development of a Language Aptitude Test*, BP Modern Languages Project Occasional Paper 2, Oxford, University of Oxford Department of Educational Studies, 1982; Ann Miller and David Phillips, 'Towards a new language aptitude test', *British Journal of Language Teaching*, Vol. 20, No. 2, 1982; Peter S. Green (ed.), op. cit., 1975.
14 Burstall et al., op. cit.
15 Assessment of Performance Unit (APU), *Foreign Language Performance in Schools. Report on 1984 survey of French*, DES/Department of Education for

Northern Ireland/WO, 1986; APU, *Foreign Language Performance in Schools. Report on 1985 survey of French*, London, HMSO, 1987.

16 APU, *Foreign Language Performance in Schools. Report on 1983 survey of French, German and Spanish*, DES/Department of Education for Northern Ireland/WO, 1985.

17 APU, *Foreign Language Provision. Survey of Schools, Autumn 1982*, Occasional Paper 2, London, DES, 1983.

18 APU, op. cit., 1985, p. 395.

19 Ibid., p. 394.

20 The question of designing comparable attainment tests in different languages is, of course, not simply a linguistic problem. Other factors such as the content and sequencing of course books used and teaching method would need to be taken into account in order to reflect adequately and fairly in a test the work covered by pupils in each language. Suzy Roessler describes the complexities of designing listening comprehension tests in three languages, which are comparable in format and demands, in: 'Listening comprehension in three first foreign languages: A study of beginners in two secondary schools', unpublished M.Litt. thesis, University of Oxford, 1989.

21 APU, op. cit., 1986; APU, op. cit., 1987.

22 These projects are described in greater detail in: Caroline Filmer-Sankey, 'Attitudes towards first foreign languages in the early stages of secondary school: An investigation into French, German and Spanish', unpublished M.Litt. thesis, University of Oxford, 1991.

23 R.C. Gardner and W.E. Lambert, *Attitudes and Motivation in Second Language Learning*, Massachusetts, Newbury House, 1972.

24 Burstall *et al.*, op. cit.

25 See, for example: H.H. Stern, *Fundamental Concepts of Language Learning*, Oxford, Oxford University Press, 1983; R.C. Powell, *Boys, Girls and Languages in School*, London, CILT, 1986; S. Krashen, *Second Language Acquisition and Second Language Learning*, Oxford, Pergamon Press, 1981.

26 Michael Buckby *et al.*, *Graded Objectives and Tests for Modern Languages: An evaluation*, London, Schools Council, 1981.

27 R.C. Powell and J.D. Batters, Pupils' perceptions of foreign language learning at 12+: Some gender differences', *Educational Studies*, Vol. 11, No. 1, 1985, pp. 11–23.

28 Rosalind M.O. Pritchard, 'Boys' and girls' attitudes towards French and German', *Educational Research*, Vol. 29, No. 1, February 1987, pp. 65–72.

29 APU, op. cit., 1985; APU, op. cit., 1986; APU, op. cit., 1987.

30 Buckby *et al.*, op. cit., p. 22.

31 Burstall *et al.*, op. cit..

32 APU, op. cit., 1985, p. 391.

33 P.D. Morris, 'Children's attitudes to French at 13+', *Modern Languages*, Vol. 59, No. 4, 1978, pp. 177–183.

34 R. Powell and P. Littlewood, Why choose French? Boys' and girls' attitudes at the option stage', *British Journal of Language Teaching*, Vol. 21, No. 1, 1983, p. 37.

35 Pritchard, op. cit..

36 David Phillips and Veronica Stencel, *The Second Foreign Language: Past development, current trends and future prospects*, London, Hodder & Stoughton, 1983, p. 37. Phillips and Stencel point out, in fact, that there is no *direct* evidence in their research that boys regard German as being a more 'masculine' language than French, which is often seen as a 'cissy' language. They stress that the 'image' of French probably has more to do with classroom experience

and its presentation in course books and that the 'image' of German results from its association with the Second World War.

37 Pritchard, op. cit., p. 65.
38 Ibid., p. 67.
39 APU, op. cit., 1985.
40 Ibid., p. 390.
41 Ibid., p. 391.

4 The Oxford project

INTRODUCTION

Chapter 3 has examined research to date which relates to the provision of various FL1s and to pupils' experience of them, in order to set the Oxford Project on Diversification of First Foreign Language Teaching (OXPROD) in context and to identify a number of issues which must be considered when decisions are made about which languages to offer as FL1s. Knowledge of previous research enabled a framework for the project to be drawn up, which is summarised in diagrammatic form in the introduction to this book. This chapter now considers the design of the project in some detail, describing the hypothesis on which the research was based, the research questions which were investigated, the sample of schools and pupils, and the way in which the research was carried out.

OXPROD, which began in January 1987, is a six-year longitudinal research project funded primarily by the Leverhulme Trust and based at the Department of Educational Studies of Oxford University. The first part of the project, which forms the core of this and the following two chapters, focused on the first three years of secondary schooling, and was completed in December 1990. The second part of the project, which began in 1991, focuses particularly on aspects of diversification related to the fourth and fifth years of secondary schooling.

The overall aim of the project is to present a complete picture of pupils', teachers' and schools' experience of diversification in the five years of compulsory secondary education, set in the context of local and national developments in language policy and provision. As described in the Introduction, the hypothesis which the project aims to test is that *there is nothing in the nature of German and Spanish as subjects in the school curriculum that makes these languages unsuitable as first foreign languages for the whole ability range*. There are three main strands to the research, and these were formulated in the following questions:

1 What *attitudes* do children have to French, German and Spanish at various stages of their learning?

2 What *difficulties* do children experience in French, German and Spanish and at which stages of their learning?

3 What *organisational problems* are evident in the project schools that result from teaching a language other than French as first foreign language?

In the area of attitude the aim is to examine which aspects of French, German and Spanish pupils find most difficult, useful and enjoyable, what they think about the activities in which they are involved in their language lessons and what they think about the people and the country of the language they are learning. Changes in pupils' attitudes towards the languages over the first three years of the course are examined, as are attitudinal differences related to the ability and sex of the pupils. While pupil attainment in the three languages is not measured in the project itself, the eventual aim is to tie in attitudinal data with GCSE results at the end of the fifth year.

In the area of difficulty the aim is to examine what pupils perceive to be easy or difficult in the languages they are learning in terms of the language-learning skills (listening, speaking, reading and writing), the topic areas covered in the course, and the grammatical structures, as far as they are aware of them.

In the area of organisation the aim is to document problems encountered in schools when languages other than French are FL1s and to set the information gathered in context by relating it to the wider issue of diversification. This entails looking at various patterns of provision over the country and following the development of diversification policy at all levels.

Work on pupils' experience of learning various FL1s has been concentrated in six 'project' schools where languages other than French are taught alongside French as FL1s. Work on organisational issues associated with a policy of diversification has been carried out with the same six schools and a further number of 'associated' schools nationwide which are operating a similar system of provision to that in the project schools. These schools will be described later in this chapter.

THE PROJECT SCHOOLS

The selection of the project schools was made on the basis of a number of criteria: firstly, the schools had to be teaching languages other than French under the same conditions as French; that is, as FL1s, with the same time allocation and resources, and to pupils of the same age and experience. It was felt that the ideal conditions under which comparisons between languages could be made would exist in co-educational schools where the first-year intake was split into two or more 'cohorts' with a number of teaching groups in each. Pupils entering the schools would be allocated immediately to a language, whether French, German or Spanish, and would continue to study it until at least the end of the third year, if not to the end of compulsory schooling; secondly, the schools had to be within easy travelling distance of Oxford, where OXPROD was based, as the staffing and resources of the project would not stretch to long hours of travelling or periods of absence from Oxford; finally, with ever-increasing demands on teachers' time, schools had to be willing and able to participate over at least three years.

In fact, it was extremely difficult to find more than a handful of schools in 1987 which fulfilled these requirements and which were prepared to be committed to participation in the research as project schools over a number of years, and so the six schools which were chosen should be taken as an opportunity sample rather than a representative sample. They are all, except one (a west London school) in country areas in the south of England, and three of them are in Oxfordshire itself. This naturally diminishes the generalisability of the results, but it was felt at the outset that while this might be a disadvantage there would be benefits in terms of closer association with pupils and teachers in the schools.

The schools chosen to be project schools were coded A to F, and were all, except one (school F), 11–18 mixed comprehensive schools teaching a language (or languages) other than French as FL1(s) in addition to French from the first year. School F, a girls' school, was included in the sample because it was unusual in offering Italian as one of its FL1s.

School A is a large split-site voluntary-controlled school in a country town. It was founded as a grammar school and took its first comprehensive entry in 1970. Now it has a nine-form intake with approximately 1700 pupils on roll, including about 250 in the sixth form. A policy of diversification was introduced in 1983 by a new headteacher, a French specialist, who felt that the size of the school warranted the provision of two FL1s and that there was no 'natural' order of priority for languages. Previously all pupils had taken French, and German had been offered as FL2; but take-up of German had been low, and girls had predominated in languages overall. French and German are now taught as parallel FL1s and remain compulsory until the end of the third year when pupils may opt for one, two or no languages. About 60 per cent usually opt to continue with a language.

School B is a large split-site school in a country town. It was established in 1967 by the merger of four local secondary schools and reorganised in 1987 into a lower school for years 1–3, an upper school for years 4–5, and an area sixth-form centre. It now has a nine-form intake with approximately 1,600 pupils on roll, including about 270 in the sixth form. A policy of diversification was introduced in 1976. Previously, French had been taught as FL1, with German, Spanish, Russian and Latin as FL2s further up the school. The impetus for change came from the head of faculty and was strongly supported by the principal, also a linguist. They felt that diversification would expand pupils' language experience and preserve teachers' skills in languages other than French. French, German and Spanish are now taught as parallel FL1s and remain compulsory until the end of the third year, when pupils may opt for one, two or no languages. About 60 per cent usually opt to continue with a language.

School C is a rural comprehensive school and community college in a small country town. It has a six-form intake which increases to seven forms in the third year with the addition of boarders and specialist agricultural pupils. There are 1,100 pupils on roll, with approximately 350 students in the sixth form (including pupils from another local secondary school). The school diversified in September 1987 in order to ensure the survival of German and Spanish. Previously French had been taught as FL1, and German or Spanish had been offered as FL2s. The impetus for change came from the head of department, and the final decision was made by the headteacher in consultation with the heads of lower school. The system of diversification adopted was the 'split-wave' model operating over two years: in the first year of the scheme (1987–8) French or Spanish were offered as FL1s with German or French as FL2s; and in the second year (1988–9) French or German were offered as FL1s, with Spanish or French as FL2s. In 1989, however, on the arrival of a new head, the school reverted to French as sole FL1, primarily because of timetabling problems. At the end of the third year, pupils can opt to continue with one, two or no languages. About 60 per cent of pupils usually opt to continue with a language.

School D, situated in a country town, was established in 1958 as a secondary modern school and reorganised as a comprehensive school in 1972. It has a wide catchment area, including a local RAF base, and an eight-form intake with 1,500 pupils on roll. Diversification was introduced in 1972. At the time of comprehensivisation, the head of languages, with support from the headteacher, decided to develop the interest in German shown by local service children by introducing it as FL1 in parallel with French. Until 1987 pupils joining the school took either French or German as FL1. Since September 1988, and largely because of the success of the diversification programme, all first-year pupils study French and German in half-termly modules, and take a language awareness course which includes Latin. In years 2 and 3, a similar curriculum continues, with all pupils taking two languages from French, German or Latin. Languages are in the core curriculum, and so pupils continue with one or two languages in years 4 and 5.

School E, situated in a small country town, has a four-form intake, with approximately 700 pupils on roll and about sixty in the sixth form. A policy for diversification of FL1s has been running since September 1987. Its introduction was actively encouraged by a new headteacher who was very sympathetic towards languages, and the change came at a time of curricular reorganisation across the school. A faculty of language was created in 1988. This incorporates the English department, and most staff in the faculty teach English as well as a foreign language. Previously all pupils took French as FL1 in years 1–3 with the option of taking German as FL2 in year 4. All pupils now take both French and German in years 1–3 and can opt to continue with one, two or no languages in years 4 and 5.

School F is a girls' voluntary-aided Anglican school situated in inner London. Founded in 1791, it has a four-form intake with approximately 450 pupils on roll, including about thirty in the sixth form. Some 26 per cent of the pupils are bilingual, mostly in non-European languages. The decision to diversify language provision was taken in 1987 in the hope that good option groups in several languages would be produced in years 4 and 5. French, German and Italian are now taught as parallel FL1s in the first year. In the second year each of the four teaching groups stops work on the first language and starts another of the three languages. By the end of the year most pupils have achieved a 'level one' certificate in two languages from the Lancaster Institute of European Education. In the third year, pupils choose to continue with one of the languages they have already studied. An options system is in operation and in theory pupils can opt for one, two or no languages in years 4 and 5. In practice about 90 per cent of pupils find themselves required to choose a language, and a small proportion does two languages.

When the project started in 1987, schools A, B, C, D and F were operating a system of *split* or *parallel* provision; that is, offering French *or* another language to all first-year pupils. School E was operating a system of *dual* provision; that is, offering French *and* German to all pupils. It was included in the sample because it afforded the opportunity to investigate pupils' attitudes when they were learning two languages at the same time and were thus in a position to make comparisons between the two based on simultaneous experience of each language. In all but school F, where pupils experienced two different languages in the first two years, pupils continued with the same language (or languages in the case of school E) in the second and third year (1988–9 and 1989–90). Table 4.1 shows the pattern of FL1 provision in the project schools in the first year of the project (1987–8).

In the four largest schools, A, B, C and D, pupils were setted from the second year on the basis of progress in class and performance in end-of-year tests, and some pupils began their FL2. Setting procedures and provision of the FL2 varied considerably from school to school: in school A, for example, the nine form-groups were reorganised into eleven sets (six French and five German) within three blocks. From these, three top sets were formed (two French and one German) and these pupils, representing 30 per cent of the year-group, were offered French or German as FL2. The other eight groups remained mixed-ability until the end of the third year, but at the beginning of the third year the six French sets were rearranged again, since staff felt that pupils had not been setted

Table 4.1 FL1 provision in the project schools

School	Number on roll (first-year intake)	FL1 provision (Number of first-year groups)	
A	1,700 (250)	Split provision:	French (5) German (4)
B	1,600 (240)	Split provision:	French (4) German (3) Spanish (2)
C	1,100 (150)	Split provision:	French (3) Spanish (3)
D*	1,500 (200)	Split provision:	French (4) German (4)
E	700 (110)	Dual language: (total = 4 groups)	French (4) German (4)
F	450 (100)	Split provision:	French (2) German (1) Italian (1)

* *School D changed to a system of dual language provision in September 1988.*

satisfactorily in their second year. In school B, where the nine groups were arranged in two blocks on the timetable, three German and two French sets were created in the first block and two Spanish and two French sets in the second block. An FL2 was offered to all pupils: the original intention had been to operate a carousel system of five 'taster' courses over two years whereby a child who began French as FL1 in the first year would add a term of German, Spanish, Urdu, Russian and Latin in rotation. In fact, for a number of administrative reasons and with the arrival of a new head of faculty, this programme was abandoned after one year. In September 1989 the present system of FL2 provision was adopted, with French, German and Spanish offered as FL2s in the third year. In school C three French and three Spanish sets were formed from the six first-year groups and the top two sets in each language, representing approximately 60 per cent of the ability range, began either German or French as FL2. At the beginning of the third year the composition of the French sets remained the same, but the Spanish sets were slightly rearranged to tie in with the banding system for other subjects. In school D the eight groups were rearranged into four upper and four lower sets and all pupils started either French, German or Latin as FL2.

As can be seen, setting arrangements varied considerably from school to school and even within schools pupils were setted differently for the individual languages because of the way in which groups were blocked on the timetable. It was decided, therefore, that the effects of setting on pupils' experience of learning the various languages would be impossible to assess, and that details of the setting information should be used as background information only.

THE PUPIL SAMPLE

As described above, the pupils participating in the research in the project schools were those from the 1987 intake. Over the first three years a total of 1,091 pupils were involved: some of these left the schools in the course of the study, and some transferred-in from other schools in the course of the project. Almost half the pupils (49 per cent) in the whole sample were concentrated in schools A and B, and there was an overall imbalance in favour of girls as a result of the inclusion of school F; in the other five schools, however, approximately equal proportions of girls and boys (495 and 500 respectively) took part. Owing to the fact that schools E and F operated different systems of language provision from schools A, B, C and D, the pupil samples at these schools are described separately below and analysis of data from these schools is also considered separately in the next chapter.

Table 4.2 shows the distribution of pupils across the three languages in schools A to D. In the four schools, 53 per cent of pupils over the three years were learning French, 32 per cent were learning German and 15 per cent were learning Spanish. As Table 4.3 shows, there were slight imbalances between the numbers of boys and girls within each language cohort.

Some 114 pupils took part in school E and all of these were learning French and German. When attitudinal data were collected, about half the pupils completed a French version of the questionnaire and about half completed a German version of the questionnaire, and so for the purposes of analysis the sample was as shown in Table 4.4. In this school the imbalance between boys and girls was marked, with 67 girls in the sample as opposed to 47 boys.

Table 4.2 Distribution of pupils across languages, schools A to D

School	Numbers of pupils	Numbers learning French	Numbers learning German	Numbers learning Spanish
A	291	168	123	
B	244	115	79	50
C	160	81		79
D	186	106	80	
Total	881	470	282	129

Table 4.3 Distribution of boys and girls across languages, schools A to D

	Girls	Boys	Total	% of pupils
French	220	250	470	53
German	148	134	282	32
Spanish	60	69	129	15
All languages	428	453	881	

Table 4.4 Pupil sample at school E

	Girls	Boys	Total
French	32	24	56
German	35	23	58
Total	67	47	114

Table 4.5 Pupil sample at school F

	Numbers learning French	Numbers learning German	Numbers learning Italian	Total
Year 1	49	24	23	96
Year 2	47	24	25	96
Year 3	44	21	22	87

Some ninety-six girls took part in school F over the three years, but the overall numbers studying each language cannot be tabulated since pupils were studying different languages from year to year. Table 4.5 shows the numbers for each year separately (numbers given for each year in each language represent different pupils).

COMPOSITION OF THE LANGUAGE COHORTS

In order for valid comparisons to be made between pupils' experience of learning the various foreign languages, it was important to ensure from the outset that the composition of the groups in the French, German and Spanish cohorts was similar in terms of pupils' ability, previous language learning experience and socio-economic background, and that there were approximately equal numbers of boys and girls in each cohort. At the school selection stage, therefore, detailed enquiries were made to ascertain exactly how pupils were allocated to form-groups in the first year and how it was decided which pupils should study French and which pupils a language other than French. Informal discussions with those in charge of the allocation of pupils to first-year groups, usually heads of lower school or first year, and with heads of modern language departments, revealed that procedures differed very little from school to school. Teachers in charge of allocation consulted at length with primary schools in the summer term prior to entry and were provided with a standard transfer form for each pupil which gave information on their background, attendance record, health and general attitude. In most cases the forms also included information on pupils' ability as shown by their progress at primary school in Mathematics and English and in their performance on various reading and non-verbal tests. While the information was not standardised across all pupils because feeder schools completed the forms in different ways, the information did enable secondary-school teachers to distribute pupils according to sex, ability and background among the first-form groups. Most schools also took into account friendship groups, ensuring that at least two pupils from each primary school were allocated to each class, and in schools A and D, where a house system was in operation, pupils with siblings were allocated to the same house. School E was the only school where ability range was not taken into account in the formation of the groups, although information on this was available; the head of first year was convinced, however, that the groups emerged as mixed-ability groups without recourse to such information. For the purposes of the research, then, it can be assumed that first-year groups were, to all intents and purposes, mixed-ability, and balanced in terms of the sexes. In all but school D, the first-year tutor groups were also the first-year language groups in which special-needs pupils were fully integrated. In school D, however, special-needs pupils were allocated to extra tutor groups from the outset and the remaining pupils were divided among eight house groups. These groups were paired, and within the pairs the head of languages allocated half the pupils to a French group and half to a German group, taking care to ensure parity in terms of ability in the two language groups.

The question as to which language each group would take within a school was determined in the same way in all schools except school B. On the whole, parents were informed in an explanatory letter or at parents' evenings in the summer term about language provision in the secondary school and were told that their child would be studying one of the languages on offer. Parents with strong preferences for any one language were invited to respond by a certain date with their reasons. This is the way in which the letter was worded at school D:

It may be worth noting that all children begin either French or German in the first year with the opportunity for most to be taking both languages by the second year.

Whether your child studies French or German first is decided on whole-class designation to use teaching resources most effectively and is certainly not dependent on the ability of pupils nor status of either subject. If there is a strong preference by yourself for your son or daughter to start with French or German in Year 1 please write to me by 1st May 1987 and your request will be given my sympathetic consideration.

In fact, hardly any parents responded to this or to the letter sent out by school A, which was worded as follows:

In September 1987 [House A] and [House B] pupils will take French as first foreign language; [House C] and [House D] will take German. There will be the opportunity to learn the other language in Year 2 where this seems appropriate to the pupil's general ability and linguistic aptitude. Parents who have a particularly strong reason for wanting their child to start one language rather than the other are asked to send a letter with this admission form, giving details of their preference. We cannot guarantee to meet all requests.

School B encountered some problems, however, owing to the wording of its general admissions form (reproduced in full in Chapter 6), which included a section in which parents were invited to choose between French, German and Spanish by ticking one of three boxes. The majority expressed a preference for French and very few parents chose Spanish. Parents' wishes could not be accommodated within timetabling and staffing constraints and so many of the pupils eventually allocated to German and Spanish classes were those who had not chosen to study these languages. Further discussion of sample letters to parents about the allocation of their children to various language groups is provided in an occasional paper of the project,[1] and we shall return to the subject in Chapter 6.

There was some concern that pupils in school B would be less positively motivated than pupils whose parents had chosen French and who were in French groups. In fact, while results from the research showed this not to be the case, analysis of ability levels in the three language cohorts at this school indicated, as will be seen below, that pupils in the Spanish groups were of lower ability, on average, than those in the French and German groups.

ABILITY LEVELS OF PUPILS IN THE LANGUAGE COHORTS

At the beginning of the project, information on ability was gathered from the whole of the pupil sample. There were two reasons for this. First, it was necessary to assess the comparability of the three language cohorts in terms of ability levels in order to interpret the data which would be collected, and second, one of the aims of the research was to compare the experience of pupils of different abilities across the three languages. Two main kinds of tests were used: a test of verbal ability and a language aptitude test. It was not possible to use a further test for non-verbal ability since most schools were unwilling for pupils to be overburdened by tests in their first year.

In order to gain information on verbal ability across the sample it was decided to use a test developed and well validated at the National Foundation for Educational Research (NFER).[2] This was already used at schools A and D, and schools B, C and E were quite happy to administer the same test in November 1987 and to return the scripts to OXPROD for marking. At school F, which was under the jurisdiction of the Inner London Education Authority (ILEA) at the time, verbal scores from a test administered through ILEA were gathered, which it was felt would be approximately comparable with data from the other five schools, but data from school F were analysed separately, in any case, because a different pattern of language provision was in operation there.

In October 1987 the whole sample was also tested for language aptitude using the York Language Aptitude Test, described in Chapter 3, which has been widely used in schools since 1975.[3] The test has, in fact, been criticised for its concentration on grammatical form, which does not relate closely to the kinds of learning strategies used in today's language classrooms. It is in Swedish with forty-two items where candidates attempt by analogy to work out definite and plural forms of Swedish nouns and present tense forms of verbs. However, as the aim of administering such a test was to provide standardised information on another facet of ability across the pupil sample rather than to predict attainment, it was felt that the test was well suited to the project's requirements. The fact that the test was in Swedish was an advantage in that pupils in all three cohorts were unlikely to have encountered the language before, and, on a practical level, the test was easy to obtain, administer and mark.

The scores for verbal ability and language aptitude were used independently to divide the pupil sample into four groups: 'high ability' pupils, pupils of 'average ability and above', pupils of 'average ability and below', and 'low ability' pupils. Each group represented approximately 25 per cent of the ability range and there was considerable similarity in the two groupings, but the scores could not be pooled because a pupil coded as 'high ability' on the verbal score was not necessarily coded as 'high ability' on the language aptitude score. When data from the project were analysed separately for each ability measure, however, similar results emerged. In what follows, therefore, and for reasons of clarity, only data from the analyses using the verbal test scores are presented. Table 4.6 shows the numbers of pupils in each ability grouping in the language cohorts (excluding those for whom no information was available) and the proportion of each cohort that these represent, according to the verbal scores.

Despite schools' attempts to create comparable mixed-ability groups in the first year, there were considerable differences between the distributions of pupils of different abilities across the languages, the most significant being the large proportions of pupils in the German cohort and

Table 4.6 Pupil grouping according to verbal score

	French	*German*	*Spanish*
High ability	119 (24.1%)	106 (32.4%)	21 (17.8%)
Average ability and above	118 (23.9%)	85 (26.0%)	31 (26.3%)
Average ability and below	136 (27.5%)	67 (20.5%)	40 (33.9%)
Low ability	121 (24.5%)	69 (21.1%)	26 (22.0%)

the relatively small proportions of pupils in the Spanish cohort who were designated 'high ability'. In addition to this there was a high proportion of Spanish learners in the 'average ability and below' group.

RESOURCES

Resources were another factor to be considered when attempting to assess the comparability of the three language cohorts. In order to ensure that potential project schools would not be following entirely divergent courses, information on the course books used for French, German and Spanish was gathered at the selection stage. It was ascertained early on that there would be at least superficially a high degree of consistency in that all the schools under consideration would be using the *Tricolore* [4] course for French and the *Deutsch Heute* [5] course for German. For Spanish, the two schools were hoping to use a new Spanish course *¡Vaya!*,[6] due to be published in September 1987, and until then they would use the ILEA course *¡Claro!*[7] On the whole, languages other than French were not as well resourced in the project schools as French because they had been introduced more recently. In this respect OXPROD was very generously supported by the Goethe-Institut, the Spanish Institute and the Italian Cultural Institute, which provided funding to enable schools to equip each pupil in the sample with a course book for each of the three years so that rough comparability with the resource provision for French was attained.

Table 4.7 Course books used in schools A to D

School	Year 1	Year 2	Year 3
A	*Tricolore 1*	*Tricolore 2*	*Tricolore 3*
	Deutsch Heute 1	*Deutsch Heute 1*	*Deutsch Heute 2*
B	*Tricolore 1A*	*Tricolore 1B*	*Tricolore 2/Escalier*
	Deutsch Heute 1	*Deutsch Heute 1*	*Deutsch Heute 2/Einfach toll*
	¡Claro!/¡Vaya! 1	*¡Vaya! 2*	*¡Vaya! 2*
C	*Tricolore 1*	*Tricolore 2*	*Tricolore 2*
	¡Claro!/¡Vaya! 1	*¡Vaya! 2*	*¡Vaya! 2*
D	*Tricolore 1A*	*Tricolore 1B*	*Tricolore 2*
	Deutsch Heute 1	*Deutsch Heute 1*	*Deutsch Heute 2*

As can be seen from Table 4.7, schools A to D used the same course books throughout the three years of the study, with some variation in the pacing of the courses. School B was alone in using *Escalier*[8] for French and *Einfach toll*[9] for German with low-ability pupils in the third year. These are beginners' courses developed for graded objectives work.

School E also used *Tricolore* for French throughout and *Deutsch Heute* for German in the first two years, but switched to *Zickzack*[10] in the third year. School F used *Escalier* for French, followed by *Hexagone 2*,[11] and

Einfach toll! 1 and *2* for German. Resourcing Italian proved to be a problem throughout the three years, and no one book was found on which the course could be based. For most of the time, the Italian teacher made her own materials, which was extremely time-consuming and, on her own admission, less motivating for the pupils.

The three main course books used by the language cohorts, *Tricolore*, *Deutsch Heute* and *¡Vaya!*, all reflect the trend of recent years towards 'communicative' teaching methods by providing materials which encourage pupils to use actively the language they have learnt. They aim to give pupils clearly specified and attainable goals which they can see will have relevance to everyday life, so that they feel a sense of achievement, whatever the level of their ability. Pupils are presented with the language they need in order to be able to cope in social or public situations. These include, for example, giving information about themselves and their families and asking others about themselves, expressing wishes, needs and preferences, performing simple transactions such as shopping, eating out and making enquiries, interpreting different sources of public information and making travel arrangements. In addition to the topical or situational approach, each course provides a structural/grammatical progression.

The fact that all schools were using from the outset the same course books for each language ensured a degree of comparability within the language cohorts and across the schools in terms of what was taught in each language. Similarly, an examination of the aims and content of each course revealed common ground in terms of the topics covered, the emphasis on aural/oral skills, and general presentation. However, while information on the resources available provided a framework for *what* was taught over the three years of the project, it did not provide an insight into *how* the languages were taught. Inevitably the teacher and his or her teaching style were among the most important factors affecting pupils' experience of learning the various languages. This was certainly corroborated by pupils' comments on the attitude questionnaires administered over the three years, which will be described in the next chapter.

THE TEACHERS AND THEIR TEACHING STYLE

It was quite clear from talking to pupils in pilot schools and from discussing the proposed project with their teachers that there would be considerable variation in teaching styles within the sample, and that the effects of the teacher variable[12] on pupils' experience of learning the three languages would be very difficult to assess. There were several reasons for this, the first of which was a purely practical problem. In order to collect comprehensive information on the teaching style of all the teachers it would have been necessary to approach the matter from a number of angles, by interviewing pupils and teachers and by carrying out a period of systematic lesson observation each year. With fifty-seven teachers involved in teaching the pupils in the six schools over the three years, there was simply not enough time to observe teachers in a systematic and concentrated way, or to interview all of them and their pupils.

From the outset it had been hoped to impose some control on the variations in teaching style by ensuring that some teachers would take two groups in the first year, teaching French to one and a language other than French to the other, so that fewer teachers would be involved and more direct comparisons between languages could be made. For timetabling reasons, however, this was only possible in school C where the six-form intake was divided into three French and three Spanish groups, with three teachers taking one group in each language. In almost every other school, each first-year group was taught by a different teacher.

Another problem was the considerable variation between the schools in the levels of staff mobility. In school A, for example, fourteen teachers were involved in the first three years of the project and there was very little continuity from year to year; in school B seventeen teachers were involved, with only one teacher remaining throughout the project; in school E staff illness and frequent changes ensured that there was little continuity in the German teaching. By way of contrast, the situation in schools C, D and F was relatively stable: in school F, for example, only three teachers were involved throughout.

A further problem was that in schools A to D pupils were setted by ability in the second year. This meant that, even if the teachers had remained the same over the three years, the composition of the groups and thus their group dynamics and relationship with the teacher would have changed. In some schools there was even a reshuffling of the groups in the third year which would have complicated matters even further. Thus, it was impossible to gauge pupils' responses to individual teachers and differing teaching styles.

Finally, there was the problem that, even if it were possible to describe accurately exactly how pupils were taught, it would not be possible to relate the information directly to pupils' experience of the three languages, because the teacher variable, important as it is, was only one of many interacting variables affecting pupil attitudes. After much consideration, therefore, it was decided to gather information on the teachers and teaching style by questionnaire and to treat the whole question as 'illuminating' background information rather than as a focus for the research. Over the three years teachers completed a number of questionnaires, which provided information on their views on diversification and on their approach to teaching languages, interviews were conducted and many informal discussions with teachers took place.

THE ASSOCIATED SCHOOLS

In order to set up links with schools where language provision was already diversified or which were contemplating diversification in the near future, an information sheet about the project was drafted and circulated in spring 1987 to a wide variety of people who would be in contact with language teachers. These included the Centre for Information on Language Teaching and Research (CILT), the three cultural institutes and county language advisers. Anyone with an interest in the research was invited to respond, indicating whether they wished to be kept informed about OXPROD and its findings, if they had direct experience of diversification, and if they currently taught in a school with a policy of diversification which might be interested in becoming an associated school of the project. At the same time a number of introductory articles and news bulletins about OXPROD were published in the language journals.[13] The response to the publicity was enthusiastic, and from the replies it was possible to establish a list of about 500 people, many of them teachers, who wished to be kept informed of the progress of the project. Some of these expressed an interest in becoming more closely involved, and gradually a list of about thirty schools interested in being connected with the research as 'associated' schools was built up. Dissemination of information on the project via newsletters at an early stage also ensured that schools nationwide were aware of the project's work and pleased to exchange information and that OXPROD was invited to work on a number of INSET programmes connected with diversification. This was of tremendous benefit to the project's work.

While the thirty associated schools could not be viewed as representative, in that they were selected from those which had seen the OXPROD information sheet or through personal links, there was a wide variety of schools in the sample: two in Scotland, eight in London and its environs, six in the south of England, five in the north of England and nine in the Midlands and East Anglia, including three schools in Oxfordshire which were used to pilot some of the research instruments. Of the thirty schools, the majority were mixed comprehensives, but five independent schools (two girls', two boys' and one mixed school) were also included in the sample. The comprehensives were either 11–18, 11–16 or 12–18 schools and mixed, except for one 11–18 girls' comprehensive. In the sample were also one Catholic and one Church of England comprehensive. Most of the schools had an intake of between six to eight forms in the first year, but the independent schools were on the whole smaller. Some seventeen schools were offering French or German as FL1, two schools French, German or Spanish, one school French or Spanish and one school French, German or community languages. Among the remaining nine schools there was a variety of provision. One school was teaching both French and German to all pupils, one school French in the first year and German in the next, two schools French or German one year and French or Spanish the next, one school French *and* Spanish to all pupils one year then French *and* German the next, and one school French or German the first year followed by the other language in the second year and then a choice between the two. In addition to this, one school was offering German as sole FL1 and two schools were offering French (the two pilot schools). More detailed descriptions of individual schools will be given in Chapter 6 when the research conducted there is described.

METHODOLOGY

Information was gathered for the project primarily by means of question-naires and interviews. In the project schools the pupil sample completed attitude questionnaires and individual pupils were interviewed annually. Teachers in the project and associated schools completed questionnaires about organisational problems in their schools and were interviewed in the first and second years of the project. In addition to this, information was gathered more informally throughout the project on frequent visits to project schools and in conversations with their language teachers.

The research programme for the first three years of the project can be briefly outlined as follows:

1986–7   Identification of the project and associated schools
           Pilot study in school A

                          Year 1: 1987–8

Autumn   Collection of data on ability from first-year pupils (1987 intake) in the six project schools

Spring   First administration of pupil attitude questionnaire to first-year pupils

Summer   Pupil interviews

           Questionnaire sent to project and associated school teachers to investigate their attitudes towards diversification and their per-ceptions of organisational problems

                          Year 2: 1988–9

Autumn   Correspondence with LEA advisers nationwide to investigate their diversification policies

Spring   Follow-up questionnaire sent to heads of department in the project and associated schools on the problems of 'transfers-in'

           Second administration of pupil attitude questionnaire to second-year pupils

Summer   Pupil interviews

           Administration of questionnaire on the FL2 to second-year pupils

           Interviews with heads of department in project and associated schools on the problems of 'transfers-in'

Questionnaire on the FL2 sent to heads of department in project and associated schools

Year 3: 1989–90

Spring Third administration of pupil attitude questionnaire to third-year pupils

Summer Pupil interviews

Teacher assessment of pupil attainment

In the fourth year of the project the emphasis was on data analysis and writing-up, but pupils were also interviewed about the options choices they had made. In the fifth year the aim was to collect further information on teachers' attitudes towards diversification in the light of policy developments and to collect GCSE results for pupils in the language cohorts who had chosen to continue with their study of one or two languages. At the time of writing (1991) pupils had not yet reached this stage.

The core of the research programme in the first three years was the work on pupil attitudes in the project schools and in what follows the development of the research instrument used to test this, the pupil attitude questionnaire, is described in some detail. The research instruments used to collect qualitative data on organisational problems from the associated schools are described in less detail but are reproduced in OXPROD Occasional Papers 1 and 4.[14]

THE PUPIL ATTITUDE QUESTIONNAIRE

The pupil attitude questionnaire was designed to test areas of attitude which had been isolated by examining other research on attitudes to language learning and by talking to teachers in the pilot phase of the project about what they felt to be the factors influencing pupils' attitudes.[15] Four areas emerged:

(*i*)   pupils' enjoyment of French, German and Spanish;
(*ii*) their perceptions of the difficulty of the various languages;
(*iii*) their views on the usefulness of the various languages;
(*iv*) their attitudes to the country and people of the languages they were learning.

As in other research studies concerned with attitudes, it was decided to use a questionnaire incorporating Likert-type scales. Pupils would be required to respond to a number of statements relating to each of the four areas of attitude by indicating to what extent they agreed or disagreed with them, on a scale of 1 to 5 ranging from 'strongly agree' to 'strongly disagree'. The sum of their responses to statements in each area (or on each 'attitude scale', as they are commonly known) would be a measure of their attitude. By calculating the mean scores for groups of pupils (for example the mean scores of all pupils learning German and of all pupils learning French, or of all girls and of all boys), it would be possible to make comparisons between, for example, attitudes towards the various languages and between the attitudes of girls as opposed to the attitudes of boys.

In designing a questionnaire, it was decided to look first at other attitude questionnaires used successfully in research of this kind, in order to see if a questionnaire already existed which tested similar areas and which might be adapted for the project. The advantage of this approach was that information on the reliability and validity of an existing questionnaire would be available. Two questionnaires were found which could be used as the basis for the OXPROD questionnaire. The first of these, a questionnaire designed for the Schools Council project on Graded Objectives in 1981,[16] was adapted for the OXPROD pilot study in 1986–7 and administered to pupils from the 1986 intake in school A. This questionnaire had already been well validated with second- and third-year pupils in Yorkshire schools and covered the areas which the project aimed to investigate, except for pupils' perceptions of the difficulty of the languages they were learning. The second model for the OXPROD questionnaire was an instrument developed at the NFER for the Assessment of Performance Unit (APU), which was used in their surveys of foreign language performance and attitude.[17] This questionnaire covered all four areas that OXPROD aimed to examine and also gathered information on pupils' enjoyment of various language-learning activities. In fact, there was considerable comparability between the two questionnaires and after the pilot study they were combined to produce a shorter questionnaire laid out in the format of the APU questionnaire but with many individual items preserved from the Schools Council questionnaire. This procedure is described in detail elsewhere.[18] The resulting questionnaire consisted of four sections: Part A contained questions on pupils' contact with the foreign community, Part B contained statements about pupils' feelings about language learning and contact with the foreign country, Part C contained questions about pupils' enjoyment of language-learning activities, and Part D was a written section in which pupils were given the opportunity to give reasons for their responses to three questions from Part B and to express any thoughts about language learning that they had not been able to express elsewhere in the questionnaire. Part B was the section on which much of the analysis of pupils' attitudes in the project was based. It consisted of thirty-two items which it was anticipated would relate to the four attitude scales of enjoyment, usefulness of languages, difficulty and contact.

A first version of the questionnaire was pretested with first-year French learners in two of the associated schools in order to ensure that the questionnaire would work in practical terms with first-year pupils and to validate the questionnaire statistically. On the basis of the information gathered on pretests a final version of the questionnaire was then drafted for use in the first year of the study, and this was adapted for French, German, Spanish and Italian. Part B in the French version consisted of the following items:

1 I'm glad I'm learning French rather than another language.
2 French is one of my favourite lessons.
3 I'm not interested in meeting French people.
4 I think my parents are pleased I'm learning French rather than another language.
5 I would like to visit France (if you have already visited France, please answer whether you would like to go again).
6 I find French too hard.
7 I don't like learning French.
8 I would like to stay with a French family.
9 French will be useful to me after I leave school.
10 French is usually boring.
11 Next year I would like to start learning another foreign language as well as French.
12 I find French more difficult than other subjects.
13 There are more useful languages to learn than French.
14 I don't like French because I'm no good at it.
15 I want to go on learning French next year.
16 I am better at French than at other subjects.
17 My parents think that learning French is a waste of time.
18 I am not interested in going to France.
19 French is one of the easiest lessons.
20 I don't need French for what I want to do.
21 I think there are many jobs where French would be useful.
22 I enjoy French because it seems easy.
23 I think there are more important things to learn in school than French.
24 I enjoy other lessons more than French.
25 I understand most things in the French lesson.
26 I would like to make friends with some young French people of my own age.
27 French is no use to me as I don't want to go to France.
28 I enjoy learning French.
29 Knowing French will help me get a job I like.
30 I would like to have a French boy or girl to stay.
31 Learning foreign languages is a waste of time.
32 I'm quite good at French.

The complete questionnaire is included as an appendix in OXPROD's Occasional Papers 3 and 5,[19] and the contents of Parts A and D will be found in the next chapter. Very minor alterations were made to the questionnaire to accommodate changes in language provision in the second and third years, and it was still possible to compare data from year to year.

A separate version of the questionnaire was devised for school E where all pupils were learning French *and* German. It was necessary to change a few items in Part B which were inappropriate for pupils learning two languages and to redraft the written section, Part D, in order to give pupils the opportunity to compare the two languages they were learning.

The questionnaire was administered for the first time in the project schools over a period of two weeks in March 1988. Where possible, the research officer administered the questionnaire herself, but otherwise the administration of the remaining questionnaires was carried out by language teachers who had been able to watch the administration of the questionnaire by the research officer. It took about thirty-five minutes to complete. Pupils completed the same questionnaire in the second and third years of the project; that is, in March 1989 and in March 1990.

Factor analysis of Part B from the first year enabled the statements correlating most highly with each other to be formed into the four attitude scales, which formed the basis of the statistical analysis.[20] Alpha coefficient statistics for the attitude scales in the first year indicated high levels of internal consistency:[21]

Enjoyment – 0.8925
Difficulty – 0.8467
Usefulness – 0.8268
Contact – 0.8616

and these remained high in the second and third years of the project. When correlations between the scales were also calculated, the highest correlations were between the scales of enjoyment and difficulty and between the scales of enjoyment and usefulness. This indicated that where pupils enjoyed the language, they also found it easy and perceived it to be useful, and vice versa.

When the questionnaires were analysed each pupil was given a six-figure identification number to record his/her school, teaching group, pupil number within the group, language and sex. This enabled the pupils in the sample to be divided up into smaller groups, and also made it possible to compare the attitudes of boys and girls, the attitudes of pupils in different schools and in different teaching groups, and the attitudes of pupils learning different languages. More complex divisions of the pupil sample were also possible: for example, the attitudes of boys learning German could be compared with the attitudes of girls learning German, and the attitudes of different ability groups learning the various languages could be analysed. The pupil attitude questionnaire forms the basis of the next chapter.

THE PUPIL INTERVIEWS

Data on pupil attitudes were also collected in a series of pupil interviews which were carried out in the first three years of the project with a subsample of approximately 100 pupils chosen in the first year. The pupils were selected randomly within their teaching groups, care being taken to ensure that there was a balance of boys and girls and that they were spread across all six schools. They were interviewed in single-sex groups of four as it was felt that this would put them at their ease, and the interviews were taped and transcribed. It was intended to interview the same pupils from year to year so that changes in attitude could be monitored as pupils progressed up the school, but in practice reshuffling of groups in the second year and absenteeism meant that not all pupils were interviewed every year. A semi-structured interview schedule was drafted which covered the same areas as the pupil attitude questionnaire: enjoyment, difficulty, usefulness and contact. This was pretested in three of the associated schools and discussed with language teachers before use in the project schools, and the same schedule was used from year to year. Data from the interviews will be discussed in relation to the pupil attitude questionnaire in the next chapter.

THE QUESTIONNAIRES ON ORGANISATIONAL PROBLEMS

In the first two years of the project a number of questionnaires were devised to collect qualitative information on organisational problems associated with diversification and teachers' attitudes. The first two of these were sent out in the summer of 1988 to all language teachers in the project and associated schools. The questionnaires, which drew, among other things, on the work of the DES on teacher qualifications in modern languages[22] and the Hadley Report,[23] were designed to gather information on modern language provision in the schools and on the experience of the individual teachers. After discussions with members of OXPROD's steering and advisory committees two separate questionnaires were constructed, one for heads of modern languages in each school and one for the language teachers in their departments. These were pretested in one of the associated schools and then sent to a total of thirty schools. The heads of department questionnaire requested information on staffing, the number of first and other languages provided, how pupils were allocated to language groups, time allocation to modern languages, contact with the foreign country through exchanges, visits and native speaker assistants, and the history of diversification within the school. The teacher questionnaire elicited information on a wide range of issues including teacher qualifications, timetabling, resources, teaching methods and views on diversification. The results were published in 1988 as OXPROD's first occasional paper.[24]

One of the problems associated with diversification which emerged from returns to the first-year questionnaires was the transfer of pupils into diversified schools, and in the second year a further questionnaire was devised to investigate specifically the problem of transfers-in. This questionnaire was designed to allow teachers to comment in detail on the problems encountered in their schools, including those related to the provision of the FL2, to describe the solutions adopted, and to include examples from their own experience. The results were written up as OXPROD's fourth occasional paper[25] and the whole issue of transfers-in is discussed in Chapter 6 of this book.

Finally, drawing on earlier work carried out in Oxford, two questionnaires were compiled to examine provision of the FL2 in the project and associated schools. The first of these, sent to heads of department in June 1989, investigated the nature of FL2 provision in 'diversified' schools[26] and the problems associated with the FL2. At the same time, the second of these, a short questionnaire for pupils learning an FL2, was completed by pupils in schools A, C and D. As in the main pupil attitude questionnaire, the FL2 questionnaire included a written section where pupils were invited to respond to a number of statements, in this case comparing their FL1 with their FL2, and to give reasons for their response. Reference will be made to the findings from these questionnaires in the next two chapters.

A wealth of information was gathered from both the project and the associated schools in the first three years of the project. Chapters 5 and 6, on pupils' experience of learning languages other than French as FL1s and organisational problems respectively, will present the findings of the project and assess the extent to which the project's research questions have been answered.

NOTES

1 David Phillips and Georgina Clark, *Attitudes towards Diversification: Results of a survey of teacher opinion*, OXPROD Occasional Paper 1, Oxford, University of Oxford Department of Educational Studies, 1988, pp. 45–50.
2 Olive Wood and Valerie Land, *Verbal Test EF* (Test 128), Windsor, NFER-Nelson, 1971.
3 This test was developed at the University of York by Peter Green and is described in Peter S. Green (ed.), *The Language Laboratory in School: Performance and prediction*, Edinburgh, Oliver & Boyd, 1975.
4 Sylvia Honnor, Ron Holt and Heather Mascie-Taylor, *Tricolore*, Stage 1, 1984 (revised edition), Stage 2 1981, Stage 3 1982, Leeds, Arnold-Wheaton.
5 Duncan Sidwell and Penny Capoore, *Deutsch Heute 1*, 1983, *Deutsch Heute 2*, 1984, Walton-on-Thames, Thomas Nelson.
6 Marie Anthony and Michael Buckby, *¡Vaya! Libro 1*, Walton-on-Thames, Thomas Nelson, 1987; Michael Buckby, Michael Calvert, Christine Newsham and Brian Young, *¡Vaya! Libro 2*, Walton-on-Thames, Thomas Nelson, 1988.
7 ILEA Learning Materials Service, *¡Claro!*, Level 1, 1980, Level 2, 1981, London, Mary Glasgow Publications.
8 J. Hall, *Escalier 1*, 1986, *Escalier 2*, 1987, Cheltenham, Stanley Thornes.
9 Patricia M. Smith, *Einfach toll! 1*, 1985, *Einfach toll! 2*, 1986, Cheltenham, Stanley Thornes.
10 Bryan Goodman-Stephens, Paul Rogers and Lol Briggs, *Zickzack*, Stage 1, 1987, Stage 2, 1988, Leeds, Arnold-Wheaton.

11 K. Foden, *Hexagone 2*, Oxford, Oxford University Press, 1984.

12 As in similar investigations to that undertaken by OXPROD it was expected from the very beginning that the 'teacher variable' would probably prove to be the most significant factor in pupils' evaluation of their school learning experiences.

13 David Phillips, 'Diversification of FL1 teaching: A new research project', *Modern Languages*, Vol. 68, No. 1, 1987, pp. 29–31; David Phillips, 'OXPROD – An Oxford research project on diversification of first foreign language teaching', *British Journal of Language Teaching*, Vol. 25, No. 1, 1987, pp. 50–1; David Phillips, 'A language of "unusual simplicity and facility": Spanish as first foreign language', *Vida Hispánica*, Vol. 37, No. 2, 1988, pp. 11–12.

14 Phillips and Clark, op. cit.; David Phillips and Hazel Geatches, *Diversification and 'Transfers-in'*, OXPROD Occasional Paper 4, Oxford, University of Oxford Department of Educational Studies, 1989.

15 The construction of the attitude questionnaire was discussed regularly with an advisory committee of local teachers, who met once a term during the pilot phase of the study to advise on OXPROD's research. Members of OXPROD's steering committee, which has wide representation, were also consulted.

16 This is reported in: Michael Buckby *et al.*, *Graded Objectives and Tests for Modern Languages: An evaluation*, London, Schools Council, 1981.

17 These surveys are reported in: Assessment of Performance Unit (APU), *Foreign Language Performance in Schools. Report on 1983 survey of French, German and Spanish*, Department of Education and Science (DES)/Department of Education for Northern Ireland/Welsh Office (WO), 1985, *Foreign Language Performance in Schools. Report on 1984 survey of French*, DES/Department of Education for Northern Ireland/WO, 1986, and *Foreign Language Performance in Schools. Report on 1985 survey of French*, London, HMSO, 1987.

18 A full description of the development of the pupil attitude questionnaire may be found in: Caroline Filmer-Sankey, 'Attitudes towards first foreign languages in the early stages of secondary school: An investigation into French, German and Spanish', unpublished M.Litt. thesis, University of Oxford, 1991.

19 Caroline Filmer-Sankey, *A Study of First-year Pupils' Attitudes towards French, German and Spanish*, OXPROD Occasional Paper 3, Oxford, University of Oxford Department of Educational Studies, 1989; Caroline Filmer-Sankey, *A Study of Second-year Pupils' Attitudes towards French, German and Spanish*, OXPROD Occasional Paper 5, Oxford, University of Oxford Department of Educational Studies, 1991.

20 The composition of the attitude scales may be found in Filmer-Sankey, op. cit., 1989, p. 10.

21 Perfect correlation would be indicated by an alpha coefficient statistic of 1.0; no correlation at all would be shown by an alpha coefficient statistic of 0.

22 See Tables 1 and 2 in: DES/WO, *Foreign Languages in the School Curriculum: A draft statement of policy*, DES/WO, 1986; and in: DES/WO, *Modern Languages in the School Curriculum. A statement of policy*, London, HMSO, 1988.

23 C.G. Hadley, *Languages other than French in the Secondary School: An exploratory study of other languages as first or equal first foreign languages*, London, Schools Council, 1981.

24 Phillips and Clark, op. cit.

25 Phillips and Geatches, op. cit.

26 This is reported in: David Phillips and Karen Chidwick, *In Defence of the Second Foreign Language*, OXPROD Occasional Paper 6, Oxford, University of Oxford Department of Educational Studies, 1992.

5 Pupils' experience of learning languages other than French as first foreign languages

INTRODUCTION

This chapter is concerned with the work carried out with pupils in the six project schools during the first three years of the project. It reports primarily on the findings from the language attitude questionnaire completed by pupils each year, but also describes views expressed by a small sample of pupils in a series of group interviews. The focus is on their experience of learning languages other than French as FL1s, as formulated in the first two of OXPROD's research questions:

(*i*) What attitudes do children have to French, German and Spanish at various stages of their learning?

(*ii*) What difficulties do children experience in French, German and Spanish and at which stages in their learning?

FINDINGS FROM THE PUPIL ATTITUDE QUESTIONNAIRE

As described in some detail in the previous chapter, the pupil attitude questionnaire completed by pupils in the project schools each year was divided into four sections to provide information of various kinds on their attitudes to and experience of learning the three languages. The first section, Part A, provided factual information about pupils' contact with the country and the people of the language they were learning. The second section, Part B, examined pupils' attitudes towards learning French, German and Spanish. Part C provided information on pupils' enjoyment of various language-learning activities, and Part D allowed pupils to comment more freely on their attitudes towards the three languages. Findings from Parts B and D form the core of this chapter and are described in detail. First, however, information gathered on Part A of the questionnaire is described briefly in order to provide background information on pupils' contact with France, Germany and Spain. Full details of the procedures adopted for the analysis of Part B are reproduced elsewhere.[1]

Analysis of Part A

Part A gathered simple factual information on pupils' previous experience of the country and people of the language they were learning. It contained five simple yes/no questions which were adapted for each language. These were the items on the French version of the questionnaire:

1 Have you been to France (or any other French-speaking country) with your family?
2 Have you been to France (or any other French-speaking country) on a school visit?
3 Have you ever stayed with a family in France (or any other French-speaking country)?
4 Do you have a French-speaking penfriend?
5 Have you ever had a French-speaking person staying at your house?

Pupils' responses in this section, as might be expected, showed an increasing level of contact with the foreign country over the three years, and by the end of the third year more than half the sample had been to France, Germany or Spain. It was clear that the project schools had organised more visits to France and Germany than to Spain in the first three years and school links with these countries were generally well established. On the other hand, many more pupils had been to Spain and to France with their families than to Germany, which is probably an indication of the popularity of Spain as a holiday destination and of the proximity of France.

At the same time, a simple computation of responses to the first three questions in this section enabled the sample to be divided into two groups: pupils who had been to the country of the language they were learning and those who had not. This provided another dimension on which the results from Part B of the attitude questionnaire could be analysed.

Analysis of Parts B and D

As described in Chapter 4 the items in Part B were formed into four attitude scales – enjoyment, difficulty, usefulness and contact – and the sum of pupils' responses to all the items on a scale indicated whether they held positive or negative views in that area. By calculating mean scores and distributions on each attitude scale for selected groups of pupils, it was possible to analyse and compare the attitudes of French, German and Spanish learners, the attitudes of boys and girls, and the attitudes of pupils who had been to the foreign country and those who had not (using information supplied in Part A). With the additional data on language aptitude and ability collected in the first year of the study, it was also possible to carry out analyses to examine differences between the views of high- average- and low-ability pupils towards learning the various languages. Finally, as the questionnaire was administered to the same pupils three times, it was possible to compare their responses from year to year.

Part D provided qualitative information on pupils' attitudes towards the various FL1s to complement the quantitative data collected from Part B. The section consisted of four statements from Part B to which pupils were first asked to respond by circling either STRONGLY AGREE, AGREE, UNCERTAIN, DISAGREE or STRONGLY DISAGREE and then to give a reason for their response. The first three statements related closely to the attitude areas of enjoyment, difficulty and usefulness. In addition to this there was a final open-ended item where pupils were invited to express any opinions they had not been able to express elsewhere in the questionnaire.

On the French version of the first-year questionnaire the five items were:

1 French is one of my favourite lessons;
2 I find French more difficult than other school subjects;
3 French will be useful to me after I leave school;
4 I'm glad I'm learning French rather than another language;
5 If you have any thoughts or feelings about learning French which you have not put in Parts A, B and C, please write them below.

For each year of the study a simple quantitative analysis was carried out for each item in each language to ascertain how many pupils had agreed with the statement, how many had disagreed and how many were uncertain. The written comments were then coded in order to calculate the main reasons why pupils agreed or disagreed with the statements.

As schools A, B, C and D were operating similar systems of language provision, data from their questionnaires were analysed together throughout. Data from school E were analysed separately because pupils there had completed a different version of the questionnaire, and data from school F were analysed separately in the second and third years of the project because they were operating different systems of provision from that in the other project schools.

In the description of the findings the four areas of attitude covered by the questionnaire will be examined in turn, and then differences between pupils' attitudes towards the three languages, in particular, between boys' and girls' attitudes and between the attitudes of pupils of different abilities will be described. Pupils' comments on the three languages are quoted extensively, with spelling and punctuation improved. The sex of the pupil and the year the pupil was in are indicated after the comment in brackets (B = boy, G = girl, 1 = year 1, etc.).

Pupils' enjoyment of French, German and Spanish

Statistical analysis of the questionnaires revealed that higher proportions of pupils, in general, were enjoying the language they were learning rather than not, but that enthusiasm was at its greatest in the first year. When pupils' attitudes towards French, German and Spanish were compared, however, interesting differences between the languages were revealed: in the first year, for example, German learners achieved significantly higher scores than French learners, which indicated that they were enjoying their language much more than pupils learning French. This imbalance between French and German had evened out by the second year, but by this stage higher proportions of pupils learning Spanish thought it was enjoyable than of pupils learning French. In the third year French still appeared to be the language least enjoyed by pupils, with both German and Spanish learners achieving significantly higher scores than those learning French. Closer examination revealed these differences to be mainly attributable to boys' attitudes, that is, boys learning German and Spanish scored more highly than boys learning French, which indicated that they enjoyed these languages more. When pupils' attitudes over the three years were compared it was found that French and German learners were significantly less positive about their languages by the third year, whereas Spanish learners were enjoying Spanish just as much as they had been in the first year.

Unfortunately it was difficult to establish from pupils' responses to the first question in Part D (French/German/Spanish is one of my favourite lessons), exactly why pupils were most positive about Spanish, because the main reasons given for enjoying or not enjoying each language were the same. For example, approximately half the pupils overall, regardless of the language they were learning, mentioned factors related to their language teacher and lesson content. As might be expected, pupils who enjoyed their lessons also liked their teacher and the way they were taught, and those who found their lessons boring disliked their teacher and the way they were taught. Moreover, pupils who said that they did not like their language as much as in the previous year, or who were enjoying it more, often mentioned that they had had a change of teacher. Here is a selection of positive and negative comments which illustrate how influential the teacher is:

> I really like French. . . . My teacher is really great. She helps me and I understand her (G 1)

> I think whether you enjoy French lessons or dislike them depends on what teacher you have. You're learning a new language and you're uncertain and need someone to approach the lesson in a fun way and help you enjoy it (G 1)

> I don't like our teacher and if you don't like the teacher you don't like the lesson (G 1)

It depends whether you have a good teacher or not. If the teacher is boring, German is boring. If the teacher is good, German is good. It just so happens our teacher is boring (G 1)

Sometimes it's very interesting and we play games. But sometimes our teacher gets cross and bad-tempered in the lesson before us and takes it out on us (G 1)

I enjoy French because my teacher is fun to work with and listen to. She makes drab lessons fun and interesting (G 2)

I don't look forward to French – the class are not controlled by the teacher. The work we do is boring. We never play games or stuff like that which makes learning easier (G 3)

This year we've got a bad teacher and I just don't enjoy it because it's boring (B 3)

The teacher we have in the third year isn't very good although I enjoyed it more in the other years because the teacher taught it better (G 3)

I have lost a lot of interest this year because of the change in teacher and the speed the teacher teaches (B 3)

In their comments pupils mentioned the kinds of language learning activities they liked and disliked. 'Communicative' activities, such as games, songs, acting, pair work, oral work, films and flashcard work, were those which pupils appeared to enjoy:

I like German because we don't just sit writing all the time. We play games and sing German songs (G 1)

In German we do lots of things – watching slides, playing number games, looking at cards and saying what's on them (B 1)

French is one of my favourite lessons because we do lots of good things with [our teacher] like drawing, standing out and talking to a partner. In French we do puzzles, acting out things and working in our book from the textbook (B 2)

I think French is good because it is something different altogether and it is very interesting. It can be a lot of fun sometimes when we do acting or puzzles and games (B 2)

We have to do lots of different things instead of say writing or taking notes all the time. We might read or watch a film which stops you getting bored with the subject (G 2)

French is one of my favourite lessons because we do a lot of oral work and we're not just chained to our seats (G 2)

Activities which pupils did not like included copying from the board or overhead projector, learning verbs, listening to tapes, written exercises and tests:

> I don't like listening to some of the tapes (G 1)

> I don't like Spanish because you have to do tons of writing (B 1)

> I find French boring because they don't do enough fun activities. We don't watch any films or anything. We just write in our books and learn about clothes etc. We sometimes play games but it makes me think that French people are boring and I usually forget what we learn (G 2)

> We never do anything interesting like watching films or slides, nothing like that. We just learn words all the time and that's why people don't try – they've lost interest (B 2)

> I don't like German because it's very boring. I hate learning verbs and so I hate most of the lessons 'cos we do verbs a lot. I'd much rather learn French as German is a more masculine language than French (G 2)

> German is very boring because we usually copy off the board or from our textbooks and look at things on the overhead projector. We sometimes do acting out but not very often (B 2)

> I do not like German because I find it boring doing exercises, orals and just having tests. It might be made more interesting by teachers (B 3)

> I think it is boring most of the time and we don't do enough fun things e.g. games, drawings, and all we do every lesson is listen to tapes and do exercises. I really liked it in the second year (G 3)

Many pupils disliked listening to their teacher talking in the foreign language:

> I wasn't very fond of our old teacher. She only talked in German and if you asked her to explain, she would explain in German (G 1)

> The teacher blabbers on in German through the whole lesson (B 1)

> It's quite boring when you sit down and the teacher's talking away most of the time. I don't even know what she's going on about (G 1)

> I don't like it when the teacher talks in French. If she told us what the words meant instead of waiting for us to guess it would be much quicker (B 3)

Surprisingly there were very few comments on any of the textbooks used.

As can be seen from the above comments, a large measure of pupils' enjoyment was derived from factors such as the nature of the lessons and the teaching style of their teachers rather than factors associated with the languages themselves. Yet statistical analysis of the questionnaires revealed high correlations between pupils' enjoyment and their perceptions of the difficulty of the languages they were learning, which were substantiated in some of the pupils' comments:

> I do find French very hard to learn and it gets more boring every lesson. I don't see what use it will be. I don't like learning the language (B 1)

> I like French because I find it quite easy (G 1)

> I find French hard and boring and find it hard to learn French. It's complicated with all of the verbs (G 2)

> I do not like French very much because it is complicated (B 2)

> I don't like French because of the foreign words and things that are not easy. I would prefer to be doing sport or German (B 2)

> Spanish is one of my favourite lessons because I feel it is fun and interesting to learn and I find it quite easy (G 3)

In pupils' comments in Part D variations in the perceived difficulty of the three languages were identified which must account at least in part for the differences in pupils' motivation.

Pupils' perceptions of the difficulty of French, German and Spanish

Statistical analysis of the questionnaires revealed that higher proportions of pupils in general were finding the languages they were learning easy rather than difficult, but pupils were finding them more difficult on the whole by the third year. When pupils' perceptions of the difficulty of the three languages were compared, interesting differences between French, German and Spanish were found. In the first year, pupils learning German achieved significantly higher scores than pupils learning French, which indicated that they thought it was easier, and in the second and third years this trend widened to include Spanish learners as well, with French learners still finding the language most difficult. Boys in particular learning German and Spanish appeared to find these languages easier than boys learning French. By their third year French and German learners perceived the languages to be significantly more difficult than in the first year, whereas Spanish learners were finding the language just as easy as in the first year.

French, German and Spanish learners gave similar reasons for finding the languages difficult. These included the fact that they had not studied the language at primary school, that learning a language was hard work, that lessons were conducted in the foreign language, and that they had a bad teacher. Reasons for finding the languages easy covered the same areas, including the fact that they had previous experience of language learning, that lessons were relaxed and easy, and that they had a good teacher.

A large proportion of pupils made some comment on how easy or difficult they thought the language itself was. Some pupils were tempted to compare the language they were learning with other languages merely on the basis of vicarious impressions gained, for example, from discussion with pupils learning other FL1s in the school. Here are a few of their comments:

> I would rather learn German because you don't have two words for everything if it's a man or lady (G 1 French learner)

> German is an easy language compared with French and Spanish (B 1)

> [German] is supposed to be easier than French (B 1)

> My brother says German is easier than French (B 1)

> Learning German is easier than French because you don't have to put so many dittos above the letters (G 1)

> From what I've seen and what other people tell me, French is harder with all the signs above their words (G 1)

> People say that other languages are harder than Spanish (G 1)

> I'm glad I'm doing Spanish because it's the easiest language (B 1)

> I'm glad I'm learning German and not French because all my friends who do French say that it's difficult (G 3)

From the pupils' comments difficulties specific to the three different languages emerged. French learners, for example, mentioned from the outset grammatical difficulties, particularly with gender, vocabulary and accents, and problems with pronunciation and spelling:

> I think some things are easy like numbers and some hard like verbs and all the different meanings and spellings for one word (B 1)

> I find French more difficult than other subjects because of all the verbs and the little squiggles above and below words (B 1)

> All the verbs and dots and dashes puzzle me. I put them in the wrong place (B 1)

> I don't like the idea of male and female in everything, even rulers. It's silly and confusing (G 1)

> The *le, la, un* and *une* are confusing, so are other male and female things (G 1)

> There are too many verbs and masculine and feminine words to learn. It is a bit much to make a beginner learn that (G 1)

I find French quite difficult because of all the verbs and *le, la, les*, or *mon, ma, mes* (G 2)

There's much more to learning French like learning verbs and the difference between plural feminine and masculine (G 2)

I find French more difficult because of the verbs and the different words for we, they, you, etc. (G 2)

I agree because of having to learn all the verbs and the new system of spelling and saying the words. In all your other subjects you know a bit because it's in English (B 2)

French is quite hard because it is difficult to remember where accents go and also I can never remember spellings or verbs (G 3)

I think it's hard to say and when you hear it on tape it sounds different in writing (B 1)

I don't like French because of the way they write and the accent (B 1)

I don't find French difficult, but some of the pronunciation is hard and a lot of words are also difficult to spell (G 3)

In the third year in particular, when pupils were more articulate about the difficulties they encountered with French, verbs were mentioned most frequently. Here are just a few of their comments:

I find French harder than other subjects because of all the verbs and perfect tenses we have to learn. French is also a lot different to English. German is quite alike to English and so I find this easier (G 3)

Learning verbs, pronouns and vocab is sometimes very hard and quite a few times I do not understand the thing talked about. I think the teacher should spend more time explaining it to the class instead of just reading it out of a book (B 3)

I find French more difficult because of verbs and the future tense (G 3)

I don't understand it because there are so many verbs which have to be learnt (G 3)

I'm not very good at French as I get verbs mixed up and then everything seems really hard. And it's also difficult learning about verb endings and learning the past, present and future verbs (G 3)

French is more difficult than other subjects because we have to learn lists of verbs and vocab (B 3)

I expect there are very few people who find French easy. It's difficult to learn the verbs etc. and really get into the subject and get to know it well (G 3)

It takes a lot more thinking and to understand the changing verb endings isn't easy so it is more difficult (G 3)

I like French but it is hard to learn verbs and their endings (G 3)

Even pupils who said that they did not find French more difficult than other subjects mentioned problems with spelling and verbs. German and Spanish learners, on the other hand, mentioned that the languages were spoken as written, that pronunciation was straightforward, and that vocabulary was easy to learn, in some cases because it seemed similar to English. Here are some of their comments:

I don't think German is hard at all, you sound out the letters in the words and often the words are similar to English words (G 1)

German is quite an easy lesson because quite a lot of German words sound the same or look the same (G 1)

I find German easy and the words are easy to pronounce (B 1)

I think that German is very easy to understand and I have found that many of their words are very much like ours (G 1)

German is easy because there are rules for the words and Germans stick to them and there are no exceptions (B 1)

I think that German is nearly the same as English because the Anglo-Saxons came from Germany (B 1)

Spanish is quite easy because most of the words are not unlike our own (B 1)

Learning German vocab is easy to remember and pronunciation is quite easy too – unlike French (G 2)

German words are quite like English words so they are easier to learn (B 2)

[Spanish] is easy to learn because half of a word means the same thing in English (G 2)

Now that I'm in the second year I'm finding it [Spanish] easier and most of the words are like English words (B 2)

I don't find Spanish easy but it isn't hard because most of the words in Spanish sound how you spell them (B 2)

I think [Spanish] is quite easy because the words are easy to pronounce and I understand most things in the lesson (G 3)

Spanish is quite easy because so many of the words are like the English. It is quite logical and a nice language to learn (G 3)

By the third year, however, German learners appeared to be those most troubled by grammatical difficulties. These included problems with gender, the case system and verbs:

> You have to listen hard and there's a lot to learn and remember. We have spellings every other night to learn and it's hard work. Also remembering all the *der*, *die* and *das*'s is confusing and we are expected to learn them (G 1)

> I'm not sure about my verbs. It's like learning your alphabet *a ber ker dur* and then learning it *ay bee cee dee*!!! There are so many *zum*'s *zur*'s *der*'s *die*'s, *das*'s and then *den* comes from *der*. WHY CAN'T GERMAN PEOPLE HAVE ONE WORD LIKE 'THE' instead of about twenty words? (G 1)

> I don't really like the way she sets us on *einen*, then *der*, *die*, *das*, then *zum*'s and *zur*'s and now *ein*, *eine*, *einen* again. It's confusing! (G 1)

> I find German difficult because of the verb endings and the three words for 'the' (G 1)

> I don't find German hard but some things are a bit hard like *der*, *die* and *das* words (G 1)

> It is not like History where you just learn it in your own language. In German you have to learn verbs and the three 'the's' etc. (G 2)

> It is difficult learning the sentence constructions and the sex of objects (G 2)

> I find learning the *der*, *die*, *das* and past tenses very difficult as the teachers give us very little help (G 2)

> German is much harder than other subjects because you have so many genders and different words for things (G 2)

> German is confusing, with all the weird verbs etc. German is also fairly complicated (G 2)

> Learning German is quite hard especially learning verbs, i.e. *kann*, *will*, etc. (G 2)

> Sometimes German is more difficult than other subjects when we do sentences because it is hard trying to find the *the*, *a*, *on*, *if* words (G 2)

> German can be very difficult at times, but at others it can be very easy. I don't understand accusative and dative (G 3)

> German can be an easy subject at times. The only confusing bit is all the different words for 'the' and 'a' (B 3)

Spanish learners also mentioned difficulties with accents, gender and verbs, particularly in the third year, but on the whole they were more positive about grammatical difficulties in the language:

Some parts of Spanish are confusing like masculine and feminine (G 1)

Spanish is quite easy to learn. It's remembering where words go and when writing accents on words, e.g. *esta, está* (B 1)

You have one word that means a lot more than one word and you have a lot more endings for one word than you do in English (G 3)

I find Spanish difficult because there is a lot of vocabulary to learn and all the verb endings make life difficult (B 3)

I find it quite easy but I sometimes get in a muddle with verbs (G 3)

Doing verbs is very hard but most words are close to English words and it's not too bad (B 3)

It is probable that the linguistic difficulties encountered by French learners from the beginning, and by German learners increasingly over the three years, account for the fact that French learners found the language most difficult throughout and that German learners' initially positive attitudes gradually declined. As the statistical analysis of the questionnaire has shown that pupils' enjoyment and perceptions of the difficulty of the languages are closely related, linguistic reasons may also be assumed to account for the fact that French and German learners' enjoyment of the languages decreased over the three years. The Spanish learners, who mentioned fewer linguistic problems, were positive throughout.

Pupils' perceptions of the usefulness of French, German and Spanish

Another factor which appeared to affect pupils' enjoyment of the languages was how useful the languages were perceived to be. Results from the questionnaires revealed that higher proportions of pupils overall thought their languages were useful rather than not, and that, on the whole, the three languages were perceived to be equally useful. The exception to this was in the third year, when German learners, particularly boys, thought their language was more useful than French or Spanish learners did. Over the three years French learners' attitudes did not change, but German and Spanish learners were more positive by the third year about the usefulness of the languages to them.

The two main reasons given for finding the languages useful or not were related to whether pupils would use them in future careers and whether they would have contact with the foreign country and its people. Some pupils listed jobs where the languages would be useful (including chef and fashion designer for French learners, engineering and commerce for German learners and footballer for Spanish learners!), while others saw the importance of languages as good qualifications for careers in general. The following comments represent a variety of views:

If you want a good job which needs languages or good qualifications French would be useful (G 1)

When I go for an interview and someone else who wants the same job has a German O or A level and I haven't and they have the same other qualifications as me, they are more likely to get the job (G 1)

I agree because I want to be a football player and if I do I might get bought from Spain, so it would be helpful to know the language (B 1)

I would like to work abroad and knowing a language might help me get a job (about half of the world speaks Spanish) or something like that (B 3)

It will be useful as almost every job now you have to know a Spanish language or any other language before you can apply (B 3)

In many centres of further education you cannot get in without GCSE in one modern language. I wish to go on to further education and therefore French, being my first foreign language, will be of use to me. Also with 1992 coming up, job prospects will be better with French (B 3)

It will be especially useful to me, because even though I haven't got an exact idea of what I want to be when I grow up, I know I want to go to university and travel, work in languages and with people. Maybe a journalist, maybe a teacher in a foreign country. Anyway with Germany reuniting and the European market very strong, I think it is increasingly more important for us to be able to communicate in French and German (G 3)

Because of Europe coming together people who speak different languages will be preferred to others who can't (B 3)

Second- and third-year pupils, particularly French and German learners, were clearly aware that languages would become increasingly important in the context of 1992 and the Single European Market:

I will be able to market my products or designs abroad and in 1992 a lot of trade barriers will be broken and it may be needed (B 2)

If I get a good job I might have to do talks or entertain French clients. Also if I go on holiday, especially with 1992 (B 2)

More and more jobs nowadays will involve France and French-speaking, especially after 1992 when we will be involved even more (G 2)

With the breaking down of trade barriers in 1992 and the opening of the Channel Tunnel in 1993 it will be very important business-wise and politically-wise to speak another foreign language (B 3)

French will be useful because of the EC and all the business and companies that will come to England and the Channel Tunnel (B 3)

With 1992 coming up more firms will need people to speak French and other languages (G 3)

In 1992 when Europe joins together people will be going over to France and the French will be coming over here so it would be useful if I knew some French so I could communicate (G 3)

Even though I do not like it, I know as soon as 1992 has started I will need to know German and French (B 3)

German will be very useful in finding a job as in 1992 many people will want German speakers to help with EC work (G 3)

When the 1992 free market comes along customers will want you to speak their language plus I want to be an engineer and a lot of top European car engineering companies come from Germany e.g. Mercedes Benz, Porsche and BMW (B 3)

With 1992 on the horizon, having German will be an extreme advantage, when coming to get a job over a person who hasn't a language. This is very important in the area where I would like to work . . . industry (B 3)

It will be useful when I leave school because most of Europe either speak German as a first language or a second language, so it will be helpful after 1992 (B 3)

I don't know yet what I want to do but with Germany being reunited it would form a big country and the language would be more helpful in more jobs (G 3)

I think with the reunification of Germany soon, Germany will become a major power in the world of Economics, so being able to speak German will be very useful (B 3)

I think that Spanish will be useful to me after 1992 when I expect there will be a lot more Spanish trade in England (G 3)

German, in particular, was viewed as important in industry and commerce, and this must account for the increasingly positive attitudes of German learners over the three years, but it is interesting to note that very few pupils mentioned the then imminent reunification of the two Germanies. While career motives were also strong with French and Spanish learners, a higher proportion of these were inclined to think that their language would be useful for holidays and foreign travel, with French learners viewing the construction of the Channel Tunnel as something which would make the communication with France easier and French, therefore, more useful:

The Channel Tunnel is being built so more French will be needed to communicate with the French (B 1)

The Channel Tunnel will open and it will provide access to France (B 2)

When I leave school the Channel Tunnel will be open so there will be more French and European people in England and more English people in France (B 2)

We are over in France a lot and when the Channel Tunnel is built you will understand what they are saying (B 2)

I'm glad I'm learning French because France is the nearest foreign language country plus when the Channel Tunnel comes we will be nearer to France (B 2)

By the time I leave school and get a decent job the Channel Tunnel will be finished, so I can pop over to France for the day. I may even be able to get some work out there (B 3)

Pupils perceived Spanish as being particularly useful for foreign travel and many had direct experience of the country or were hoping to go there in the near future:

We have a time-share in El Capistrano for life (G 1)

Whenever the English go abroad they never seem to speak in the countries' language, so it will be good if you can understand posters and conversations (G 1)

I went to the country and I could not speak a word. We are going this year and I will be able to speak a lot (G 1)

In Spain we have a really nice apartment and I would like to learn Spanish for when we go there and my Dad would like me to as well (G 1)

I am glad I'm learning Spanish because the first time we went to Spain my Dad ordered two ham sandwiches instead of cheese ones and I would like to learn about other places and what Spanish people eat, etc. (G 2)

A few pupils were motivated to learn the language for its own sake, as these comments from French learners show:

I enjoy French because it is a challenge to learn another language and always new parts are being introduced. It is satisfying to know another language, so you can understand a group of people you couldn't before (B 2)

Learning a language is more interesting than English or Maths. It is something totally new. When you start you know nothing of the language at all but slowly you build up your French/German vocabulary (G 2)

It is always different and I am continuously learning new things. I find it interesting and hope I will do well in the year (G 2)

It is interesting to learn and also interesting to learn about the country and different foods and customs that the French have (B 2)

French is one of my favourite lessons because I love learning languages. I also like German. I love the country France and love to be able to speak French to my penfriend or other French people. French will be useful for what I want to do and also it sounds very feminine (G 2)

French is definitely one of my favourites, if not my favourite. Not just because it is a language, but because it is so feminine and flowing. Also I have been to France many times and have a French friend so there is a target to work for (G 3)

It is interesting to learn about another country and its language because you learn something about the country, and the language part helps you communicate to a wider variety of people than just knowing English would allow you to (B 3)

But, as can be seen, careers were the main reason why all three languages were perceived to be useful. While pupils' attitudes towards French might have been affected by the traditional status of French as FL1 and their perceptions of it as a widely-spoken language, pupils saw German and Spanish as just as important to them, particularly after they had been studying them for some time.

Pupils' attitudes towards the people and country of the language they were learning

In general, pupils were found to be well disposed towards the country and people of the language they were learning, although pupils learning French were less keen on contact with the foreign country than pupils learning German or Spanish. Attitudes were coloured by parents' views, past experience of the foreign country or people, and alarmingly, in-built prejudices about the three countries and their languages. Previous contact with the foreign country was shown to have a positive effect on attitudes: pupils who had already been to the foreign country (about 60 per cent by the third year) were, not surprisingly, found to have better attitudes towards the country and people than those who had not. They appeared to enjoy learning languages more, perceived the languages to be easier and more useful to them, and wanted to visit the foreign country again. Pupils' attitudes towards French, in particular, appeared to be significantly improved in those who had been to France or who knew French people.

Differences between the attitudes of girls and boys

Experience of the foreign country was clearly an important variable affecting pupil attitudes, but two other factors, the sex of the pupils and their ability, were also found to be influential. Comparison of boys' and girls' attitudes revealed that by the third year girls were enjoying the languages much more and were more convinced than boys that languages would be useful to them later on. In addition to this girls were more positive than boys throughout the study in their attitudes towards the country and people of the language they were learning. On the other hand, boys and girls appeared to find the languages equally difficult. When the attitudes of boys and girls towards the different languages were compared, interesting variations in perception of the different languages were detected, which suggested that boys were generally less positive in their attitudes towards French than in their attitudes towards German and Spanish. Over the three years boys appeared to enjoy French the least and to find it more difficult than boys learning German or Spanish, and from the second year onwards boys learning French were also less positive in their attitudes towards France. The boys' preference for German and Spanish over French may account for the fact that girls appeared to be more positive than boys about languages generally, as higher proportions of pupils in the sample were learning French than were learning German or Spanish. Nonetheless, the questionnaire did provide interesting evidence to suggest that boys on the whole responded more positively to German and Spanish than to French, whereas girls were equally positive in their attitudes to all three languages.

Differences between the attitudes of pupils of different abilities

Interesting differences between languages were also found in the area of ability. For example, in all three years high-ability French and German learners perceived their languages to be easier than low-ability learners and were more positive in their attitudes towards the foreign country than low-ability learners, whereas there were no differences in the attitudes of Spanish learners across the ability range. Similar, but not so distinct, trends also emerged in pupils' enjoyment of the three languages and in their perceptions of the usefulness of the language to them. It is also interesting to note that pupils in the lower half of the ability range were enjoying French less by the third year than pupils learning Spanish, and finding it more difficult than pupils learning Spanish or German.

Differences between pupils' attitudes in the six schools

While absolute comparisons between pupils' attitudes in the six schools could not be made owing to minor variations in the questionnaires completed, pupils in schools A to D, where a system of parallel language had operated since the first year, were shown to be more positive in all respects than pupils in schools E and F, where different patterns of provision had operated (school E – dual languages, school F – different languages for years 1 and 2, and a choice in the third year). This may be an indication that a system of one FL1 throughout the three years encouraged more positive attitudes, but it is more likely that other factors adversely affected attitudes in schools E and F. In school E a few pupils mentioned that they found two languages on the timetable too much to cope with, but interviews with pupils and teachers there revealed that negative attitudes had been fostered by considerable staffing changes over the three years, particularly for German. In the case of school F attitudes deteriorated in the second year when all pupils changed to a different FL1 but were taught by the same teacher, a factor which was acknowledged to have diminished enthusiasm for the new language.

Summary observations on the pupil attitude questionnaire

A few summary observations about pupils' attitudes towards the three languages can be made. First, a higher proportion of pupils overall enjoyed the languages they were learning, found them quite easy, thought they would be useful to them later on and were keen to visit the foreign country rather than not, but enthusiasm for languages among French and German learners declined over the three years. While it was possible to identify linguistic features of the three languages which influenced pupils' perceptions of them, classroom experience was found to be the overriding factor determining how much pupils enjoyed their lessons and how easy they found their FL1: about half the pupils made some reference to their teacher, the content of their language lessons and the way they were taught.

The perceived usefulness of the language to pupils later on was also important. Some pupils were 'intrinsically' motivated to learn the foreign language out of interest in the language itself or in the foreign country and its people, but a far greater number were 'extrinsically' motivated by a desire to gain a qualification or skill which would enable them to find a job they liked after leaving school. Over the three years there appeared to be a growing awareness of the importance of languages as good qualifications for obtaining an interesting and/or lucrative job. The advent of the Single European Market in 1992 was mentioned particularly as a reason why languages would be of use in careers. French learners were conscious of the proximity of France and increased opportunities afforded by the Channel Tunnel, while German learners stressed the advantages of a knowledge of German in the economic and commercial world.

A few further trends emerged: parents' and siblings' attitudes towards languages and experience of language learning, for example, were found to have a strong influence on pupils' perceptions of the languages they were learning. Pupils, particularly those in the first year, mentioned whether their parents or siblings knew the language and could help them with their homework. Comments of this kind were inevitably more frequent with French learners, since French tended to be the language that their parents had learnt at school:

> I am glad I am doing French because if I get stuck my Mum or brother can help me, but I don't usually need their help (G 1)

> My Mum and Dad want me to learn French and some people in my family speak French (B 1)

> I like French and my sister does French so we can help each other (G 1)

> If I don't understand my homework my sister will help me but not tell me the answers (B 1)

> I am glad I am learning German because my family can help (B 1)

> My Dad has done German and my uncle lives in Germany so I can get help when I need it which makes me more confident (B 1)

> My sister learnt French at school and it would have been nice to learn (B 3 German learner)

German and Spanish learners, on the other hand, whose families were less likely to have experience of these languages, mentioned how pleased they were to be learning something different from the language which their parents knew or which their brother or sister was learning:

> I am the only one in the family that is learning German and I think German is better than French (G 1)

> All my uncles, aunties and cousins learnt to speak French so I thought I would be different (B 1 German learner)

> Nobody in my family learns [Spanish] and I like to be different (B 1)

> I agree because I am the only person in my family that knows any Spanish (B 2)

> I'm glad I'm learning Spanish because I like it and I'll be the only person in the family that can speak it (B 3)

There was also a certain novelty value in learning a language other than French at school: many pupils were aware that it was a new departure in their schools for German or Spanish to be taught as FL1 and they felt that they were somehow 'special'. Comments on this from Spanish learners were particularly frequent:

> [Spanish] is a different language to ours and not many other schools do it in the first year (G 1)

[Spanish] is different to French and French is a common language to learn in the first year (G 1)

I think I like Spanish better than any other language because everyone does French and it gets boring. I wouldn't have minded doing German (G 1)

Spanish is a new language taught in schools and we got the chance to study it for the first time (B 1)

I like learning Spanish because it is different and new. Also when you are in France most people know English but in Spain it's less (B 1)

I prefer German to French because it's easier and more unusual than French which is what most people learn and I like to be different (G 2)

At most secondary schools all the students learn French and I think it is better to learn something that is different to everyone else (G 2 German learner)

We are the only pupils in this school to do Spanish from being first years (G 2)

I'm pleased I'm learning Spanish because it's fun like other languages and when I say I'm doing Spanish they say that's different (B 2)

I enjoy Spanish a lot and it's nice to learn a different language from other groups (B 2)

Everyone expects us to learn French, so when you say you are learning Spanish it surprises them (G 2)

I am glad we are doing Spanish because so many other schools learn French and German and it is nice to do something different for once (G 2)

I am glad I'm learning Spanish because it's something different. I am more likely to be going to Spain than say Germany (G 3)

Spanish is better than French because it is a bit easier and I like it because it is different (B 3)

At the same time pupils held differing opinions on the relative importance of the three languages in the world. Many of the French learners were convinced that French was the most widely spoken language:

I think people speak French in more countries than any other language apart from English (G 1)

I think it's the second most used language in the world (B 1)

It is a more universal language than German or Spanish (B 1)

French like English is an international language which will come in handy on holidays or business trips (B 1)

France is nearer and a wider-spread language than German (G 1)

French is a very widely spoken language so, as we have to do a language, I'm glad it's French (G 2)

French is the next biggest language next to English and Japanese (B 2)

I know why French is taught but why Spanish? People are more likely to go to France than Spain (G 3)

A similar point was raised by Spanish learners, but, of course, with more justification:

Spanish is spoken in more places than French and German and also it's OK (G 2)

I am glad I'm learning Spanish because it's the second most spoken language in the world and that could help a lot (B 2)

A lot of other countries speak Spanish like South America (B 2)

It's a new language and lots of foreign countries speak it and if I ever go to South America or Spain it is useful. More countries speak Spanish than French or German (B 2)

It is such a wildly [*sic*] spoken language and it is interesting (G 2)

There are lots of countries where Spanish is a first language. I would rather learn Spanish than French because Spanish is easier to understand and pronounce (G 2)

A third of the world's population speaks Spanish, so it would help if we spoke Spanish too (B 2)

It is easier than French to learn and it is spoken in more countries than French (G 2)

On a negative note there were many comments from French and German learners which revealed deep-seated prejudices against French and German people:

I've never liked the French and I've always liked the Germans (B 1)

I'm glad I haven't been to France. I hate the smell there. I hate French a lot (B 1)

I hate French and the people who boil live crabs and lobsters (B 3)

I would like a clean person if they came to stay at my house if they came from abroad (G 1)

I'm glad I'm not learning German because after what Adolf Hitler did I wouldn't want anything to do with Germany (B 1)

I've always wanted to speak in French because I hate Germans and the German language (G 1)

A comparison of pupils' attitudes towards the three languages produced valuable evidence to support the hypothesis on which the research was based, namely that *there is nothing in the nature of German and Spanish as subjects in the school curriculum than makes these languages unsuitable as first foreign languages for the whole ability range.* Pupils in the sample perceived the three languages to be equally useful, and by the third year they were found, in fact, to be enjoying German and Spanish more, to be finding them easier and to be more receptive to contact with Germany and Spain than with France. On closer examination, boys in particular were revealed to be more positively disposed towards German and Spanish than towards French. At the same time it was found that pupils in the lower half of the ability range were less positive towards French than towards German and Spanish, and furthermore there were no differences in the attitudes of pupils learning Spanish right across the ability range. While only a small sample of Spanish learners were involved in the study, this is perhaps an indication of the greater suitability of Spanish for the whole ability range.

While these results may be attributed at least in some part to linguistic differences between French, German and Spanish, it is acknowledged, of course, that a number of other factors will have considerable influence on pupils' attitudes towards the three languages and on the generalisability of the results from the attitude questionnaire. These include, among other things, the fact that the sample of schools was not geographically or socially 'representative', that ability levels in the language cohorts were not identical (despite random allocation to the teaching groups in the first year), and that pupils were setted by ability in different ways in each school from the second year. By far the most influential factor, however, was the teacher and his or her teaching style, which pupils in the sample mentioned more frequently than the language itself. While attempts were made from the outset to ensure that teachers were using the same materials for each language in the schools and that the course books used were approximately comparable in content and style, it was of course not possible to ensure that pupils were taught in the same way across schools and languages, desirable as this might have been for the research. The findings are presented here on the assumption that the various teaching styles were evenly distributed across the language cohorts and as such will not have influenced the results in favour of any one language. Over the three years interviews with pupils and teachers in the six schools certainly indicated that, despite differences between individuals' teaching styles, teaching approaches were similar in each language, and statistical analysis of the data for each school separately revealed similar differences between the languages within the schools. This suggests that the teacher variable has not skewed the results from the attitude questionnaire overall.

The pupil interviews

The pupil interviews, carried out in June for the first three years of the project, revealed much to corroborate the findings from the pupil attitude questionnaire. As far as enjoyment of the languages is concerned, for example, pupils gave similar reasons for liking or disliking language lessons. These included, as expected, the teacher and the way the languages were taught:

> It's brilliant because mainly it's the teacher, we've got a really nice teacher. He comes out with funny jokes . . . he did this joke like, what do you call two Spanish firemen? Hose a and Hose b! (B 1)

Pupils were very aware of the fact that it was important to have a good teacher and many attributed changes in how much they enjoyed their languages from year to year to the fact that they had had a new teacher. Games and activities involving interaction were those most enjoyed throughout, and many pupils disliked listening to tapes because of the speed of native speech and poor audio equipment. There were no clear differences between pupils' enjoyment of the three languages but the Spanish learners in both schools where Spanish was taught (B and C) were particularly positive about Spanish and became increasingly enthusiastic over the three years. Most pupils liked the textbook they were using. French learners found *Tricolore* helpful, clearly laid out and easy to understand. German learners liked *Deutsch Heute* but found the German explanations difficult to understand. Similarly, Spanish learners liked *¡Vaya!* but again expressed reservations about the Spanish instructions, which made homework difficult.

In the area of difficulty, as on the questionnaire, it was easier to identify differences between pupils' attitudes towards the three languages. In French the main problems mentioned were spelling, pronunciation and grammatical difficulties, including gender, verbs and adjectival agreement. Pupils throughout recognised that French was not phonetic or spoken as written, as these comments show:

> A lot of letters that you have to pronounce are a lot different to what we say so you have to get used to that (G 1)

> Spelling just makes it harder because you're going to pronounce it how the word was spelt but you're not really meant to (G 1)

> Not having to pronounce the last letters is difficult (B 1)

On paper it's a lot different to how you actually spell it (G 2)

The actual written language is a lot easier but when it comes to speaking it's so difficult . . . because German is, where you speak, you can actually speak the word, but in French you need to know all the accents as to how it's pronounced (B 3)

When you see it written down and then you pronounce it, you pronounce it wrong because you pronounce it the way it looks (B 3)

At the same time there was a growing feeling among the French learners interviewed that the French accent was hard to reproduce and that it was embarrassing to try to pronounce French words:

Some words are really hard to pronounce. You need a special way and it's hard to do it (B 3)

I can't get my tongue and that around words so when I say it it comes out differently from what I wanted to say (B 3)

It's embarrassing (G 3)

If you say it wrong, everyone sort of just shrieks out laughing (G 3)

Most of it's tongue-twisting (B 3)

Sometimes we just say it for fun and it comes out properly. We just put on a French accent just for fun and she says it's good so we just do that (B 3)

Among third-year boys there was also the feeling that voice-breaking could compound this problem:

You do find it very difficult because you've got such a deep voice (B 3)

I think their [girls'] voice sounds better because . . . their voice is always broken (B 3)

In addition to this, French learners described French as a complex language:

Some things are the same but they've got more words added on to a sentence (G 2)

They've put more words in when we don't need them (B 2)

You have lots of words, whereas in English you have just the one (G 2)

A short sentence would probably be really long in French because they seem to say lots more than we do (G 2)

It's back to front (G 2)

The majority of German learners interviewed found German easy on the whole but many expressed reservations about grammar, spelling and pronunciation. While German was generally viewed as similar to English and thus a fairly easy language to learn, some pupils thought this was a source of confusion rather than an advantage:

> It sounds like English but the spelling isn't the same, it's slightly different (B 3)

> You've got the English words in there and you know them and also it might be confusing because you might slip in an English word instead of a German one (B 3)

> I just do what it sounds like. I'm mostly wrong (G 3)

> It sounds the same but the spelling turns out wrong (G 3)

Many pupils also found difficulties with 'the long words' in German:

> The strings of words are very difficult to spell (B 1)

> The long words are really hard (G 1)

> They join a lot of the words up together and they're hard to learn (B 3)

> They never have short words. They always seem to be long and then you have to put 'g' in front of them or 'p' on the end or something like that, so you get really confused (G 3)

> They join a lot of words up together and they're hard to learn (B 3)

And, as on the attitude questionnaire, pupils mentioned problems with word order and gender:

> If you translate it straight into English it doesn't make sense (B 3)

> If you're translating bits of it into English they don't sort of go properly (B 3)

> It's a bit stupid because you've got things that you think are masculine which are feminine (B 3)

On the whole, however, the pupils interviewed found fewer difficulties with German than with French. Spanish learners, too, were fairly positive in this respect. Most of those interviewed said that the language was similar to English, and that it was easy to spell and pronounce because the words were spoken as written:

> You pronounce all the letters in the words so it's quite easy to read them and to say them (B 3)

> The alphabet's easy, like French I can't pronounce it, like 'a' or 'e' you don't normally pronounce it as 'a' or 'e' (G 3)

Reading's quite easy because we pronounce virtually every letter, unlike French, which sometimes you only pronounce letters on the end of the words and also the accent in French is different, totally different than English, unlike Spanish which is similar to English, so it's easy to pronounce the words (G 3)

Pupils were questioned each year about the relative difficulty of the four language-learning skills – listening, speaking, reading and writing – and in all three languages their opinions were very much the same. Listening was found to be the most difficult skill by the majority of pupils, irrespective of the language they were learning, and they complained about the poor quality of tape-recordings and the impossible speed of the language when spoken by natives. Pupils also found writing difficult, but reading and speaking were thought to be easier skills to acquire.

Most learners felt that their language would be useful to them after leaving school. French learners thought French was the most useful language because France was nearer and they would be more likely to go there, and some pupils believed French to be a more widespread language than German or Spanish. German learners, on the other hand, thought German would be useful in their careers and for business, but not as useful as French for holidays, as Germany was further away. Some Spanish learners were aware of the importance of Spanish as a world language, but others still said that French would be a more useful language to learn because it was more widely spoken. On the other hand, a few were aware that it would be an advantage to have a qualification in Spanish rather than one in French because Spanish was more unusual. Many of the pupils interviewed had been to France, Germany or Spain, but a few had never been abroad.

Interviews with pupils learning Italian at school F revealed very positive attitudes towards the language which generally compared favourably with French for enjoyment and ease. Pupils mentioned in particular that Italian was spoken as written and no reference was made to problems with grammar or vocabulary. They were also aware that it was unusual to be learning Italian as an FL1 and were pleased to be different from pupils in other schools learning French. On the negative side many pupils bemoaned the lack of a textbook for Italian and very few had been to Italy or anticipated ever going there. Overall, however, pupils were found to be as positive towards Italian as they were towards other languages.

As can be seen, the conversations with pupils over the three years produced much to support the evidence gained from the pupil attitude questionnaire. The nature of the exercise was such, however, that direct comparisons could not be made between the attitudes of the various groups interviewed each year or from one year to the next.

SUMMARY OF THE MAIN FINDINGS

The main points to emerge from the pupil attitude questionnaire and interviews may be listed as follows:

1 Over the three years French learners, particularly boys, enjoyed their language less than German or Spanish learners. German was found to be most popular in the first year, and Spanish in the second year.
2 Spanish learners were as well-motivated by the end of the third year as they had been in the first year, but French and German learners' levels of motivation decreased.
3 French learners, particularly boys, perceived their language to be more difficult than German or Spanish learners. They experienced problems with pronunciation, spelling, gender and vocabulary. German and Spanish learners commented that the languages were spoken as written and found them easy to pronounce. German learners, however, were troubled by grammatical difficulties by the third year. These included gender, cases, word order and verbs. Spanish learners mentioned fewest linguistic problems.
4 The three languages were perceived to be equally useful, particularly for future careers. Pupils were aware of the importance of languages as qualifications in the context of 1992 and the Single European Market.
5 Pupils were generally well disposed towards the country and people of the language they were learning. Those who had visited the country were more positive than those who had not.
6 High-ability French and German learners were more positive in their attitudes than low-ability learners. In Spanish, on the other hand, motivation did not decrease with ability. Low-ability learners were particularly negative in their attitudes towards French.
7 Pupils' attitudes in general were influenced by parents' and siblings' attitudes to and experience of the three languages.
8 Pupils learning German and Spanish felt that there was a novelty value in learning a less commonly taught language.
9 Classroom experience was as important an influence on pupils' attitudes as the languages themselves.

CONCLUSION

The findings from the questionnaire and the interviews together afford interesting insights into pupils' experience of learning French, German and Spanish and provide encouraging evidence from an *educational* perspective to support the wider introduction of German and Spanish as alternatives to French as FL1s in secondary schools. Pupils in general were shown to be at least as positive in their attitudes towards these two languages as they were towards French; boys in particular were found to be more positively motivated when offered German or Spanish as FL1, and pupils of all abilities were found to respond equally well to Spanish. Persuasive evidence of this kind must taken into account alongside the purely practical considerations associated with diversification of language provision, to be discussed in the next chapter, when decisions are made as to which language or languages should be offered as FL1s on the curriculum.

NOTE

1 The statistical analysis of the questionnaire is described in detail in: Caroline Filmer-Sankey, 'Attitudes towards first foreign languages in the early stages of secondary school: An investigation into French, German and Spanish', unpublished M.Litt. thesis, University of Oxford, 1991.

6 Organisational questions

INTRODUCTION

We have seen that the protracted debate about diversification and its implementation has returned again and again to the need for *policy* and *planning*. In the early 1980s, when the FL2 was perceived to be at great risk (a situation which has not noticeably improved during the past decade) it was clear that the best way to consolidate its position *nationally* was for LEAs to develop plans *locally* that would ensure a range of provision. One of the present authors, with Veronica Stencel, had called for the formulation of local policy and the development of plans for its implementation, in a study published in 1983,[1] and we have recounted in earlier chapters the steps taken to produce a national policy position which would include diversification. Policy statements by the DES, gratifyingly, have included exhortations to LEAs to make sure that provision locally is properly 'diversified'.

Those exhortations are of course made weaker by the introduction of Local Management of Schools (LMS), which has created a degree of independence from LEA control and influence that has considerably lessened, among other functions, the role of the advisory service. It was precisely the advisers who would be crucial in encouraging the development of local plans for diversification. The 'ESG authorities' did, however, provide considerable impetus, as the DES had hoped, to the need for various patterns of provision to be established in LEAs, and in what follows we shall consider the kind of arrangements made, together with evidence from other LEAs.

We shall also be concerned with individual schools and their arrangements for diversification, including such matters as timetabling, teacher reactions, resources, 'transfers-in' and relations with parents. We shall look too at the FL2, and consider in-service training (INSET) arrangements and the continuing problem of staffing.

LEA PROVISION

In October 1988 OXPROD contacted all LEAs in England and Wales not in receipt of the special Education Support Grant, and put two main questions to their modern languages advisers about diversification. The first simply requested information on current provision for languages other than French; the second asked for details of any plans to diversify FL1 teaching.

The survey was undertaken at a time of increasing awareness of diversification issues. LEAs were fully cognizant of the policy position described in HMI's *Modern Foreign Languages to 16* of 1987 and in *Modern Foreign Languages in the School Curriculum: A statement of policy*, issued by the DES in 1988. HM Inspector John Marshall had devised a 'mapping exercise',[2] made available to LEAs through CILT, and the DES had invited bids for a share of the ESG to support the development of diversification policy locally. There was therefore a clear familiarity with the particular wind of change blowing, if rather gently, across the country, and this was reflected in the responses received.

(i) Patterns of provision

The first question, concerning provision, revealed a remarkable range of available information. Some authorities could reply in great detail, and clearly had well-developed means of storing and updating information about language teaching in all their schools; at the other extreme a few LEAs seemed to hold no central information at all.

In the developments which, post-Callaghan and pre-ERA, had begun to explore what was known about curricular provision locally, a DES Circular[3] had caused considerable embarrassment in many LEAs, which had found themselves quite unable to answer some straightforward questions about the curricula of their schools. (The 1944 Education Act laid down of course that 'secular provision . . . *shall be under the control of the local education authority*'[4] [present writers' emphasis].) Among the questions on modern languages were:

> What is the authority's policy for the provision of courses in the various modern languages in secondary schools? To what extent is the present position in the authority's area in accord with that policy?

> What steps have the authority taken to help schools decide which modern languages should be taught to which groups of pupils between the ages of 11 and 16, and what should be the minimum length of language courses?

> What steps have the authority taken to promote the co-ordination of provision for modern language courses in sixth forms and in a wide variety of languages available to them?

From the sketchy information in answer to those particular questions provided ('concocted' might be a more appropriate term in some instances) by LEAs, the DES devised a bar graph (Figure 6.1) to show frequency of

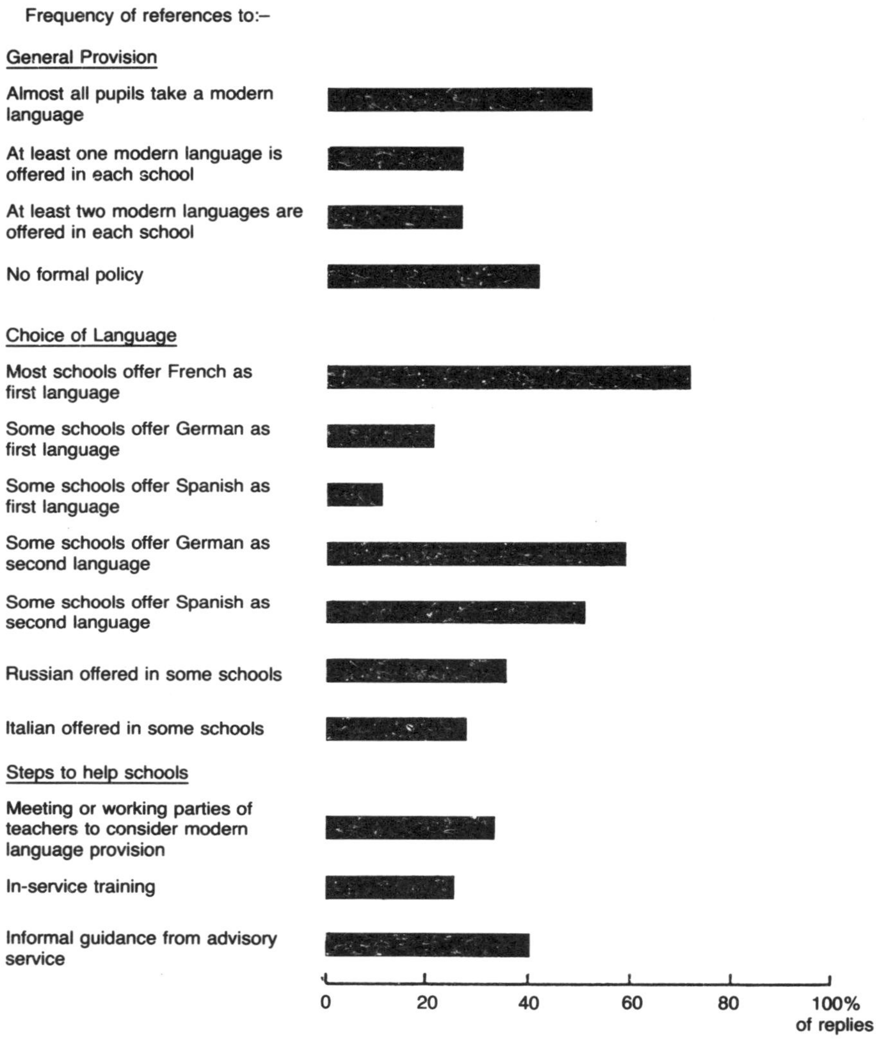

Frequency of references to:–

General Provision

Almost all pupils take a modern
language

At least one modern language is
offered in each school

At least two modern languages are
offered in each school

No formal policy

Choice of Language

Most schools offer French as
first language

Some schools offer German as
first language

Some schools offer Spanish as
first language

Some schools offer German as
second language

Some schools offer Spanish as
second language

Russian offered in some schools

Italian offered in some schools

Steps to help schools

Meeting or working parties of
teachers to consider modern
language provision

In-service training

Informal guidance from advisory
service

```
0        20        40        60        80      100%
                                            of replies
```

Figure 6.1 Frequency of reference to aspects of general provision, choice of
language and steps taken to assist schools
Source: DES/Welsh Office: *Local Authority Arrangements for the School
Curriculum*, London, HMSO, 1979, p. 101.

reference to aspects of general provision, choice of language and steps
taken to assist schools.[5] The figure of some 40 per cent of LEAs having
no formal policy on general provision is, if anything, probably rather
conservative, but the fact that four out of ten LEAs could confess to not
having such a policy was very worrying indeed.

It was not until the APU survey published in 1983[6], however, that more

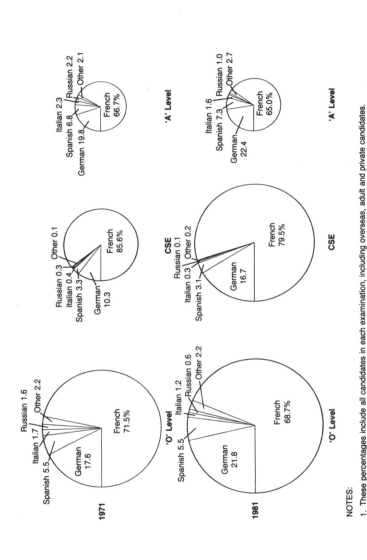

Figure 6.2 Examination entries: summer examinations of 1971 and 1981 (English and Welsh boards)

Source: DES/Welsh Office, *Foreign Languages in the School Curriculum: A Consultative Paper*, London, HMSO, 1983, Appendix, Figure C.

NOTES:

1. These percentages include all candidates in each examination, including overseas, adult and private candidates.
2. Candidates who entered examinations in more than one language are included in the percentage of each language taken.
3. Other modern languages does not include Welsh.

detailed information was made available about national provision. Figure 6.2, taken from the consultative paper *Foreign Languages in the School Curriculum*, published in the same year, demonstrates the too familiar pattern of provision (based on entries for public examination at O level, CSE and A level), with French dominating, German a poor second, and Spanish achieving observable levels, while Italian, Russian and other languages can scarcely be seen when the data are presented in the form of a pie-chart.[7]

Information from the LEAs surveyed by OXPROD in the autumn of 1988 not surprisingly reinforces this familiar pattern. But it was encouraging to hear from a number of authorities that the relatively very small number of schools with 'diversified' FL1 provision was likely to increase in the reasonably near future.

Provision in Berkshire in the summer of 1988[8] demonstrates the usual pattern, despite the rare presence of Chinese and Japanese. At that time there were fifty-five secondary schools and four middle schools deemed to be secondary schools: they produced the teaching groups per language per year shown in Table 6.1.

South Glamorgan analysed its provision, reflecting considerable diversification, as shown in Table 6.2.[9] To take a few LEAs at random: in Bury thirteen out of fourteen high schools were offering French as FL1, with the remaining one offering German; seven schools had German as FL2, six offered Spanish, with one having no FL2. Six schools in Cambridgeshire were offering a language other than French as FL1 with a few more planning to do so in September 1989. Derbyshire had one school with German as FL1, with nine others moving towards introducing the language as sole or parallel FL1. Four schools (out of forty-six) in Durham were offering German as alternative FL1; in Enfield three schools had German as parallel FL1 and one school offered German as sole FL1; in Wirral six schools (out of twenty-two) provided German or Spanish as sole or joint FL1s; the Isle of Man, Kirklees and Sefton – LEAs of varying size – each had one school offering a language other than French as FL1; Manchester calculated that some 30 per cent of its schools offered a foreign language other than French in the first year of secondary education.

Table 6.1 Language provision in Berkshire

	1	2	3	4	5	6	7
French	226	289	315	206	192	46	38
German	16	58	101	68	62	32	32
Spanish	0	4	7	5	4	11	7
Russian	0	1	1	2	1	1	1
Italian	3	3	3	0	0	2	0
Chinese	0	0	2	1	1	0	1
Japanese	0	0	0	1	0	1	0

Information supplied by F.W. Ranson, 16 December 1988.

Table 6.2 Language provision in South Glamorgan

No. of secondary schools	28
No. offering French as FL1 with German as FL2	11
No. with French FL1 and Spanish FL2	3
No. with French and German as equal FL1	7
No. with French and Spanish as equal FL1	2

Information supplied by Robert Hopkins, 22 November 1988.

Among the problems raised in response to the question about provision were: the particular situation of LEAs with middle schools ('At present French is the only language taught in Middle Schools. This will be so for the foreseeable future'; 'It would be unreasonable to expect [middle schools] to offer an alternative FL'; one LEA reported that one of its high schools had in some years received an intake from as many as thirty-seven middle schools!); unused staffing resources ('three teachers with a qualification in German not teaching it at the moment, two in the same position regarding Russian, and five with regard to Italian'; 'Russian is, sadly, non-existent now, although we have a tiny handful of FL1 teachers who could teach it, given the chance'; another authority recorded six schools not teaching Spanish which had a teacher qualified to teach the language, three teachers with a qualification in German, two with Russian and five with Italian); and the position of 'community' languages ('If Urdu is not recognised as a first foreign language we shall have difficulties, to put it mildly'; 'There is a definite trend towards providing Gujerati as a first foreign language'; 'One school [runs] a modular, "taster" programme for all which includes an Asian language'; 'three of the [fifteen] schools are experimenting with the provision of Urdu and/or "language awareness"').

One authority, reflecting the problems created by the existence of middle schools, replied in sardonic multilingual negatives to OXPROD's questions, adding that we might

> note the bilious view of the ESG project taken by an area which is three-tier in its entirety with FL1 necessarily beginning in the 9–13 institutions. For a variety of reasons, therefore, diversification assumes – for me at least – some hollowness.

The same problems, of course, affect the independent sector, where preparatory schools providing tuition in French pre-empt decisions about FL1 provision in the schools to which their products eventually transfer. There is little comfort that can be offered in these situations, since it would clearly not be advisable to allow most pupils to abandon their FL1 upon transfer in order to provide genuine diversification at the start of the upper school or independent school. One LEA reported, however, that 'at 13 . . . there is extensive diversification, with schools urged to offer a second language to some as an addition or as an alternative for all'. (The respondent in question added: 'National proposals about the second foreign language will be strenuously resisted'.)

Our LEA respondents provided information about the forms in which some schools were managing to diversify their FL1 provision. We know that there have even been two-form entry schools that have managed to offer alternative FL1s, and so it is not surprising that most schools have opted for the split-intake arrangement, with two FL1s being offered as parallel alternatives. Some schools, however, offer the so-called 'wave' model, where, say, French is offered as FL1 in one year, with German being so offered the following year; for each intake the FL2 would vary consequentially. One LEA, with some seven years of encouragement to diversify behind it, reported several schools offering six months of French and six months of either German or Spanish, with the FL2 beginning in year 2. Another LEA reported 'an increasing interest in language awareness in the first year, this leading to a choice of first foreign language', though in the light of HMI reaction to language awareness and some types of 'taster' courses this interest might prove to be shortlived.[10] No other pattern was evident from our first survey of LEAs in 1988.

(ii) Plans for diversification

At the time of our survey of LEAs there was, as we have noted, widespread awareness nationally of diversification issues, and this was resulting in various local initiatives encouraged by advisers. Many LEAs had submitted unsuccessful bids for a share in the Education Support Grant, and those proposals themselves provided blueprints for development. Of approximately forty LEAs for which we received information, about a quarter indicated they had no plan or policy for diversification currently in operation, though some of them – as did the majority of the remainder – spoke in terms of offering encouragement to schools able to diversify. Indications of 'support' or 'encouragement' in one form or another were common to several responses, and the general impression created by the returns was of enthusiasm for the now very real prospect of diversification.

One authority pointed out that LEA plans 'do not necessarily influence what schools want, or are able, to do'; another, mindful of the change of role for LEAs with the implementation of the 1988 Education Reform Act, reminded us that 'in the current climate . . . there is little more that local education authorities can do than recommend to schools to take certain courses of action. . . . The governing bodies will be taking the decisions regarding curriculum provision'. That proviso aside, however, the LEA in question was among a group of several in our sample that had overseen or were helping to implement something looking like a local policy. Let us consider some examples.

One authority presented its plans as follows:

We are in the middle of a very big reorganisation exercise, the first part of which . . . is going ahead at the moment. In their curricular plans all the Heads of the new schools are proposing first language diversification; in most cases probably French and German will be the answer, though one school, which is one of the biggest, . . . is considering French, German and Spanish. As we are inevitably limited by the teachers who are in post at the moment I cannot say which schools will be doing what and how much diversification will be achieved at the end, but eleven schools are involved in this particular exercise, and two tertiary colleges. . . . One school has diversified this year to bring French, German and Russian in as equal first languages in the first year, and there is the possibility that we may have one school next year with French and Italian.

Here is a good example of an authority using a major reorganisation exercise in order to encourage the development of a (in this case) city-wide diversification policy, involving a spread of languages, and with the larger schools aiming to offer a choice of three. Uncertainty abounds, owing largely to staffing, but the LEA reported that it had already been in contact with twelve Russian specialists locally, 'willing to restart Russian', and staffing and INSET needs were clearly receiving proper attention.

Another LEA, with just under a third of its schools offering a language other than French to first-year pupils, reported in detail on the efforts it was making to ensure adequate staffing, at the same time drawing attention to the financial constraints upon retraining on any large scale:

The preferred pattern seems now to be that of two parallel first foreign languages from the first year in the secondary school. Such a model can present some difficulties in the case of very small schools. . . . The problem which nearly every school had identified in moving over to any form of diversification is the need to have staff with the flexibility to offer the appropriate language skills. We have tried to do something about this in a very modest way by offering some retraining, on a full-time or part-time basis, in languages other than French. This has been set up as a pilot project with two local higher education establishments. Because [the authority] is in such severe financial difficulties, this has only been possible with teachers who have been employed in schools where there is over-establishment. This has meant that we have not had to undertake the cost of a replacement teacher full-time, which is obviously the most expensive part of the process. We have been pleased, however, by the feedback we have had from teachers so far who have undertaken this kind of retraining in Spanish and German.

A Welsh authority, with an already impressive record of diversification, was cautious about expanding for similar reasons:

At the moment there is no intention to steam ahead with diversification. Schools will be encouraged to diversify where the staff are already in place, but the current teacher supply situation makes a more hurried and concerted effort unwise, we feel.

A London borough reported staffing problems in a poignant way:

Sadly, the three schools [with diversified provision] did it without consultation [with the adviser] and, consequently, all ran into fairly predictable problems. One had to abandon its scheme, another is in real difficulties over staffing, and in the third there will have been two changes in [head of department] by Christmas. A fourth school has introduced a more conventional division into two equal languages this September and, hopefully, this will be more successful. Diversification is something we have worked towards over the years in anticipation of our secondary reorganisation by equipping teachers with additional languages. It was therefore a devastating blow last year to see one third of the language teaching force (30) disappear in one direction or another because of the restraints of rate capping and the consequent reduction of teaching staff generally. However, almost all of our teachers are capable of teaching two languages and many can offer three.

Another London borough reported considerable success over several previous years, with ten (out of eighteen) of its schools diversifying their provision. The schools in question are described in Table 6.3. The 'six months' provision is sometimes consecutive, sometimes concurrent, and 'even a mixture of both', with the adviser preferring the consecutive six-month intensive model.

One authority, building its diversification models on an enthusiastic commitment to the graded objectives movement (GOML) described a

Table 6.3 Diversified schools in one London borough

School	Years of diversification	Languages	Pattern
1	3	F & G	6 months F & G, yr 1; choice yr 2
2	1	F & G	Alternative years, F or G
3	1	F & S	6 months F & S, yr 1; choice yr 2
4	1	F & G	6 months F & G, yr 1; choice yr 2 or continue with both
5	4	F & G	[no current information]
6	3	F & G	6 months F & G, yr 1; choice, yr 2
7	4	F & G	placed in F & G groups from yr 1
8	3	F & G	6 months F & G yr 1; choice yr 2
9	2	F & G	6 months F & G; choice yr 2, ablest 30 continue with both
10	1	F & G	6 months F & G; then either or both in yrs 2 & 3

pattern for an individual school which was scarcely likely to fulfil the National Curriculum expectations:

> In a six-form entry school with half-year timetable blocking, half-year groups begin with a course of language awareness, followed by either French or German, following courses based on LEA Graded Objectives schemes, culminating in GOML assessment tests which may be taken whenever the groups are deemed to have completed the syllabuses. Teachers able to offer both languages in [the] lower school facilitate changeovers from FL1 to FL2 which may be at any point during the school year. The following demonstrates the type of structure offered to half-year group A, whilst half-year group B follows a similar system beginning with French:

		Year 1		Year 2		Year 3
Set 1	LA	G1	F1		G2	F2
Set 2	LA	G1		G2		F1
Set 3	LA		G1			F1

Key: Figures refer to graded test levels:
  LA = Language awareness
  G1 = German level one graded test
  F1 = French level one graded test
  G2 = German level two graded test
  F2 = French level two graded test

It is difficult to see advantages in a model of this kind, even if it were to be acceptable in National Curriculum terms. The switching from one language to the other would be likely to be wholly counter-productive of teacher energy and pupil learning, despite the clear incentive of reaching graded test levels within well-defined periods.

In the North-east another LEA had produced an action plan requiring responses from its schools, which included 'a plan for diversification of first foreign language, wherever possible, developing also, wherever possible, languages other than French and German'. Here was an authority pushing forward with the kind of guidelines or directives that would have been more common if LEAs had taken their responsibilities for the curriculum under the 1944 Act more seriously, while at the same time others were seeking not to venture beyond encouragement and advice.

We have only provided a selective snapshot of what some LEAs were managing in late 1988, by which time the ten 'ESG authorities' were completing the first term of their work. Before looking more closely at what happened in those authorities, however, we can assess what progress was being made in a number of other LEAs by mid-1989, when we followed up our initial survey with a request for authorities to update the information they had provided for us at the beginning of the school year.

EXPANDING LEA POLICY

From some thirty-one responses received in 1989 it is possible to gain an impression of how rapidly moves towards diversification were progressing. Some eighteen authorities could report considerable advances, and most of the remainder were showing obvious enthusiasm and providing evidence of policy development. Detailed analysis is difficult; we quote some of the more interesting examples.

Nottinghamshire reported the following pattern of provision:

> 76 institutions teach German, 20 Spanish, 8 Urdu, 6 Russian, 5 Italian, 5 Panjabi, and 1 Hindi

> In 3 schools, German is . . . being taught as first foreign language to all pupils

> In 1 school, Spanish has become the first foreign language

> 8 schools have a system of parallel languages from Year One. 7 split pupils between French and German. 1 splits pupils between French and Spanish

> 15 schools offer at least some experience of more than one foreign language to all pupils within Key Stage 3. The majority offer French and German. One offers French and Spanish. One offers French and Russian. One offers French, German and Panjabi

> A small number of schools offer, in Years Four and Five, the Certificate in European Languages, which requires pupils to have experience of at least three languages during their course.

West Sussex could describe quite considerable development:

No. of secondary schools (excluding middle/intermediate)	36
No. of secondary schools with FL1 other than French pre-1988	2
No. of secondary schools with 'diversified' FL1 1988/89	15
Of these: those with 'triple' FL1 (French, German, Spanish)	2
those with dual FL1 (French, German)	13

Kingston-upon-Thames, with ten secondary schools, indicated that seven of them would be diversifying FL1 provision from September 1989, with the remaining three following suit in September 1990. The authority had provided £26,000 for INSET purposes (a 30-week retraining programme, with teachers released for one half-day per week, followed by a 2–3-week immersion course in France or Germany). Wiltshire could count twenty-five out of thirty-two comprehensive schools with diversified provision; in Wirral at least eight out of twenty-two secondary schools were diversifying by September 1989; in Clwyd, which had three diversified schools, a further three were to diversify from September 1989 and five more from September 1990 (out of a total of thirty-three secondary schools); in Dorset eight schools had patterns of diversification as follows (figures indicate number of groups):

School	1	F3 + G2	(split year group)
	2	F4 + G3	(split year group)
	3	F3 + G2	(split year group) (FL2 Spanish)
	4	F4 + G1	(German to one middle-band class)
	5	F4 + G3	(split year group)
	6	F4 + Sp2	(split year group)
	7	F4 + Sp3	(One Sp group in each of three bands)
	8	F2 + G1 + Sp1	

While the general picture looked encouragingly good in most of the LEAs in the sample, some reported actual or potential difficulties. One authority, which had over 40 per cent of its schools diversified, listed 'constraints inhibiting further progress':

Uncertainty over the effect of National Curriculum policies, especially in areas of the County with Middle/Intermediate schools, where French is currently taught to all pupils from the age of ten;

the probable effect of LMS on the application in schools of non-statutory curriculum policies;

the rapidly deteriorating position over the recruitment and retention of specialist modern language staff in areas such as this, especially staff able to offer two or more languages to an appropriate level of proficiency.

the absence of LEATGS funding targeted at the training or re-training of ML staff to meet these needs.

Staffing and retraining were seen by other authorities too to create problems:

The Authority has great difficulty in finding supply teachers, therefore, even if resources were available to finance refresher courses, the issue of releasing staff for retraining would present great problems. Introduction of diversification is likely therefore to have to go hand-in-hand with the gradual appointment of staff with dual qualifications. There is no intention on the part of the Authority to promote the teaching of languages other than French unless properly qualified staff can be found. The instant crash course can never be an acceptable means of preparing effective language teachers.

Many of our teachers are moving on, either for promotion or out of teaching, which means that the plans to diversify which several of our schools were beginning to think seriously about have now been shelved for another year.

The growth of diversification has created some staffing problems. It has become difficult, in some instances, to replace dual linguists, very necessary for timetabling flexibility, when they leave for other posts. The growing shortage of language teachers will only exacerbate this.

A few schools have made a conscious effort to diversify, one or two have succeeded. We have no additional manpower or funding to support such a move, consequently we have no policy other than to encourage. Quite frankly, given the present uncertainties and pressures, most schools are clinging to what they have built up. The teacher shortage in [foreign languages] is another problem and is beginning to bite here.

Schools clearly are in some difficulty if they wish to alter their pattern of provision when they do not have the staffing flexibility in terms of linguistic expertise to carry out this operation. We have not been able to offer this year the retraining possibilities on a full-time basis which have existed on a small scale over the last two years.

Occasionally, however, a school discovers its untapped resources:

One of our high schools . . . is changing from French FL1 to joint French/Spanish on an alternating year basis – this has been made possible by the happy 'discovery' that three French specialists all held dormant qualifications in Spanish.

These comments highlight the central importance of staffing, always considered the main stumbling-block on the road to diversification, and they give little comfort. It must be a matter of some concern that *if* LEAs develop diversification at the pace which some of those in our sample indicated, and if they do so without adequate retraining and continuing INSET, they will find some schools having soon to revert to pre-diversification patterns, with a consequent knock-on effect (given uncertainties about the FL2) for languages other than French generally. A few advisers had indeed commented to us on various occasions that they had specifically advised against a particular school diversifying, when there was evidence that staffing could not be sufficient. Such comments were of the kind: 'I have advised one school against [diversifying] as they do not yet have the necessary staffing capability to take it through for the full five years'.

At the same time many schools were keen to recruit teachers able to teach more than one language as quickly as possible, fearing that if they did not do so eventual implementation of the National Curriculum would become very difficult.

Mention was made in both sets of LEA returns to the 'mapping' exercise, a 'survey instrument' devised by John Marshall to ascertain the match between teacher qualifications and availability and teaching requirements. The mapping exercise became a useful tool for schools and LEAs to determine the viability of plans for diversification, and was much used in INSET courses. For once it became common for LEAs to have an up-to-date breakdown of qualifications among its language teaching staff. Buckinghamshire (one of the ESG authorities), for example, reported the pattern shown in Table 6.4 as reflecting its teacher qualifications in September 1989. Staffing and (re)training became one of the principal concerns of those involved in the work undertaken in the ESG authorities, to which we now turn.

THE ESG AUTHORITIES

The ten 'ESG authorities' were announced in December 1987, when a grant of £30,000 was awarded, as we have seen, to Avon, Birmingham, Bolton, Buckinghamshire, Croydon, Essex, Hampshire, Havering, Lancashire and Staffordshire. The specific aim of the grants was to enable the authorities in question 'to plan and implement pilot projects . . . to help schools offer at least one language other than French as a mainstream first foreign language for secondary pupils in the first to fifth years'.[11]

Each authority was able to appoint a co-ordinator specifically responsible for diversification. Margaret Tumber[12] describes how she and a colleague set about identifying 'ten or so' schools in Essex where a language other than French might be introduced as FL1. Schools were informed of the pilot project, and were then invited to bid to take part in it. A version of Marshall's mapping exercise was used to gain a county-wide picture of actual and potential provision, and visits were made to 'diversified' schools.

In the early stages of the project, and following much discussion in the schools visited, Margaret Tumber was able to produce a checklist of criteria contributing to the successful introduction of diversification:

- availability of suitably qualified staff;
- support from senior management and parents;
- co-operation and team work within modern languages department;
- perception of diversification as a whole school policy;
- well thought-out strategy for diversification which the department is capable of delivering;
- awareness of differing needs of pupils of all abilities;
- recognition of developmental needs of staff;
- imaginative use of resources.

But not unnaturally she highlights staffing as the most crucial consideration of all, and staffing (actual and potential) was at the heart of the concerns of the ESG authorities as they set about their task.

The Centre for Information on Language Teaching and Research (CILT) worked closely with advisers and co-ordinators in the ten ESG authorities, and produced, between January 1988 and June 1990, a series

Table 6.4 Teacher qualifications in Buckinghamshire

	A	B	C	D
French	158	47	21	6
German	67	25	25	15
Spanish	21	12	9	16
Italian	8	9	5	9
Russian	1	3	2	4

Key
A: main degree subject
B: subsidiary subject or college level
C: A level or equivalent
D: O level or equivalent

Table 6.5 Ratio of diversified: non-diversified secondary schools in the ESG authorities

Avon	11:60
Birmingham	11:87 (+22 middle schools)
Bolton	5:16
Buckinghamshire	12:46 (12+ secondary schools)
Croydon	6:21
Essex	18:108
Hampshire	12:96 (+97 middle schools)
Havering	3:20
Lancashire	[no details given]
Staffordshire	19:72

of three collections of papers describing and updating the work in progress.[13] This 'open-access' material provided much useful information to other authorities as they developed their own diversification policies.

At the time of the first CILT survey (December 1988) the number of diversified schools in each authority varied considerably (from 12.49 per cent of secondary schools in Hampshire to 31.25 per cent in Bolton), though the great variation of size of the ten authorities must be borne in mind (Hampshire had ninety-six secondary schools and an additional ninety-seven middle schools; Bolton had sixteen secondary schools). Details are given in Table 6.5. Between them the ten authorities had examples of schools with split-year, 'wave model' (alternative years), 'taster' or 'carousel' courses, and dual language (for all, for one or more years) provision. Split-year provision sometimes meant that languages other than French were taken by fewer than half the first-year classes. (Hampshire, for example, reported 2/2, 3/3, 3/4 and 2/2/2 models).

LEAs were alert to training needs, and various approaches are evident in the CILT returns, including *ab initio* and refresher classes, with some authorities regarding GCSE/O level as a minimum qualification for teaching a particular language, others preferring A level or a degree as essential. There was much co-operation with higher education institutions, which offered appropriate courses. Most teacher resourcing, however, could be provided 'within the establishment' of the pilot schools.

CILT asked about the public relations dimension, and returns indicated that information leaflets, newsletters, visits to schools (discussion with governors, headteachers, heads of department, parents) had all been included in an effort to promote the notion of diversification. We return below to the question of how individual schools might communicate with parents on the matter of which language their children will be learning: 'cases [are] presented to parents carefully!', as one LEA return puts it. Essex later reported that co-ordinators were providing a standardised LEA letter on diversification to parents and guidelines to schools for their individual letters. Hampshire reported a similar arrangement, and model letters to parents were in fact produced by several authorities.[14]

The ESG authorities produced a large amount of material, including carefully researched individual reports on diversification, which has been a valuable contribution to the continuing debate and to the actual implementation of policy up and down the country. We have already noted that the pilot projects were themselves conducted both by the NFER and HMI, and this is not the place to seek to replicate those exercises. Suffice it to say that the ten authorities generated an enormous amount of expertise and enthusiasm which provided – as was intended – much stimulus to other authorities to 'go forth and diversify', as one or two of those involved put it.

By November 1989, a circular sent out to all language advisers in England, Scotland and Wales by CILT and the National Association of Language Advisers (NALA) and responded to by fifty authorities, found (with appropriate caveats), that

- French [was] sole FL1 in 69% of schools, and available as FL1 in 87%;
- It [was] not envisaged that this situation [would] change very much by 1993;
- A degree of diversification [was] being introduced in 15% of schools (varying from 0 to 89%). The main increase [appeared] to be in German, followed by Spanish. There [was] little or no diversification into other languages . . .;
- 9% of schools [had] implemented languages for all in year 10.[15]

Though by no means indicating the major breakthrough that some had been hoping for, particularly for a wide range of languages other than French, this picture at least showed a quite significant improvement in the situation as it had existed just a few years previously. Diversification was beginning to make an impression on the otherwise overwhelming uniformity of French as FL1.

IN-SERVICE TRAINING

The ESG authorities had made considerable efforts to ensure that sufficient in-service training was provided so as to secure appropriate staffing for diversification, and of course INSET, in its various manifestations must be an essential aspect of diversification policy. Staffing is the main obstacle to the teaching of languages other than French, and LEA officers, headteachers and school governors have rightly been cautious about changing a policy rooted in the relative security of expecting to recruit primarily teachers of French, to one which requires seeking out teachers with qualifications in other languages from a much less reliable pool of talent. Given this situation, it is vital that the skills of existing staff be properly exploited and developed, and that a continuous programme of training and retraining be made available locally.

One of the leading exponents of INSET in connection with diversification is Michael Calvert, whose highly successful project of 1988–9, based at the University of York, resulted in some valuable training materials.[16] These cover such matters as attitudes towards, concerns about, and benefits of diversification, negotiation with headteachers and others, and evaluation; an accompanying video recording, which presents simulated interviews with a headteacher and examples of FL1 teaching in German, Spanish, Italian and Russian, together with interviews with teachers and pupils, covers benefits of diversification, staffing, INSET, organisation, marketing (to parents, mainly) and funding.

Other authorities have been active in producing local programmes, backed up in some instances by training materials. Hampshire, for example, has issued a video-package based on the experience of a local school with a long-standing successful policy of diversification behind it.[17] The material (a video-recording and accompanying notes) provides information leading up to the key questions facing any modern languages department contemplating diversification:

- Could you diversify provision, if called upon to do so?
- What would be the implications for future resources, both human and material?
- Can you work towards a possible three-year plan for implementation of diversification?
- Which language(s) would you offer beside or in place of French?
- How would you prepare pupils, parents, governors and colleagues for a change in provision?

Teachers confronted with these questions will find support in the Hampshire package, in the York materials, and in Calvert's descriptions of language training and organisational preparation through INSET.[18]

THE SECOND FOREIGN LANGUAGE

In our 1989 survey of LEAs some concern was expressed about the potential fate of FL2s if diversified FL1 provision were not to become a reality.

Much of the motivation for diversification is coming from the pressure on FL2 and the need to retain two languages in the timetable . . .

It is . . . a concern within the Authority that the likely pattern of provision within the new legislative framework will lead to second foreign languages coming under considerable pressure. Unless schools are prepared to look at the kind of provision they offer, in particular giving careful consideration to the possibility of two parallel first foreign languages, the future for languages other than French looks somewhat precarious.

'Diversification', of course, must be taken to include provision for the FL2: the term implies variation from the norm of French FL1 plus, usually, German FL2 at a later stage, towards planned local provision of a range of languages in various combinations, aimed at various groups, and started at various times (including *ab initio* courses in the sixth form and further education).

The recommendation that the FL2 be started in year 4 (year 10 in the post-ERA numbering) rather than in year 2 or 3 (years 8 and 9) caused much anger and frustration among teachers of languages other than French. The sop that since an official policy on diversification would eventually result in vastly more pupils studying such languages as FL1s was not sufficient to allay fears that there would inevitably be an overall *decrease* in the number of children studying those languages (German and Spanish in particular). While it was only appropriate that the recommendation was eventually publicly rejected by its original supporter, the damage had already been done, and curriculum planners and timetablers would be able to point to DES and HMI statements to defend any decision to keep the FL2 out of the lower school ('key stage 3') curriculum.

In the summer of 1989 OXPROD conducted a small-scale investigation into how twenty-four 'diversified' schools associated with the project were reacting to problems relating to FL2 provision. The findings are presented in full in an OXPROD occasional paper.[19] At the same time an investigation of pupil response to the experience of learning two foreign languages was also undertaken: we shall return to this later.

Of the schools surveyed most were offering French and German as alternative FL2s (fourteen were offering Spanish, and three Italian). One school mentioned that despite its currently offering no fewer than *five* FL2s in year 2 it was not planning to provide an FL2 in either year 2 or year 3 in 1989/90 because of demands on the timetable made by the National Curriculum. There were indications from other schools that the introduction of the FL2 would have to be delayed in due course, and some were already planning for such postponement. Almost half the schools felt that the position of the FL2 was under some threat; others were hoping to treat the recommendation precisely as a *recommendation*, and thus susceptible to being ignored ('My understanding is that this delayed start is recommended, not compulsory, so I hope things will not change').

In the summer of 1988 HMI John Marshall[20] was reinforcing this point; if schools could demonstrate that they were following the principle of a broad and balanced curriculum they could indeed introduce the FL2 earlier than the recommended time, but staffing for the FL1 would have to take priority, he argued. Marshall pointed out on the same occasion that much of the criticism of the recommendation was failing to address the question of breadth and balance (which, of course, provided the rationale for the recommendation).

Our respondents expressed themselves in unequivocally outraged terms when it came to recording their comments on the DES/HMI recommendation:

- a recipe for possible disaster
- totally opposed
- not a practical possibility
- totally unrealistic
- not remotely possible
- rubbish
- back to the bad old days
- crazy! unrealistic!
- TOTALLY unacceptable
- utter nonsense
- an unmitigated disaster.

The main reason given for their clear opposition was the 'crash course' nature of provision over just two years (or rather less, since the third term of the fifth year is by no means a full teaching term). This was seen to be undesirable both in theory (a general recognition that language learning is better spread over a longer period) and in practice (with the, for many language teachers, still quite new demands of GCSE syllabuses). Here are some of the comments:

There is a great deal to be gained from a slow build-up to language competence. Crash courses are often like the seed which fell on stony ground

The course seems rushed, unsatisfactorily compressed, generates anxiety rather than a sense of enjoyment

At least a three-year course is necessary to extend pupils to their fullest potential

O level could be crammed! GCSE is too broadly based for that, quite apart from the time factor in advanced speaking/listening skills

A two-year course to GCSE does not allow for the necessary breadth of communicative practice, and leads to more traditional language teaching.

An inevitable result of postponement was seen by several respondents to be an increased elitism in the constitution of FL2 groups:

It will lead to elitist selection processes – GCSE after two years is not on, except for the very able *and* motivated

GCSE could only be covered in two years by high flyers

No point in offering FL2 to those other than more able pupils. Even so, GCSE in two years [is a] very hard task

A two-year course tends to limit the accessibility of an FL2 to more able pupils.

Others in our sample felt that the FL2 would be squeezed out of the timetable altogether by the need to accommodate the core and foundation subjects of the National Curriculum (NC), as well as other 'extra' subjects that might take priority over another foreign language, which could be dismissed as 'more of the same', thus operating against the interests of curricular breadth:

NC arrangements will squeeze the FL2 almost out of existence . . . if this regulation [*sic*] is implemented, FL2 provision, we fear, will be savagely cut

Could lead to demise of languages other than French

The position of traditional FL2s (German, Spanish) will be threatened by their introduction only at 15+ – the existence of Italian [and] Russian will be terminated in most instances

If this proposal is realised it will be an unmitigated disaster both for diversification and for adequate knowledge of FL2.

Timetabling problems could also be exacerbated – extra lessons might have to be arranged to mitigate the effects of a two-year course, some FL2 classes might have to be taught *together with*(!) FL1 pupils ('a supported self-study course, in effect'), and arguments about 'uneconomic' groups would surface. Other arguments centred on the incompatibility of the delayed start recommendation with norms in other EC countries ('not in keeping with the spirit of 1992'), on the needs of business and industry for people competent in more than one foreign language, and on reduced numbers following A level courses.

This latter point raises an issue of fundamental importance. If FL2 provision is weakened it will result in a neat but alarming circular development: fewer pupils learning two languages to GCSE will result in fewer 'double linguists' in the sixth form; fewer candidates with two A level languages will result in fewer students studying two languages at university; fewer graduates with more than one language will result in fewer trainee teachers offering two languages; and fewer trained teachers with two languages will in turn endanger the implementation of diversification policy, including provision for FL2s.[21] This danger is touched on by one of our respondents:

> We feel that the introduction of the NC may well threaten the position of the FL2, with the consequent squeeze on time in all subjects of the curriculum. In most schools the FL1 will remain French, and very few pupils will have the opportunity of studying an FL2. This will result in an even worse shortage of dual linguists to train as language teachers. Not a very solid basis on which to promote further diversification in language learning.

One of the pupils involved in the study by Phillips and Stencel[22] had remarked that 'a "linguist" can hardly be a linguist with only one language', and this view too found some resonance:

> Each student needs experience of at least two FLs to begin to be able to understand FL learning as a discipline

> I feel it is essential that children should have the opportunity to learn to communicate in at least two major European languages before 1992 is upon us, and thereafter!

In our survey of pupils' FL2 experience, undertaken at the same time, it was found that the vast majority were glad to be learning their FL2 as well as their FL1. (This was markedly the case with those who had French as FL2.) Most pupils believed that the study of more than one language was useful and interesting, and offered greater travel, communication and career opportunities, as well as increased chances of studying the language of their choice to GCSE. Some of the pupils with French as FL2 said they were glad to have been given the opportunity to learn the most traditionally taught language, a view which ties in with the Hadley committee's 1981 finding that *parents* do not object to the teaching of languages other than French as FL1 *provided that* French is available if not as joint FL1 then later as FL2.[23] Those pupils who had reservations generally expressed the view that learning two languages concurrently was confusing.

The position of the FL2 is almost as important as that of the first in the context of diversification policy and provision. Certainly neglect of the FL2 will have adverse effects on the first language and will undermine diversification generally. Accommodation of the FL2 in the post-ERA curriculum will have to be monitored closely to ensure its survival. And it will be particularly important to keep in mind the expectations in other EC countries, in which there is also some concern about the plight of particular languages when offered as FL2. A group convened by the Goethe-Institut, Nancy, for example, met in Pont-à-Mousson in November 1989 to consider the position of German as FL2 and produced a manifesto,[24] calling for systematic moves not only towards 'Zweisprachigkeit' but also towards

'Mehrsprachigkeit', moves which cannot be left to chance but in all probability will be in the UK. It is with the learning of an FL2, so the group argues, that the 'Mehrsprachigkeit' desirable in the new Europe begins.

It is worth looking in detail at the National Curriculum Working Group's final report of October 1990[25] in which a whole section is devoted to the place of the FL2 in the school curriculum. The section begins, unpromisingly, with an exhortation to schools:

> Schools will need to adopt a clear, positive policy for providing and teaching the second foreign language outside National Curriculum time in order to satisfy the country's aspirations as a competitive market leader in the global economy and to equip more of its young people with marketable foreign language skills in a wider range of languages.

And it recalls Circular 9/89,[26] which states that

> The National Curriculum requirement . . . relates only to the *first* modern foreign language; second and subsequent foreign languages may be provided outside the National Curriculum at schools' discretion, and may include languages, including classical languages, other than those specified in the Order.

The Circular went on to ask for action on the part of LEAs and schools to review their modern foreign language provision and take steps to ensure that it is in line with the requirements of the Order and its accompanying Circular.

The Working Group then proceeded to make two comments in the light of Circular 8/99 and the 1988 *Statement of Policy*, the first regarding timing, the second in connection with access:

> (*i*) We recommend a flexible approach which would encourage schools to consider the introduction of second foreign languages as early as possible;
> (*ii*) We recommend that a second language be offered to those who, in learning the first, have given evidence of enthusiasm and commitment. We see much to commend . . . in the principle . . . of 'language availability', to ensure that as many pupils as possible are offered the chance to learn a second foreign language.

In anticipating a way forward, the Working Group sees the inclusion of a foreign language as a foundation subject in the National Curriculum as helping to strengthen the position of languages other than French and regards a properly planned and resourced policy of diversification as being 'important consequences' for FL2s.

The Working Group encourages LEAs and schools to examine various patterns of provision in order to allow the FL2 to compete for available time outside of the National Curriculum. It lists the factors that need to be considered:

size of school, number of dual linguists on the staff, pupil transfers, staffing loads, setting, resources, timetabling, parental wishes, the community served, and local links abroad – either trade, such as major export or import areas, or socio-cultural, such as overseas reactions, sporting links, and twinning of towns.

But it offers little advice on the real and difficult problems of selection and accommodation of a selective (whether *selected* or *self-selecting*) group within an otherwise common curriculum consisting of non-selective groups, if the FL2 is to be started, as the Working Group hopes, earlier than year 10. On this latter point the Group argues that 'if a school feels that it can satisfy the criteria of the National Curriculum in terms of a balanced curriculum and still offer an FL2 to pupils in year 7, 8 or 9, it should be encouraged to do so'. On the former it wishes the opportunity to study a second language to be offered to pupils 'who have shown enthusiasm and commitment'. An additional point of importance made by the Working Group is that the availability of a second language outside of National Curriculum time would cater for pupils wishing, for whatever reason, to change their National Curriculum language, the subject of separate recommendations in its report.

On the subject of curriculum time the Working Group helpfully argues that, in principle, a 10 per cent share should be preserved for the first modern foreign language in key stages 3 and 4; if two languages are accommodated, the Group suggests that an additional 5 per cent of curriculum time be made available, and – and this is the crucial point – it recognises that some schools 'may need the organisational flexibility to divide [the] total [of 15 per cent] in a variety of ways between the two languages'.

In the light of the problems created by the damaging recommendation in the *Statement of Policy* to relegate the FL2 to a start in the fourth year (year 10), the Working Group's report is a most refreshing contribution, proposing a flexibility of approach which should allow schools, used to, if unhappy about, coping with the difficulties of accommodating a second language in the lower school (key stage 3), to continue to provide two foreign languages for some children for more than just two years of compulsory schooling.

The welcome message of the Working Group's discussion of the subject is reflected in the National Curriculum Council's consultation report, which contains the following section on the FL2:

The majority of respondents accepted the comments made about the second foreign language in the report. There was concern expressed, however, about the likely amount of time available for two modern languages (21%) and that the National Curriculum jeopardised the second foreign language (11%). 13% of respondents urged an early start for the second language.[27]

The relatively low percentages of responses expressing concern are likely rather to reflect general satisfaction with the way the Working Group had dealt with the difficult problems which had resulted from the DES statement of policy than complacency about the very real dangers that still exist for FL2s where they are not included as part of a co-ordinated policy on diversification.

We turn now to look at how the schools associated with the Oxford project accommodated both FL1s and FL2s.

PATTERNS OF LANGUAGE PROVISION IN OXPROD'S PROJECT AND ASSOCIATED SCHOOLS

As we have described in Chapter 4, OXPROD's work on organisational questions was carried out in the six project and thirty associated schools. Table 6.6 shows the nature of their language provision. The vast majority of schools in the sample (69 per cent) were operating a system of *split provision* whereby the first-year intake was split into two or three populations and a different FL1 was offered to each. In the OXPROD sample, nineteen schools operated this arrangement with French and German as FL1s, but three schools were teaching Spanish, one school Italian and one school community languages in addition to French and German. One

Table 6.6 Language provision in OXPROD's project and associated schools

FL1s offered	Model of provision	Number of schools
French or German	Split provision	18
French or Spanish	Split provision	1
French, German or Spanish	Split provision	3
French, German or Italian*	Variant of split provision	1
French, German, or community languages	Split provision	1
French or German in year 1, German or French in year 2, then a choice	Variant of split provision	1
French and German	Dual language	3
French or German	Wave model	1
French or German, alternating with French or Spanish	Split/wave model	3
French and Spanish or French and German	Dual language but split provision	1
French	Sole FL1	2
German	Sole FL1	1
Total		36

* In this school (project school F) French, German or Italian are taught as FL1s in the first year. In the second year pupils take a *different* language from that studied in the first year (chosen from French, German and Italian). In the third year pupils are allowed to choose which of the two languages previously studied they would like to pursue.

school was operating a system of split provision with French and Spanish. In a few of the schools operating this system two languages were taught in the first term and then pupils were allowed to choose the FL1 they would like to pursue. Other models of diversification in operation included in one school the *wave model* or alternating year system, in which all pupils in one year group take the same FL1, and pupils in the following year group take another FL1, and in three schools there was a system of *dual language provision* where all pupils are taught two FL1s, in parallel or consecutive modules. Three schools were operating a more complex *split-wave model* in which the intake is *split* into two populations, but the FL1s on offer alternate from one year to the next (French and Spanish the first year, for example, followed by French and German the next). In addition to this, one school was operating a system of *split provision* but each population took a combination of two languages: French *and* German or French *and* Spanish. Finally two of the schools were teaching French and one school German as sole FL1.

Information on language provision in the OXPROD schools and on teachers' attitudes towards diversification was gathered mainly by means of two questionnaires, one for heads of modern language departments and one for language teachers, which were sent out in the summer of 1988 to the project schools and twenty-four associated schools[28] (the number of schools associated with the project grew eventually to thirty). Replies were received from all the project schools and fourteen associated schools across the country. The FL1s on offer in this sample of schools were predominantly French and/or German, with twelve schools operating a system of split provision, three schools a system of dual language provision, one school the wave model and one school German as sole FL1. The three remaining schools (project schools B, C and F) were offering French, German or Spanish, French or Spanish alternating with French or German, and French, German or Italian respectively. From the questionnaire returns it was possible to identify some of the advantages and disadvantages of the different models in operation.

School A, for example, was operating a model of *split provision*. When OXPROD began its investigations in 1987 the school had a nine-form intake with five first-year groups starting French as FL1 and four starting German (this has since evened out to equal numbers of groups in French and German). The school has a system of four houses, and French and German are taught to two houses each in alternating years to avoid any house being labelled a 'French' or 'German' house. Language groups are mixed-ability in the first year with three 70–minute periods a week, and in the second year the top end of the ability range (30 per cent) starts French or German as FL2 in time borrowed from the FL1. In the third year the FL2 is set against design subjects. Problems mentioned in the questionnaire returns included occasional anxieties about initial placement in language groups, administrative and timetabling complications, an imbalance of numbers by the end of the third year in the two languages, with French groups substantially larger, and some difficulty in recruiting dual linguists. It was felt by most, however, that the problems were outweighed by the benefits. Teachers commented that 'German has gone from a dying minority subject to one of the strongest in the school', that the school's reputation had been enhanced, and that diversification had eliminated the idea of one language being more 'elite' than another. When asked if they had experienced negative reactions, one teacher replied: '[On] the contrary – most pupils and parents seem very positive indeed towards German as FL1'.

One of the associated schools was operating a similar system of split provision with an eight-form intake, but offered Spanish only as FL2, as the head of department explained:

> We considered we had to limit FL2 to Spanish . . . if we were to have viable setted groups in Years 4 and 5, who had studied the language for the same length of time. We did not want to be forced to have groups consisting of some who, say, had had French for 2 years and some for 3 years. This, of course, rules out the conventional combination of French and German and there was some parental objection, particularly in the early years, to this. One result of this change had been to strengthen the position of Spanish, the FL2.

Another of the associated schools was operating the *wave model*. This school has a six-form intake with French and German offered in alternating years as FL1 and FL2. Diversification was introduced in about 1966: all pupils took half a year of French and half a year of German and were then allowed to choose. This gave rise to an imbalance in numbers in the two languages, however, because transfers-in were allocated to French groups, and there were difficulties in establishing FL2 sets in two languages at the options stage. It was decided therefore to change over to the wave model, as the head of department explains:

> We have adopted the alternative year approach as an apparent solution to problems posed by diversification. We are constrained by languages available [among the] staff. As a fairly mature group of teachers we feel unable to suddenly acquire further language qualifications.

Language groups are mixed-ability in the first year and setted in the second and third years with an allocation of four 35–minute periods per week in the first year and three periods thereafter. In the third year the FL2 is offered to the top two-thirds of the ability range in two extra periods a week. The only problems this school mentioned were that not all members of the department could teach German, which led to an imbalance in teaching loads, and that there were occasional problems in accommodating pupils transferring into the school in alternate years when German was the FL1. It was felt, however, that both languages now had status within the school, and this would be jeopardised if a further foreign language were introduced. Here is a comment elicited by the transfers-in questionnaire administered in 1989:

> Diversification in our case is of long standing, well resourced and well received by all but one particularly intransigent parent! By keeping to German and French we have avoided major problems in staffing, and in pleasing the customers, as the second language is available to average and above pupils through 3rd year and beyond.

Project school C combined the two models of diversification described above by offering, for two years only, the *split-wave model*. In 1987 the six-form intake was split, three groups taking French as FL1 and three taking Spanish, with German and French as FL2s respectively. In the 1988 intake three groups were taught French and three German as FL1, with Spanish and French as FL2s. Language groups are mixed-ability in the first year and setted subsequently, with a time allocation of three 50–minute periods per week for the FL1 and time for the FL2 borrowed from other subjects. Approximately two-thirds of the intake start the FL2 in the second year. It was hoped that this system would strengthen both German and Spanish within the school and utilise expertise among the staff to the full. Unfortunately, with a relatively small intake, the model became too complex to timetable and administer. In addition to this, the school reported that it had been unable to accommodate ten new pupils in the French side in 1988/9 because the French groups were already over-subscribed. The school contemplated introducing the wave model, with French, German and Spanish offered as FL1 in a three-year cycle, but on the arrival of a new headteacher in 1989 the school reverted to French as sole FL1. This was partly because of fears that, with open enrolment, numbers would drop if French were not available as FL1.

Three of the schools in the sample, including project schools D and E and an associated school, were operating a system of *dual language* provision. The associated school, which diversified in 1985, offers French and German to all pupils in the first three years. Language groups are mixed-ability in the first term and setted thereafter. After the third year pupils can opt to continue with one or both languages. Respondents from this school were wholly positive about the effects of diversification. This is how the head of department explained the change:

> Too much concentration is a bad thing. Languages faculties should be that – a plural concept. French and German are very different languages – some pupils are more suited to one than the other – wider range of linguistic experience and opportunity. Protection and strengthening of the second language.

The headteacher had been very much in favour of languages and all changes were made with his enthusiastic support and approval. This is how another teacher at the school described the advantages of the dual language system:

> As all pupils now learn both French and German we are placing modern languages on a level with Maths/Science/English and increasing the number of children opting for more than one language and giving them greater choice.

But this teacher felt that others in the department should lower their sights, as teaching both languages in the same time allocation meant inevitably that they did not cover as much ground.

Similar positive responses were noted by teachers at schools D and E:

> I have been very pleased at the general response (both parental and pupil) to learning 2 foreign languages. Pupils have generally accepted them as a normal part of their curriculum and have scarcely raised the question of confusing the two.

Finally, one of the associated schools had changed over completely to German as sole FL1. The six-form intake school introduced German as FL1 in 1979 on the arrival of a new head of languages and in order to use teacher resources more efficiently. The only disadvantage mentioned was the problem of accommodating late entrants arriving with French. Otherwise teachers at this school were very positive about offering sole German:

> The policy at our school is language for all. German is taught as 1st foreign language to all pupils in mixed ability groups. We try to encourage an interest in language and stress the importance/usefulness of learning/knowing a foreign language. I find German easier to teach as a 1st language to pupils – various reasons, sound/symbol relationship – no surprises in German unlike French. Pronunciation closer to English. In a school such as [this] where the option take-up of a language is a large percentage of the year group, diversification to German has had tremendous success.

The advantages and disadvantages of the different models of diversification revealed by the 1988 survey are supported by other recent work on organisational issues associated with diversification,[29] and may be summarised as follows:

(*i*) *Split provision*. This model allows flexibility in that teaching resources can be used effectively, but it works best in schools with at least a six-form intake. Problems include a possible imbalance in numbers when transfers-in are allocated to French groups, and setting difficulties. If two FL2s are offered, this may lead to difficulties in years 10 and 11 in creating viable groups and to problems in merging FL2 and FL1 groups. An 'independent' FL2 (such as Spanish when French and German are FL1s) ensures a viable group further up the school. Initial liaison with parents on allocation to language groups in the first year must be handled carefully.

(*ii*) *The wave model.* This is particularly suitable for small schools. It facilitates setting and allows for more viable groups in the FL2. Potential problems include accommodating 'transfers-in' in a non-French year, coping with parental preference for French, and uneven staffing loads from year to year.

(*iii*) *The split-wave model.* This has advantages in that a number of languages have the status of FL1s on the curriculum, but it is complex to timetable and requires considerable flexibility in staffing.

(*iv*) *Dual language provision.* This allows for pupil choice, but there may be educational disadvantages arising from the reduced time allocation, and pupils may confuse the two languages. In addition to this, there will be resource implications in providing textbooks for all pupils in both languages.

(*v*) *Language other than French as sole FL1.* Schools not offering French as FL1 may encounter opposition from parents, and there may be problems in resourcing French as FL2. The advantages of this model are that it uses existing teaching resources to the full (though leaving less flexibility if a member of staff leaves), it is easy to timetable, and setting is made easier. It is particularly suitable for smaller schools.

By far the most popular model of diversification in the sample of schools surveyed was the system of split provision.

TEACHERS' VIEWS ON DIVERSIFICATION

In addition to information on the models of diversification adopted, responses from heads of department provided a wealth of information on schools' reasons for introducing languages other than French as FL1s, the position of the FL2, staffing, the allocation of pupils to language groups in the first year and parents' views. In many of the schools the decision to diversify had, in fact, come from within rather than as a result of any LEA policy. Reasons given for the change included the fact that the head of department was not a French specialist, that the school had good contacts with Germany and that better use of staffing and resources could be made if language provision were diversified. In addition to this, over half the sample mentioned the desire to move away from the traditional dominance of French and to reinforce on the curriculum the precarious position of languages not normally taught as FL1s. Here are a few of their comments:

Many reasons:

(a) better deployment of staff;

(b) taking better advantage of existing teaching skills;
(c) rationalisation of language teaching;
(d) hope of increasing numbers in option groups in years 4 and 5;
(e) desire to contribute to the national shift of emphasis away from French.

To improve the status of German, to produce more German-speaking pupils.

We have always had very keen linguists, but not enough most years to form sets of 15+ in FL2.

Very few respondents had experienced serious problems as a result of introducing diversification, but there were clearly a few areas of concern. These included the position of the FL2 in diversified schools, which OXPROD investigated further in 1989, and the issue of staffing, though the problem of finding suitably qualified languages staff is, of course, not restricted to schools which have diversified their FL1 provision. One school offering French or German as FL1s reported 'immense problems' in finding double linguists to replace teachers who had left mid-year, and similarly, another school pointed out that staff cuts affected the viability of its diversification policy. Two further issues to emerge which are specifically related to diversification policy were liaison with parents on allocation to language groups and pupil transfer, particularly from un-diversified schools. These will be examined in detail later in this chapter.

Responses to the teacher questionnaire provided information on teachers' language qualifications and use, their attitudes towards diversification policy, and their views on the suitability of languages other than French as FL1s. All in all, returns were received from eighty-five teachers, thirty in the project schools and fifty-five in the associated schools.

In the project schools it emerged that there were few staff not actively employed in teaching those languages in which they were qualified, though there was some unused expertise in French, Italian, Dutch, Portuguese and Spanish at schools A and B. A similar picture was presented by responses from the associated schools where there was some unused capacity in French, Spanish, Russian, Italian, Polish and Arabic. This is, of course, only to be expected, since most of the schools in the sample were diversifying into German. Several teachers had been called upon to teach languages which they had not used for some years, but few had received any formal preparation for this. Many felt there was a need for oral practice and for refresher courses on the resources available for languages other than French, as there was very little formal preparation in school for those reviving their language skills.

Most teachers' views on diversification were extremely positive, but two French specialists at school A, one with sole French, saw no advantages in diversification, and at school E, where a system of dual language provision was in operation, one teacher regretted the fact that language time on the curriculum was shared between French and German. Others at school E, however, were in favour of offering two FL1s to all pupils: one teacher pointed out that 'children seem to have a marked preference for either French or German', so that giving them access only to French was doing them a great disservice, and another argued:

> I think that diversification is very beneficial in that pupils do not see their foreign language in isolation. . . . I feel that diversification and the confidence it imparts (and the status it gives to foreign languages) means that children are able and willing to go abroad at an earlier age, which can only be a good thing for their education generally.

Teachers in the associated schools mentioned the fact that diversification offered less able pupils the opportunity to learn a language other than French, and one maintained that 'diversification is good for teachers: it brings the FL2 teacher out of isolation and makes the department more democratic'. Reservations included the possibility of creating timetabling and administrative difficulties, and problems of group size.

A variety of views were expressed when teachers were asked which foreign language they felt to be most suitable for pupils to learn as FL1. In the project schools there was considerable support for German and Spanish, largely on the grounds of their comparative ease of assimilation for English speakers, as the following comments illustrate:

> I can only comment on French and German as far as inherent difficulty of the language is concerned. I feel that pronunciation is very important at the early stages and this makes German far more acceptable. Difficulties can be skated over [regarding] grammar in German until a later stage.

> Ease of pronunciation – grammar is very close to English if those elements of grammar which do not affect communication are played down, e.g. case endings. Close links between pronunciation and spelling – importance of Germany to Great Britain.

> Because it is easier to pronounce than others as a first foreign language, but mainly because it is a good language from a commercial point of view. Also the English and Germans are perhaps closer culturally and this makes it easier to run successful exchanges. The Germans are generally very positive towards English people, where the French are not always.

> The grammar and pronunciation are consistent. Most children are now more likely to visit Spain than any other of the countries, which can be used as motivation.

> Simple pronunciation, easy grammar, country [Spain] most likely to be visited by English people.

In the associated schools 20 per cent of teachers indicated that, in their view, French was the most suitable FL1 to be taught, and a similar number supported German. Spanish was a less popular choice, but views here were presumably swayed by the fact that none of the fourteen associated schools in the sample was teaching Spanish as FL1. In both project and associated schools, as might be expected, a large number of respondents chose no language above any other.

Only one teacher from the schools sampled mentioned a lack of teaching materials for diversification, but this was presumably linked to the fact that all the project schools had been given extra funds by the cultural institutes for the purchase of teaching materials, and that language provision in the sample was limited almost exclusively to French, German and Spanish. The range of course books in use at the associated schools was similar, on the whole, to that in the project schools: *Tricolore*[30] for French, *Deutsch Heute*[31] or *Zickzack*[32] for German, and *¡Vaya!*[33] or *¡Claro!*[34] for Spanish. At the time of the survey, investigations by OXPROD into the availability of published materials for French, German, Spanish, Italian and Russian revealed a wide variety of published materials for French and German, and a growing amount for Spanish. In Italian and Russian, on the other hand, there were very few materials geared towards GCSE courses at secondary level. In the last two years availability of resources in these languages has improved, with the publication of course books for Italian such as *Ciao!*[35] and with initiatives such as the York–Sheffield Russian Project.[36]

To conclude: OXPROD's survey of teacher opinion in 1988 revealed teachers to be overwhelmingly in favour of diversification. There were few problems and many benefits, and only one school mentioned that diversification was expensive in terms of resources. Concerns expressed about the question of liaison with parents and problems of pupil transfer led OXPROD to investigate these matters in more detail.

LIAISON WITH PARENTS

In most schools pastoral or senior staff (rather than languages staff) allocated pupils to first-year language groups, with the aim of creating a balance of ability in the different languages. On the whole parents and pupils were not given the opportunity to choose the FL1, but few schools had experienced objections to the FL1 selected. Where a choice had been offered, there had been an imbalance in numbers in favour of French, and schools had encountered problems in accommodating pupils within their chosen languages. One respondent noted an interesting correlation between parental preference and both gender and ability:

> Since French is taught to one band of four forms and German to the other, parents are asked to inform the schools if they have a strong preference for their child to do one language or the other. Nearly all

such requests are for French and mainly for girls. . . . A consequence has been the above-average presence of able girls in the 'French' band (because of the correlation between ability and that kind of parental interest).

Similarly, project school D, with some twenty years' experience of diversification, had decided to cease soliciting parental opinion because it was felt that this had resulted in more linguistically able children being allocated to French groups.

Pupils' allocation to different languages was clearly an issue requiring careful handling and during the course of OXPROD's investigations it was possible to collect further information on how individual schools approached the task of communicating with parents about foreign language provision for first-year pupils.[37] Apart from the PR aspect of such communication, there is the equally important and sensitive issue of pupils' allocation to particular language groups.

As responses from OXPROD's teacher questionnaire show, most schools will prefer to allocate pupils randomly, but there is a strong and legitimate feeling that an element of choice should be involved, and it is here that the problems begin.

Project school B, for example, prior to the first year of its three-language diversification policy, asked parents of new entrants (due to arrive in September 1987) to complete an admissions proforma which contained the following section:

FOREIGN LANGUAGE

Please tick
one box

1) I have a strong preference of foreign language.
2) I would like a choice of language in the order of preference shown if possible.
3) I have no particular preference of foreign language my child will study.

If you have ticked Box 1 or Box 2 above please rank your order of preference.

FRENCH

GERMAN

SPANISH

But, as described in Chapter 4 this resulted in a severe imbalance of parental preference towards French, which for a time threatened the viability of the new policy and caused considerable embarrassment to the head of languages (who had not drafted the admissions form). Much sensitive negotiation was necessary to redress the balance and to ensure that the new language being introduced (Spanish) could in fact be started in viable groups in the first year. A modified version of this letter sent to parents of the 1988 first-year intake, with the language boxes in reversed order, produced the same effect:

When your child enters in September, there will be an opportunity to begin the study of a foreign language. Of the eight tutor groups in the first year, four will begin French, two will begin German and two will begin Spanish. If you wish to express your preferences for the study of language please indicate by using the space below:

Please tick one box:

1. I have no particular preference.
2. I have a strong preference for:

SPANISH

GERMAN

FRENCH

Given a free choice of the kind offered by school B, it is not surprising that many responses, preferring French, were of the kind:

Being as [*sic*] her brother and sisters have taken French, I feel they could encourage and help her through any difficulties.

Similarly, the following formulation, appended to an enthusiastic and informative letter about the nature of a change of provision in another school (moving to five classes of French and two of German) resulted in fifty-two parents expressing a strong preference for French and only five for German – but this did not affect the school's intention of introducing two German classes.

    *   I HAVE A *VERY STRONG* PREFERENCE FOR MY SON/DAUGHTER TO STUDY
    *   FRENCH/GERMAN AS HIS/HER FOREIGN LANGUAGE.
    *   Please delete as appropriate
[Mixed comprehensive school]

Two further examples from our associated schools which offer elements of positive choice and could therefore result in an imbalance of group size are these:

(i)

> I would wish my son/daughter to study (please tick):
> No preference
> French
> German
> Comments ....
> ....
>
> [Scottish school]

(ii)

> Please delete as appropriate:
> 1) I have no strong preference and will leave the School to decide whether my daughter begins French or German
> 2) I have a strong preference that my daughter should begin German in the Middle IVth
> 3) I have a strong preference that my daughter should begin French in the Middle IVth
>
> [Girls' independent school]

While it might be expected that the following example from another of our associated schools would invite objection, it provoked, in the event, little negative response:

FOREIGN LANGUAGES

When your son/daughter comes to this school next September he/she will start learning a foreign language.

In the past years *all* pupils studied *French*; and a number of them when they reached the third year began to study a second language as well, *German*.

We are considering changing this situation but before we do so we wish to hear from you.

What it means is this. Instead of all eight classes in the first year learning French, it would be possible for 4 to learn French and 4 to learn German.

Your son/daughter will then, of course, be able to study a second language, French/German, if appropriate, in the Third year.

I WISH TO ASSURE YOU THIS WILL INVOLVE NO SELECTION BY ABILITY

YOUR SON/DAUGHTER WILL STUDY EITHER FRENCH OR GERMAN BECAUSE OF THE CLASS HE/SHE IS IN; AND NOT BE PUT INTO A CLASS BECAUSE IT OFFERS FRENCH OR GERMAN.

Could I ask you for your opinion on my suggestion?

Could you please tick the correct box.

DO YOU HAVE ANY OBJECTION TO YOUR SON/DAUGHTER STUDYING GERMAN?

YES   NO
☐   ☐

IF YES PLEASE SAY BRIEFLY WHY.
....
....

[Mixed comprehensive school]

The reason for the lack of objection or 'negative choice' in this instance is probably the headteacher's care in wording the covering letter. Fears are allayed, parents are brought into the process of change, and their responses are clearly directed towards *objection*. The headteacher of this school had in fact asked parents of pupils a year or so before German was to be introduced to four first-year classes in his eight-form entry school 'Do you have any objection to your son/daughter studying German? If yes, say briefly why' and had been pleased to receive only fourteen negative responses[38] as opposed to 128 responses indicating no objection.

The following example seems to cover all contingencies:

Junior School French?   (Yes/No) :...
                        If yes, how many years? ....

Please tick one of the following boxes:

1. Strong preference for French

2. Slight preference for French (but
   would not object to German)

3. Don't mind

4. Slight preference for German (but
   would not object to French)

5. Strong preference for German

   Please add any information you consider useful,
especially if you have ticked 1 or 5.

[Boys' independent school]

Evidence from both project and associated schools suggests that a *negative* choice (i.e. the choice to *object*) offered to parents produces far fewer indications of preference – and therefore far fewer problems than a *positive* choice. Only if schools have a great degree of possible flexibility in terms of balance between numbers of first-year classes in the languages on offer, or if headteachers and others are prepared if necessary to ignore parents' stated preferences in some circumstances, might it be advisable to offer the kind of choice given in some of the examples above.

Many of the schools for which we have information have also provided covering letters that speak of the foreign language provision. Examples from project schools A and D were included in Chapter 4 and here is a further selection from our associated schools:

(i)

As you may be aware, approximately half the pupils joining . . . School in September 1989 will learn German and the other half will learn French as their main foreign language. In the Second Year almost all pupils will have the opportunity to study a second Foreign Language. I am writing to inform you that your child will be studying German as his/her first Foreign Language. If you have strong grounds for wishing your child to learn the alternative Foreign Language, for example in the case of close family relations, please write to me at the school before the end of this term to apply for a change. You should be aware, however, that a change of Foreign Language would involve a change of tutor group for your son or daughter.

[Mixed comprehensive school]

(Half the year-group received this German version, the other half received one for French)

(ii)

When your children join us in September 1988 they will learn either French or German. It must be made clear that THEY WILL NOT BE OFFERED A CHOICE. The language that they learn will depend entirely on the tutor group in which they are placed by the Head of First Year, who considers many other factors before reaching such a decision.

However, if you have any strong reason for wishing your child to learn either one or the other language, e.g. French or German parents or grandparents, then you are invited TO WRITE DIRECTLY TO THE PRINCIPAL stating clearly your reason, NOT LATER THAN TUESDAY 3rd MAY.

Whichever language your child begins, he or she will have the opportunity to participate in our Foreign Exchange Programme to either France or Germany at some stage during his/her school life.

Also the opportunity to learn a second language is offered in the third year to those who have shown the greatest aptitude. . . .

[Mixed comprehensive school]

(iii)

For some years past, modern linguists and their advisers in Education have been concerned that in this country we have allowed a serious imbalance to occur over which languages we teach our young people. Whilst French is traditionally the European language taught in schools, German deserves much more of our attention than it receives. Recent published research has shown that it is highly suitable as a first foreign language for young people. It represents in its later stages a strong and extremely influential culture, and is becoming vitally important in business and international trade.

We have created the opportunity for some boys to start German in the First Form instead of French and are now inviting you to express on the reply slip your own opinion. A number of other schools, including local ones, offer German as a subject from 11+.

Pupils who take German in the First Form will have the chance to start French in the Third Year, and thus continue both languages to GCSE level. German will remain as a major option in the Third Year for those taking French as their first language.

Clearly those boys who have already been learning French at Junior School may wish to continue French at Senior School level. On the other hand some boys in this category may wish to make a 'new start' with German. Parents of boys who have no Junior School French are encouraged to choose German as the first foreign language, unless there are good reasons for selecting French.

[Boys' independent school]

Example (ii) above is a fairly fierce version of the 'negative choice' option; examples from project schools A and D, and from (i) above rely on the fact that parents with strong views will take the opportunity to make those views explicit.

We have had access to a limited but varied range of schools' letters to parents, the most interesting of which have been cited above. The letters demonstrate clearly the need to keep parents fully in the picture as far as language provision is concerned, and may show too some of the pitfalls to be avoided in tackling the issue of language group composition in the first year.

We shall consider now the other main potential difficulty raised by teachers in the 1988 teacher questionnaire, the question of pupil transfer, mentioned by approximately a quarter of the respondents.

PUPIL TRANSFER

The problems of pupil transfer reported were associated first with lack of continuity of language study when pupils move between schools, second with organisation of timetabling and group size, and third with provision of supplementary work and help for pupils with special needs. In addition to this, comments from late entrants to the six project schools in the second and third years of the project revealed the problems pupils face when they have to pick up a language from scratch, and the demotivating effect this has upon them:

I think German is very hard, because I've only been doing it for a couple of months, and I don't understand it much.

I wish I could go back and learn the easy things in German because I missed eight months at the start so I didn't know much.

I don't really like German because I find it very hard because I missed a year of German, so it's hard for me to understand it.

I've only just started Spanish so I'm not very good at it. I don't like it so much because I can't join in most of the time.

I've only just started [Spanish]. I'm not too good at learning languages and find French easier.

The reason French is not my favourite lesson is that this is my first year of it and it is hard to say French words. I sometimes cannot understand the teacher. I wish I was in a lower French group so I could start at the beginning and learn the words you learn in the first year.

I find [German] difficult because it's a jump for me but not for people who have been here for years and are used to it, well I'm not.

I am quite new and the group is too far ahead for me to catch up and they know things I don't and I find it annoying. . . . And I am not given different homework to help me instead.

I have only recently started to learn Spanish and am having to catch up on two years' work. This becomes tedious sometimes as quite often I can't properly join in and I am always having to ask for help.

It is difficult catching up but if I had started from the beginning I am sure I would find it a great deal easier.

In view of the many comments in both the teacher and the pupil questionnaire returns related to the question of pupil transfer, it was decided to investigate the problems in more detail and to compile a list of solutions found. Findings from this investigation are reported in full in OXPROD's Occasional Paper 4[39] and will be summarised below.

The 'transfers-in' questionnaire was designed to elicit information from the OXPROD project and associated schools on their language provision, on problems encountered when pupils transfer to diversified schools, on provision made for coping with such pupils and on problems of pupil transfer specific to provision of the FL2.[40] The investigation was undertaken in February 1989 and returns were received from twenty-seven schools in all, the six project schools and twenty-one associated schools (a larger sample than that for the 1988 survey). Table 6.7 shows the nature of their FL1 provision. Returns from the questionnaire revealed that transfers-in did not present a problem in many of the schools surveyed, as these comments show:

We have encountered no new problems as a result of diversification.

Because of . . . diversification, it is reasonably easy for transfers-in to

Table 6.7 Language provision in schools responding to 'transfers-in' questionnaire

FL1s offered	Model of provision	Number of schools
French or German	Split provision	15
French, German or Spanish	Split provision	2
French, German or Italian	Split provision	1
French or German in year 1,	Variant of split	
German or French in year 2,	provision	1
then a choice		
French and German	Dual language	3
French or German	Wave model	1
French or German, alternating		
with French or Spanish	Split/wave model	1
French and Spanish or	Dual language but	
French and German	split provision	1
French*	Sole FL1	2
Total		27

* These two undiversified schools were included in the sample because their returns to the 1988 teacher questionnaires contained comments on new entrants *from* diversified schools.

> continue with their original FL1, and this has been a definite advantage of diversification (school offering French, German and Spanish as FL1s).

> Smooth transition into either French or German when pupils transfer. Pupils *never* unable to continue languages previously studied.

> We can usually find a timetable slot for pupils who have studied French and/or German. Difficulties arise only if a pupil had studied neither or has studied some other foreign language. To the best of my knowledge this has rarely happened.

And it was found that children transferring to a school not offering the language they had previously studied could usually be accommodated provided they transferred in the first two years and that teaching groups remained of mixed ability for one or two years.

On the other hand a number of problems were registered. These related in particular to group size, provision of individual tuition, the particular experience of individual pupils, 'transfers-out', pupil grouping and the FL2.

Many schools, for example, mentioned difficulties in maintaining a balance in numbers between French and languages other than French, because most transfers-in had learnt French previously and would be allocated to French groups:

> Most of the transfers-in have learned French as FL1 and . . . this can cause imbalance in the pupil numbers in teaching groups.

> Most incoming pupils have only had French. This means that in the third year (where we have French, German and Spanish groups) the French groups are becoming very large (up to 32 in a group).

But in some schools problems arose, regrettably, when French groups were already full:

> It has happened that a pupil who started French in his previous school was put into the German class because the French class was too big.

> All new pupils had to go into Spanish side as French side was full up.

In cases where transfers-in had to pick up a language from scratch some way into the course, many schools faced the problem of trying to provide individual *ad hoc* support or of encouraging parents to arrange private tuition. Other schools expressed concern about the difficulties entailed in accommodating pupils with different learning experiences and at different levels, but this was not a problem specific to diversified schools, as this teacher points out:

> There are bound to be problems with transfers-in, whether to the same language or a new one.

Two schools mentioned the problem of 'transfers-out':

> Problems arise when pupils leave this school, to transfer to schools which do not offer German as FL1 (or indeed French!).

> Diversification has proved to be an advantage, except possibly for a pupil who transferred out, having chosen German FL1, to a school where no German was taught.

And many teachers commented on problems related to pupil grouping, such as the difficulties of setting when more than one language was on offer, allocation to teaching groups by non-linguists with pastoral responsibilities, social composition of groups, and banding arrangements.

Finally, some schools commented on problems related to the FL2. While FL2 provision in a particular language often provided the only opportunity for a transferring pupil to continue a language previously studied, problems arose with ability levels in the FL2 groups and the timing of the FL2 start, as these comments illustrate:

> In years 2/3 we sometimes have pupils who, as far as ability is concerned, should be in the top (i.e. FL2) set, but because they have not started an FL2, have to be placed in [the] second set (roughly mixed ability).

> Up until now pupils have opted for FL2 in year 4, while other schools may have given pupils exposure to the FL2 in year 3.

It was found, in fact, that many potential transfer problems could be reduced by offering FL1s in parallel, by always offering French on the timetable and by keeping French group numbers smaller than those for other languages on offer at the beginning of the school year. A number of schools, however, commented on specific organisational strategies that helped them cope with transfers-in, giving detailed explanations of aspects of timetabling and language provision that offered flexibility and alleviated problems. These included in particular blocking of language lessons on the timetable and mixed-ability teaching in the early years.

For those pupils who did not transfer smoothly and had to pick up a new language part way through the course, schools adopted a variety of strategies. In many schools parents paid for private tuition; others reported that support from parents at home and other pupils at school had proved useful; and a large number of respondents commented on the necessity of extra help and support from the language teacher, usually outside the lesson. It was stressed, however, that the success of extra help varied considerably because of the pressures of time, and depended on the motivation of the pupil and goodwill of the teacher. Very few schools were able to provide extra staff to help transfers-in, and only a small number gave details of the assistance given, reporting that teachers were usually able to respond individually to a new pupil's needs, ability and attitude. A few, however, were more specific:

> If they are beginners in say year 2 German . . . we set up a supplementary programme to enable them to catch up quickly.

> Simplified books will generally be given in addition to the normal textbook, with the pupil probably starting with Book 1 of any given course.

> We provide supplementary worksheets, checklists, etc., as necessary.

> Carefully chosen teaching materials can be used for individual study.

> Pupils are provided with worksheets and given informal assistance.

OXPROD's Occasional Paper 4 provides more detailed examples of specific problems and strategies adopted for solving them.[41]

The findings from the questionnaire were encouraging: the real difficulties that were identified had not proved to be a disincentive to diversification within the schools and most had devised strategies to cope with them. It was felt, however, that there would be more need to address the problem of pupil transfer as diversification of the FL1 became more widespread.

We have devoted considerable space to organisational problems, since they have loomed so large in the considerations of headteachers, curriculum designers and timetablers. From the mass of evidence now available it should be possible for the questions of sceptics to be answered, and for a way forward to be suggested for most institutions, provided that staffing problems are not insurmountable. We shall now attempt to draw the threads of this study together, but first we must rehearse the arguments that have been put in favour of those modern foreign languages which make the most frequent claims upon time in the curriculum of British schools.

NOTES

1 David Phillips and Veronica Stencel, *The Second Foreign Language: Past developments, current trends and future prospects*, London, Hodder & Stoughton, 1983.
2 *Mapping Foreign Languages Provision in Schools: An instrument for surveying existing class provision and available teacher resources, and for costing planned requirements*, London, Centre for Information on Language Teaching and Research (CILT), 1988.
3 DES, *Local Education Authority Arrangements for the School Curriculum*, Circular 14/77, London, HMSO, 29 November 1977.
4 1944 Education Act (7 & 8 GEO.6.Ch.31), para. 23(i).
5 DES/WO, *Local Authority Arrangements for the School Curriculum: Report on the Circular 14/77 review*, London, HMSO, November 1979, p. 105.
6 Assessment of Performance Unit (APU), *Foreign Language Provision. Survey of schools, autumn 1982*, Occasional Paper 2, London, DES, 1983.
7 DES/WO, *Foreign Languages in the School Curriculum. A consultative paper*, London, HMSO, 1983.
8 Information supplied to OXPROD, 16 December 1988.
9 Information supplied to OXPROD, 22 November 1988.
10 See: DES, *A Survey of Language Awareness and Foreign Language Taster Courses* (a report by HM Inspectorate), London, 1990. The survey was kinder to 'taster' courses than to language awareness courses *per se*: 'Foreign language taster courses were diverse in structure, intent and effectiveness. Some had no connection whatever with language awareness and simply sought to provide pupils with a basis for choosing the first foreign language. Short, straightfor-wardly structured courses of this type operated effectively and were consistent with the policy of diversification' (para. 16).
11 DES News, 387/87, 17 December 1987.
12 Margaret Tumber, 'Diversification: A co-ordinator's account', *German Teaching*, Vol. 2, No. 3, December 1989.
13 'Diversification of first foreign language: Education [*sic*] Support Grant pilot project', summary sheets, London, CILT, January 1989, March 1989, June 1990.
14 See also the model letters described below. These are included as an appendix to OXPROD's Occasional Paper 1: David Phillips and Georgina Clark, *Attitudes towards Diversification: Results of a survey of teacher opinion*, Oxford, University of Oxford Department of Educational Studies, 1988.
15 'CILT/NALA (National Association of Language Advisers) Survey on Diversification', 3-page report, undated.
16 Michael Calvert, *Towards Diversification: Activities and notes for INSET leaders and teachers*, York, Language Teaching Centre, University of York, 1989 (plus accompanying video).
17 Hampshire Education Authority, *Modern Languages: Partners – Diversifying first foreign languages*, Winchester, 1987.
18 Michael Calvert, 'INSET and Diversification', in David Phillips (ed.), *Which Language? Diversification and the National Curriculum*, London, Hodder & Stoughton, 1989; 'Towards Diversification: INSET materials', *Language Learning Journal*, Vol. 1, No. 2, September 1990.
19 David Phillips and Karen Chidwick, *In Defence of the Second Foreign Language*, OXPROD Occasional Paper 6, Oxford, University of Oxford Department of Educational Studies, 1992.
20 Speaking at a CILT conference on 'Languages in the National Curriculum 11–16', York, 5–7 July 1988.

21 This circular argument has been used by Phillips in: 'Diversification: current developments and future outlook', *Language Learning Journal*, Vol. 1, No. 1, March 1990.

22 David Phillips and Veronica Stencel, op. cit., 1983, pp. 54–5.

23 C.G. Hadley, *Languages other than French in the Secondary School*, London, Schools Council, 1981, p. 49.

24 'Thesen und Empfehlungen zu den Besonderheiten des Lehrens und Lernens von Deutsch als zweiter Fremdsprache', in K.-Richard Bausch and Manfred Heid (eds), *Das Lehren und Lernen von Deutsch als zweiter oder weiterer Fremdsprache: Spezifika, Probleme, Perspektiven*, Bochum, Brockmeyer, 1990.

25 DES/WO, *Modern Foreign Languages for Ages 11 to 16*, London, HMSO, October 1990, particularly pp. 86–8.

26 DES, *Modern Foreign Languages in the National Curriculum*, The Education Reform Act 1988, Circular 9/89, 19 May 1989.

27 NCC, *National Curriculum Council Consultation Report: Modern Foreign Languages*, London, May 1991, p. 12 (para. 2.19).

28 Results from the 1988 survey are reported in full in David Phillips and Georgina Clark, *Attitudes towards Diversification: Results of a survey of teacher opinion*, OXPROD Occasional Paper 1, Oxford, University of Oxford Department of Educational Studies, 1988. The head of department and teacher questionnaires are included as Appendix I, pp. 29–42.

29 See, in particular: Michael Calvert, op. cit., and Peter Dickson and Barbara Lee, *Diversification of Foreign Languages in Schools: The ESG pilot programme*, Slough, NFER, 1990.

30 Sylvia Honnor, Ron Holt and Heather Mascie-Taylor, *Tricolore*, Stage 1 1984 (revised edition), Stage 2 1981, Stage 3 1982, Leeds, Arnold-Wheaton.

31 Duncan Sidwell and Penny Capoore, *Deutsch Heute 1* and *2*, Walton-on-Thames, Thomas Nelson, 1983 and 1984.

32 Bryan Goodman-Stephens, Paul Rogers and Lol Briggs, *Zickzack*, Stage 1 1987, Stage 2 1988, Leeds, Arnold-Wheaton.

33 Marie Anthony and Michael Buckby, *¡Vaya!*, Libro 1, Walton-on-Thames, Thomas Nelson, 1987; Michael Buckby, Michael Calvert, Christine Newsham and Brian Young, *¡Vaya!*, Libro 2, Walton-on-Thames, Thomas Nelson, 1988.

34 ILEA Learning Materials Service, *¡Claro!*, Level 1 1980, Level 2 1981, London, Mary Glasgow Publications.

35 Jenny Jackson, Kathy Wicksteed and John Israel, *Ciao! Primo libro*, Walton-on-Thames, Thomas Nelson, 1990.

36 The York–Sheffield Russian project is described in: David Rix and Robert Pullin, 'Russian Renaissance', in David Phillips (ed.), *Which Language? Diversification and the National Curriculum*, London, Hodder & Stoughton, 1989, pp. 32–43.

37 The letters reproduced in this chapter are also described in an appendix to Phillips and Clark, op. cit., pp. 45–50.

38 Ibid., pp. 1–2.

39 David Phillips and Hazel Geatches, *Diversification and 'Transfers-in'*, OXPROD Occasional Paper 4, Oxford, University of Oxford Department of Educational Studies, 1989.

40 Ibid., pp. 28–9.

41 Ibid., pp. 17–25.

Conclusions

IN DEFENCE OF VARIOUS LANGUAGES

We have argued in Chapter 1 that no one foreign language has a logically better claim to be taught as first foreign language in UK schools than any other. The dominant position of French is being challenged – rightly, we believe – precisely because, as an 'historical accident', it now appears to be so anachronistic.

French will continue, however, to be the most widely taught modern foreign language in British schools by virtue of the sheer momentum it has gained through staffing, resources and popular expectation. But beyond that, there are of course many arguments that can be put in defence of the language of one of the world's great cultures.

With approximately seventy million mother-tongue speakers, French ranks only eleventh among the main languages of the world,[1] but it is an official language of the United Nations alongside the more widely spoken Chinese, English, Spanish and Russian, and is spoken in a number of European countries. French is particularly important in European politics and business, and much of Britain's export trade involves countries where French is spoken. A nationwide survey of the need for different languages in British business conducted by Hagen in the mid-1980s[2] revealed that French and German were the languages most used by the staff of the firms in the sample, and nearly 23 per cent of firms were found to need French. In addition to this, France is Britain's nearest neighbour and a popular holiday destination for British tourists. Indeed with the opening of the Euro Disney theme park outside Paris and the Eurotunnel project, French is likely to prove even more attractive for the British holidaymaker. As far as the language itself is concerned, French has a long history as the language of diplomacy. Its close association with English over the years accounts for a shared word-stock and exchange of expressions between the two languages, and knowledge of French permits access to a rich and varied literature. Westgate, who considers the claims for and against teaching French as a first foreign language, feels that

> French will . . . probably retain a first-among-equals status, because it scores highly on key criteria: the proximity of France, the high profile

of French in European politics and business, the abundantly available teaching and support materials, and especially the number of teachers qualified to teach it. French is also a language, which, together with the people who speak it, their culture and beautiful country, continues to command special affection in many English hearts.[3]

The arguments in favour of French are certainly persuasive, but no stronger than the claims for teaching many other languages. German, for example, ranking tenth in the pecking order of languages, has as many as 100 million mother-tongue speakers and, according to the Goethe-Institut, is learnt as a foreign language by a further sixteen million people worldwide, over nine million of whom live in the Soviet Union.[4] It is still the *lingua franca* of Eastern Europe and a major language of the European Community, all the more so since the unification of the two Germanies in 1990. In business terms Germany is one of Britain's major trading partners, and studies of language use in industry show it to be as much needed by British firms as French. While it has been considered a grammatically 'difficult' language in the past, German has benefited from modern communicative methodology and it is widely acknowledged that the close association between the spoken and written language facilitates learning in the early stages. In addition to this, as with French, a knowledge of German allows access to a rich cultural heritage.

Spanish, the third most widely taught language in secondary schools, outstrips both French and German in terms of numbers of mother-tongue speakers, ranking third in the list of world languages. An official language of the United Nations, Spanish is the mother-tongue language in most of South America, as well as in Spain, and is widely spoken in the United States. A knowledge of Spanish, therefore, introduces the learner to a wide variety of cultures. A promotional leaflet produced by the Association of Teachers of Spanish and Portuguese, *Learn Spanish*,[5] categorises the arguments in favour of teaching Spanish under four main headings:

A world language
Some 300 million people in twenty-one different countries speak Spanish. Its spread throughout the world makes it enormously important. There are almost three times as many native speakers of Spanish as there are of French. Spanish is third in the list of the world's most spoken languages.

A useful language
Spanish is so widely spoken that it is extremely useful in the field of international relations – commercial, cultural and diplomatic. Many firms have subsidiaries in Latin America and Spain so trade is extremely important – even more so now that Spain is a member of the EC.

The language of your holidays
6.5 million British people visit Spain every year. Spain is the most visited country on earth.

An attractive language
No foreign language is easy to learn – it needs time and effort – but Spanish does have features which make it easier to learn in the early stages than French, German or Russian.

Despite the document's clear bias towards Spanish, the reasons it gives for the wider teaching of Spanish are all valid. Spain is an ever-important holiday resort for British tourists, British trade with Spain is considerable, and trade links with South America are growing in importance. The accessibility of the language, particularly in the early stages, which is derived from phonetic simplicity and orthographic regularity, suggests that it should be widely taught at secondary school level, and resources are now available to teach it. At the same time, advanced study of the language provides a challenging experience for more able linguists.

The linguistic claims for Spanish are matched by those for Italian. In C.V. James's scale of linguistic distance, described in Chapter 3,[6] in which the relative distance of French, German, Italian, Russian and Spanish from English is assessed, Italian is estimated to be closest to English. Italy is an attractive country and a popular destination for British tourists, and a knowledge of Italian opens up a diverse world of literature, music, painting, sculpture and architecture. According to Crystal, Italian has approximately sixty million speakers and ranks only fifteenth in the list of world languages, but it is an important community language in Britain. A selection of arguments in favour of Italian from a recent CILT resource guide for teachers of Italian show that the case for Italian as first foreign language is no less convincing than that for other languages:

- A survey of school visits abroad revealed that Italy is the most popular destination after France;
- Italian is one of Europe's major languages and by the year 2000 Italy will have the largest population in Western Europe (with all the economic implications of this . . .);
- There are approximately 170,000 native speakers of Italian living in the United Kingdom;
- Italy's considerable literary, musical, artistic and archaeological heritage should be accessible to people in the United Kingdom through the medium of Italian;
- Under the single market European economy, employment opportunities will be lost unless many people are proficient in Italian. For example, a major company with dealings in both Italy and the United Kingdom may seek staff who can speak both English and Italian. Such jobs will go to Italian nationals who are fluent English speakers if there are no British candidates who are fluent in Italian.[7]

In terms of linguistic difficulty, C.V. James places Russian, the fifth most widely taught modern language in British schools, at the opposite end of the scale to Italian, that is, as most distant from English. However, Joan Macrae and David Rix point out, among other things, that:

- the difficulty of Russian is greatly exaggerated;
- Russian does not have to be restricted solely to the linguistically gifted élite;
- in the past it has been taught mostly (but not exclusively) to older and academically gifted pupils simply because opportunities to teach it earlier and across the ability range have largely been denied;
- the Cyrillic alphabet is not nearly the terrible stumbling block that many suppose, and young children can have great fun in picking it up;
- the degree of difficulty in learning any modern language depends to a large extent on the methods by which it is taught, and Russian is no different in this respect.[8]

They stress that Russian has benefited from modern communicative methods and can be taught to mixed-ability classes with great success. Other claims for Russian are powerful: it is an official language of the United Nations, has approximately 150 million mother-tongue speakers and ranks seventh in the list of world languages. The recent improvement in relations with the former USSR and resurgence of Western interest in its affairs all suggest that more people should be learning its language. Cultural and educational contacts have increased and trade prospects improved. Teaching materials are becoming available: the York–Sheffield Russian Project, for example, has established a network of teacher-based materials development groups nationwide for the production of GCSE and ancillary Russian materials.[9] Knowledge of Russian, as with the four languages described above, affords access to a vast cultural heritage.

The arguments advanced in favour of French, German, Spanish, Italian and Russian above relate to similar areas: the numbers of mother-tongue speakers, the importance of trade links with the countries where these languages are spoken, the most frequent holiday destinations for British tourists, and subjective views on the difficulty of the languages. Claims of various degrees of similarity might of course be made for any one of the EC or non-EC languages listed by the DES as potential National Curriculum modern languages. To compare the claims of various languages for the place of FL1 on the curriculum on the basis of such criteria, however, would be to overlook more fundamental considerations of the kind we have examined in this study.

FINAL REMARKS

We have rehearsed the various arguments in favour of particular foreign languages mainly for the sake of completion. It is clear, as we have argued at the beginning of this study, that no one modern foreign language has an overriding claim to be taught as the first foreign language in British schools.

The best defence of any decision as to which language to offer has in our view to be an educational one. Which language, or languages, given the needs and ability of the pupils, the interest and availability of staff, and the support of parents and governors, would make educational sense in a particular institution? By 'educational sense' we imply taking into consideration such evidence as there is, of the kind collected by OXPROD and other research projects, on pupil motivation and on the 'accessibility' of the language(s) concerned, as well as those organisational problems that might inhibit success.

As far as OXPROD is concerned, and taking into account the necessary caveats about what can be concluded from a limited investigation of this kind, it is clear that there is every reason to suppose that the wider teaching of German and Spanish (in particular) as FL1s would be at least as successful as the teaching of French. There is some evidence that those languages would be more likely to result in success at certain levels and with certain pupils, as we have indicated in Chapter 5 of this study.

We have attempted to show:

– that over many decades the case for the more widespread teaching of languages other than French has been argued with great conviction, and that until recently it has met with little response, either of a negative or a positive kind;
– that government attitude towards diversification developed rapidly in the late 1980s and culminated in the first proper policy statement encouraging its development;
– that there is considerable evidence that pupils in what is now key stage 3 react at least as positively to German and Spanish as they do to French; and
– that the many organisational problems associated with diversification may be overcome, despite major (and as yet unresolved) questions about staffing.

Diversification, thanks to great enthusiasm among linguists at all levels, to LEA initiatives all over the country, and to clear statements of policy from HMI and the DES, has gained remarkable momentum since we embarked on the project described in this study. It has been gratifying to see so much ground gained in a short time-span of some five or six years.

In order for that momentum to be sustained, it will be necessary to ensure that the main issues are kept alive. We conclude with a checklist of considerations and action that must now continue to inform moves towards diversification and enable implementation to flourish.

(1) Diversification must be taken to include the teaching of a *variety* of different languages at different levels; it should include second and third foreign languages and cover provision for 16–19 pupils in school and further education, as well as those in key stages 3 and 4.

(2) Where permissible, National Curriculum arrangements should be used flexibly, so that decisions about *the* National Curriculum foreign language in a given school can be made in terms of pupil needs and abilities, as well as staffing provision.

(3) Linguists should be aware of the real danger still facing the second foreign language in schools. A wary eye should be kept on curricular policy which facilitates FL1 diversification and regards that alone as solving the problems for languages other than French: diversified FL1 provision can become an excuse for simply abandoning the second foreign language.

(4) The Section 3 Order needs to be looked at closely by schools wishing to teach non-EC languages. It requires that pupils must be offered an EC language as an alternative, but of course some schools could still – and quite legitimately – find themselves in the position of teaching a non-EC language to the vast majority of pupils with the full approval of all concerned.

(5) Though the powers of LEAs have been considerably diminished since the passing of the 1988 Education Reform Act, LEA advisers and inspectors remain in the best position to co-ordinate local provision and to advise schools about what is possible. The development of local plans for language provision – which has been on the agenda for an unconscionably long time – should still be of vital importance.

(6) INSET arrangements should be continued beyond the phase of initial enthusiasm for a new policy of diversification within LEAs: the arrangements should include:

– classes for the learning of languages *ab initio*;
– refresher courses in teachers' 'dormant' languages;
– teaching methodology in teachers' 'new' languages;
– tactical training in the issues involved in implementing diversification policy in schools.

(7) Staffing should be a priority for those responsible at national level. Training institutions will need extra support to produce young teachers with competence in and confidence to teach more than one language. In universities those who have already decided upon a career in teaching should be encouraged to study two languages, rather than combined subjects which *could* well prove to be less useful. This is a consideration that would apply also in schools when it comes to making A level choices.

(8) Publishers and other providers of teaching materials (the BBC and the independent television authorities) should continue to ensure that languages other than French are given prominence, and courses and

programmes aimed both at FL1 and FL2 learners. In particular it is important to produce accelerated FL2 courses, especially in French.

(9) The professional organisations, and the UK-based cultural and other institutes representing the countries of the languages to be taught in a 'diversified' system, have an important role in monitoring progress and keeping awareness of the advantages of learning individual languages alive.

(10) Schools should keep parents and the local community informed about developing policy, and make sure that the issues are fully explained and understood. Communication with parents over language choice should be handled with care and sensitivity.

(11) Pupil interest should be taken into account; there is considerable evidence available that pupil motivation can be language-specific, and there should certainly be little excuse for arguing that languages other than French (particularly German and Spanish) will be less popular.

(12) If the main argument for including the study of a modern foreign language in the curriculum is *educational* rather than purely *functional* or *utilitarian*, then a decision as to which language to teach ought to be based on the potential success of *learning* in the various languages: language *accessibility* ought to be a key factor in decision-making, and if that is accepted, then the evidence in favour of languages deemed to be more accessible than French, at least in the early stages, should be an important consideration.

This checklist attempts to cover the main issues. Diversification is one of the most exciting aspects of recent policy development, and at last there is a real chance to fulfil the hopes that have been expressed for languages other than French for so many years. The progress that has been achieved must now be properly developed. Not to take up the present challenge would be a tragedy for the UK unthinkable in the Europe envisaged after the introduction of the Single Market.

Let us finish with Allison Peers. A year after the publication of *Spanish – Now*, his summing up, in *'New' Tongues*, of the inevitable conclusions to be reached from a study of the various languages taught in British schools still sounds an appropriate warning:

> It is hard to see how any unprejudiced person, after weighing the claims of each [of the five languages] can ever again acquiesce in the present state of affairs, in which French has had an almost complete monopoly . . ., German has been taught very little, Spanish much less, and Italian and Russian hardly at all.[10]

We hope that this present study will have helped to provide further challenge to such acquiescence.

NOTES

1 Estimates for numbers of mother-tongue speakers of the various languages described are taken from David Crystal, *The Cambridge Encyclopedia of Language*, Cambridge, Cambridge University Press, 1987, p. 287.

2 Stephen Hagen (ed.), *Languages in British Business: An Analysis of Current Needs*, Newcastle upon Tyne Polytechnic Products, in association with the Centre for Information on Language Teaching and Research (CILT), 1988.

3 David Westgate, 'French – first among equals', in David Phillips (ed.), *Which Language? Diversification and the National Curriculum*, London, Hodder & Stoughton, 1989, p. 11.

4 Peter Boaks, *German*, Resource Guide for Teachers, London, CILT, 1991, p. 2.

5 The *Learn Spanish* leaflet is available to teachers from: ALL Spanish Section, 16 Regent Place, Rugby CV21 2PN.

6 This is described in C.V. James, 'Foreign languages in the school curriculum', *Foreign Languages in Education*, NCLE Papers and Reports 1978, London, CILT, 1979.

7 Jenny Jackson, *Italian*, Resource Guide for Teachers, London, CILT, 1990, p. 5.

8 Details of these may be found in: Joan Macrae and David Rix, *Russian*, Resource Guide for Teachers, London, CILT, 1991.

9 Ibid.

10 E. Allison Peers, *'New' Tongues*, London, Pitman, 1945, p. 87.

Bibliography

Anthony, M. and Buckby, M., *¡Vaya! Libro 1*, Walton-on-Thames, Thomas Nelson, 1987.

Assessment of Performance Unit (APU), *Foreign Language Provision. Survey of Schools, Autumn 1982*, Occasional Paper 2, London, Department of Education and Science (DES), 1983.

—— *Foreign Language Performance in Schools. Report on 1983 survey of French, German and Spanish*, DES/Department of Education for Northern Ireland/Welsh Office (WO), 1985.

—— *Foreign Language Performance in Schools. Report on 1984 survey of French*, DES/Department of Education for Northern Ireland/WO, 1986.

—— *Foreign Language Performance in Schools. Report on 1985 survey of French*, London, HMSO, 1987.

Association of Assistant Mistresses in Secondary Schools, *Memorandum on Modern Language Teaching*, London, University of London Press, 1956.

Bausch, K.-Richard and Heid, M. (eds), *Das Lehren und Lernen von Deutsch als zweiter oder weiterer Fremdsprache: Spezifika, Probleme, Perspektiven*, Bochum, Brockmeyer, 1990.

Bello, J., 'Spanish as a first foreign language in British schools: Past development and present practice', unpublished Special Diploma dissertation, University of Oxford, 1988.

—— *Spanish as First Foreign Language in Schools: Past and Present Perspectives*, OXPROD Occasional Paper 2, Oxford, University of Oxford Department of Educational Studies, 1989.

——'The teaching of Spanish in secondary schools, 1900–1950', unpublished M.Litt. thesis, University of Oxford, 1990.

Boaks, P., *German*, Resource Guide for Teachers, London, Centre for Information on Language Teaching and Research (CILT), 1991.

Board of Education, *Modern Languages*, Circular 797, London, HMSO, 1912.

—— *Memorandum on the Teaching of Modern Languages in Secondary Schools*, London, HMSO, 1912.

—— *Position of German in Grant-aided Secondary Schools in England*, Educational Pamphlets, No. 77, London, HMSO, 1929.

—— *Foreign Languages in 'Modern' Schools*, Educational Pamphlets, No. 82, London, HMSO, 1930.

—— *Report of the Consultative Committee on Secondary Education* (The Spens Report), London, HMSO, 1938.

—— *Curriculum and Examinations in Secondary Schools* (The Norwood Report), London, HMSO, 1943.

Breul, K., *The Teaching of Modern Foreign Languages and the Training of Teachers*, fourth edition, Cambridge, Cambridge University Press, 1913.

Buckby, M. *et al.*, *Graded Objectives and Tests for Modern Languages: An evaluation*, London, Schools Council, 1981.

Buckby, M., Calvert, M., Newsham, C. and Young, B., ¡*Vaya! Libro 2*, Walton-on-Thames, Thomas Nelson, 1988.

Burstall, C., Jamieson, M., Cohen, S. and Hargreaves, M., *Primary French in the Balance*, Windsor, National Foundation for Educational Research (NFER), 1974.

Calvert, M., 'INSET and diversification', in Phillips, D. (ed.), *Which Language? Diversification and the National Curriculum*, London, Hodder & Stoughton, 1989.

—— *Towards diversification: Activities and Notes for Inset Leaders and Teachers*, York, Language Teaching Centre, University of York, 1989.

—— 'Towards diversification: INSET materials', Language Learning Journal, Vol. 1, No. 2, September 1990.

Central Advisory Council for Education (England), *Half Our Future* (The Newsom Report), London, HMSO, 1963.

Clark, G., 'Diversification and the National Curriculum: Policy and provision', in Phillips, D. (ed.), *Which Language? Diversification and the National Curriculum*, London, Hodder & Stoughton, 1989.

Committee on Education for Salesmanship, *Modern Languages*, Second Interim Report, London, HMSO, 1930.

Crystal, D., *The Cambridge Encyclopedia of Language*, Cambridge, Cambridge University Press, 1987.

Department of Education and Science (DES), *Modern Languages in Comprehensive Schools, HMI Series: Matters for Discussion 3*, London, HMSO, 1977.

—— *Local Education Authority Arrangements for the School Curriculum*, Circular 14/77, London, HMSO, 1977.

—— *An Inquiry into Practice in 22 Comprehensive Schools where a Foreign Language forms part of the Curriculum for all or almost all Pupils up to Age 16*, London, HMSO, 1987.

—— *Modern Foreign Languages to 16, HMI Series: Curriculum Matters 8*, London, HMSO, 1987.

—— 'Increasing teachers of modern languages', Teacher Training Circular letter 8/88, 1988.

—— *Modern Foreign Languages in the National Curriculum*, The Education Reform Act 1988, Circular 9/89, 1989.

—— 'National Curriculum Modern Foreign Languages Working Group: Terms of Reference', *DES News*, 261/89, 1989.

—— *National Curriculum Modern Foreign Languages Working Group: Initial Advice*, London, 1990.

—— *A Survey of Language Awareness and Foreign Language Taster Courses*, A report by HMI, London, 1990.

—— *Diversification of the First Foreign Language in a Sample of Secondary Schools*, spring and summer terms 1990; a report by HMI, London, 1991.

—— *National Curriculum: Draft Order for Modern Foreign Languages*, London, 1991.

DES/Welsh Office (WO), *Local Authority Arrangements for the School Curriculum: Report on the Circular 14/77 Review*, London, HMSO, 1979.

—— *A Framework for the School Curriculum*, London, HMSO, 1980.

—— *A Survey of Modern Languages in the Secondary Schools of Wales*, Education Survey 11, Cardiff, HMSO, 1983.

—— *Foreign Languages in the School Curriculum: A Consultative Paper*, London, HMSO, 1983.

—— *Foreign Languages in the School Curriculum: A Draft Statement of Policy*, 1986.

170   *Diversification in modern language teaching*

—— *Modern Languages in the School Curriculum: A Statement of Policy*, London, HMSO, 1988.
—— *Modern Foreign Languages for Ages 11 to 16, Proposals of the Secretary of State for Education and Science and the Secretary of State for Wales*, London, HMSO, 1990.
Dickson, P. (DES/APU), *Assessing Foreign Languages: The French, German and Spanish Tests*, Windsor, NFER-Nelson, 1986.
Dickson, P. and Lee, B., *Evaluation of ESG Programme of Diversification of First Foreign Language*, Slough, NFER, 1990.
—— *Diversification of Foreign Languages in Schools: The ESG Pilot Programme*, Slough, NFER, 1990.
Education Act (7 & 8 GEO.6.Ch.31), 1944.
Education Reform Bill, London, HMSO, 1987.
Education Reform Act, London, HMSO, 1988.
Filmer-Sankey, C., 'Diversification: The OXPROD project', in *Coloquio 40. Proceedings of the Colloquium on the Teaching of Spanish, December 1987*, Association of Teachers of Spanish and Portuguese, 1988.
—— *A Study of First-year Pupils' Attitudes towards French, German and Spanish*, OXPROD Occasional Paper 3, Oxford, University of Oxford Department of Educational Studies, 1989.
—— *A Study of Second-year Pupils' Attitudes towards French, German and Spanish*, OXPROD Occasional Paper 5, Oxford, University of Oxford Department of Educational Studies, 1991.
—— 'The basis of choice', in Phillips, D. (ed.), *Which Language? Diversification and the National Curriculum*, London, Hodder & Stoughton, 1989.
—— 'Attitudes towards first foreign languages in the early stages of secondary school: An investigation into French, German and Spanish', unpublished M.Litt. thesis, University of Oxford, 1991.
Foden, K., *Hexagone 2*, Oxford, Oxford University Press, 1984.
Gardner, R.C. and Lambert, W.E., *Attitudes and Motivation in Second Language Learning*, Massachusetts, Newbury House, 1972.
Goodman-Stephens, B., Rogers, P. and Briggs, L., *Zickzack*, Stage 1, Leeds, Arnold-Wheaton, 1987.
—— *Zickzack*, Stage 2, Leeds, Arnold-Wheaton, 1988.
Green, P.S. (ed.), *The Language Laboratory in School: Performance and prediction*, Edinburgh, Oliver & Boyd, 1975.
Green, P.S., 'Testing for language aptitude', *Journal for the National Association of Language Advisers*, No. 8, 1977.
Hadley, C.G., *Languages other than French in the Secondary School: An Exploratory Study of Other Languages as First or Equal First Foreign Languages*, London, Schools Council, 1981.
Hagen, S. (ed.), *Languages in British Business: An Analysis of Current Needs*, Newcastle upon Tyne Polytechnic Products, in association with CILT, 1988.
Hall, J., *Escalier 1*, Cheltenham, Stanley Thornes, 1986.
—— *Escalier 2*, Cheltenham, Stanley Thornes, 1987.
Hall, K. and Clayton, J., *Spanish,* Resource Guide for Teachers, London, CILT, 1991.
Hampshire Education Authority, *Modern Languages: Partners – Diversifying First Foreign Languages*, Winchester, 1987.
Hawkins, E., *Modern Languages in the Curriculum*, Cambridge, Cambridge University Press, 1981, revised edition, 1987.
Hawkins, E. and Lawrence, G., 'Modern language teachers – an endangered species', *Education*, 24 June 1988, pp. 537–8.
—— 'Survival course for language teachers', *Education*, 1 July 1988, pp. 10–11.

Her Majesty's Inspectorate (HMI), *Mathematics, Science and Modern Languages in Maintained Schools in England: An appraisal of problems in some key subjects by HM Inspectorate*, London, HMSO, 1977.

Honnor, S., Holt, R. and Mascie-Taylor, H., *Tricolore*, Stage 1, Leeds, Arnold-Wheaton, revised edition 1984.

—— *Tricolore*, Stage 2, Leeds, Arnold-Wheaton, 1981.

—— *Tricolore*, Stage 3, Leeds, Arnold-Wheaton, 1982.

Hopkins, E.A., 'Contrastive analysis, interlanguage and the learner', in Lohnes, W.F.W. and Hopkins, E.A., *The Contrastive Grammar of English and German*, Michigan, Karoma, 1982.

ILEA Learning Materials Service, *¡Claro!*, Level 1, London, Mary Glasgow Publications, 1980.

—— *¡Claro!*, Level 2, London, Mary Glasgow Publications, 1981.

Incorporated Association of Assistant Masters (IAAM), *The Teaching of Modern Languages*, London, University of London Press, 1949.

Jackson, J., *Italian*, Resource Guide for Teachers, London, CILT, 1990.

Jackson, J., Wicksteed, K. and Israel, J., *Ciao! Primo libro*, Walton-on-Thames, Thomas Nelson, 1990.

James, C.V., 'Foreign languages in the school curriculum', *Foreign Languages in Education*, NCLE Papers and Reports 1 1978, London, CILT, 1979.

Keene, A.E., 'German as joint or sole first foreign language in the secondary school', unpublished M.Sc. dissertation, University of Oxford, 1984.

Krashen, S., *Second Language Acquisition and Second Language Learning*, Oxford, Pergamon Press, 1981.

Macrae, J. and Rix, D., *Russian*, Resource Guide for Teachers, London, CILT, 1991.

Marshall, J., *Mapping Foreign Languages Provision in Schools: An instrument for surveying existing class provision and available teacher resources, and for costing planned requirements*, London, CILT, 1988.

Miller, A., *Report on the Pretesting of a Language Aptitude Test*, BP Modern Languages Project Occasional Paper 1, Oxford, University of Oxford Department of Educational Studies, 1980.

—— *The Development of a Language Aptitude Test*, BP Modern Languages Project Occasional Paper 2, Oxford, University of Oxford Department of Educational Studies, 1982.

Miller, A. and Phillips, D., 'Towards a new language aptitude test', *British Journal of Language Teaching*, Vol. 20, No. 2, 1982.

Ministry of Education, *Modern Languages*, Pamphlet No. 29, London, HMSO, 1956.

Modern Studies (The Leathes Report), London, HMSO, 1918, reprinted 1928.

Morris, P.D., 'Children's attitudes to French at 13+', *Modern Languages*, Vol. 59, No. 4, 1978, pp. 177–83.

National Curriculum Council (NCC), *Modern Foreign Languages in the National Curriculum* (a report to the Secretary of State for Education and Science on the statutory consultation for attainment targets and programmes of study in modern foreign languages), York, NCC, 1991.

National Foundation for Educational Research (NFER), *Diversification of First Foreign Language in Schools* (Interim Report on the NFER Evaluation of the ESG Pilot Programme), Slough, n.d.

Nettleship, H., 'A brief statement of the case for the proposed final honour school of modern languages and literature, 1887', in Firth, Sir Charles, *Modern Languages at Oxford, 1724–1929*, London, Oxford University Press, 1929.

Nottinghamshire County Council, *Guidelines for the Teaching of Modern Languages: A document for discussion*, Nottinghamshire County Council, 1978.

Nuffield Foundation, Modern Language Materials: *En Avant*, E.J. Arnold; *Adelante*, Macmillan; *Vorwärts*, E.J. Arnold; *Vperyod!*, Macmillan/Lund Humphries, 1967–75.

Oman, Sir Charles, *Memories of Victorian Oxford*, London, Methuen, 1941.

Oxfordshire County Council, *A Working Party Report on Modern Language Teaching in Oxfordshire; Some notes of guidance for language departments*, Oxfordshire County Council, 1980.

OXPROD, *Newsletter No. 1*, Oxford, University of Oxford Department of Educational Studies, 1987.

OXPROD, *Newsletter No. 2*, Oxford, University of Oxford Department of Educational Studies, 1988.

OXPROD, *Newsletter No. 3*, Oxford, University of Oxford Department of Educational Studies, 1988.

Peers, E.A., *Spanish – Now*, London, Methuen, 1944.

—— *'New' Tongues*, London, Pitman, 1945.

Phillips, D., 'A thoroughly respectable language – pupils' views on German and other 'second' foreign languages', *British Journal of Language Teaching* Vol. 20, No. 1, 1982, pp. 23–9.

—— 'Diversification of FL1 teaching: A new research project', *Modern Languages*, Vol. 68, No. 1, 1987, pp. 29–31.

—— 'OXPROD – An Oxford research project on diversification of first foreign language teaching', *British Journal of Language Teaching*, Vol. 25, No. 1, 1987, pp. 50–1.

—— 'A language of 'unusual simplicity and facility': Spanish as first foreign language', *Vida Hispánica*, Vol. 37, No. 2, 1988, pp. 11–12.

—— 'From complacency to conviction: Thirty years of language teaching theory, practice and policy', in Phillips, D. (ed.), *Languages in Schools: From complacency to conviction*, London, CILT, 1988.

—— (ed.), *Which Language? Diversification and the National Curriculum*, London, Hodder & Stoughton, 1989.

—— 'Chances for German', in Phillips, D. (ed.), *Which Language? Diversification and the National Curriculum*, London, Hodder & Stoughton, 1989.

—— 'Diversification: Current developments and future outlook', *Language Learning Journal*, Vol. 1, No. 1, 1990, pp. 18–21.

Phillips, D. and Chidwick, K., *In Defence of the Second Foreign Language*, OXPROD Occasional Paper 6, Oxford, University of Oxford Department of Educational Studies, 1992.

Phillips, D., and Clark, G., *Attitudes towards Diversification: Results of a survey of teacher opinion*, OXPROD Occasional Paper 1, Oxford, University of Oxford Department of Educational Studies, 1988.

Phillips, D. and Filmer-Sankey, C., '*Vive la différence*? Some problems in investigating diversification of first foreign language provision in schools', *British Educational Research Journal*, Vol. 15, No. 3, 1989, pp. 317–29.

Phillips, D. and Geatches, H., *Diversification and 'Transfers-in'*, OXPROD Occasional Paper 4, Oxford, University of Oxford Department of Educational Studies, 1989.

Phillips, D. and Stencel, V., *Second Foreign Languages: An investigation into organisation, teaching methods and pupils' attitudes in Oxfordshire schools*, Oxford, University of Oxford Department of Educational Studies, 1982.

—— *The Second Foreign Language: Past developments, current trends and future prospects*, London, Hodder & Stoughton, 1983.

Powell, R.C., 'Sex differences and language learning: A review of the evidence', *Audio-visual Language Journal*, Vol. 17, No. 1, 1979, pp. 19–24.

—— *Boys, Girls and Languages in School*, London, CILT, 1986.

—— 'Italian in school, college and university', in Phillips, D. (ed.), *Which Language? Diversification and the National Curriculum*, London, Hodder & Stoughton, 1989.

—— 'Foreign language teacher supply: Continuity, opportunity and quality control', *Language Learning Journal*, Vol. 1, No. 1, March 1990.

Powell, R.C. and Batters, J.D., 'Pupils' perceptions of foreign language learning at 12+: Some gender differences', *Educational Studies*, Vol. 11, No. 1, 1985, pp. 11–23.

Powell, R. and Littlewood, P., 'Why choose French? Boys' and girls' attitudes at the option stage', *British Journal of Language Teaching*, Vol. 21, No. 1, 1983, pp. 36–40.

Pritchard, R.M.O., 'Boys' and girls' attitudes towards French and German', *Educational Research*, Vol. 29, No. 1, 1987, pp. 65–72.

Radford, H., 'Modern languages and the curriculum in English secondary schools', in Goodson, I.F. (ed.), *Social Histories of the Secondary Curriculum: Subjects for study*, London, Falmer Press, 1985.

Rees, F., 'The Wrong Gender', *Modern Languages*, Vol. 68, No. 3, 1987, pp. 183–7.

—— *Languages for a Change: Diversifying foreign language provision in schools*, Windsor, NFER-Nelson, 1989.

Report on the Teaching of Russian (The Annan Report), London, HMSO, 1962.

Rivers, W.M., *A Practical Guide to the Teaching of French*, New York, Oxford University Press, 1975.

Rivers, W.M., Dell'Orto, K.M. and Dell'Orto, V.J., *A Practical Guide to the Teaching of German*, New York, Oxford University Press, 1975.

Rix, D. and Pullin, R., 'Russian renaissance?', in Phillips, D. (ed.), *Which Language? Diversification and the National Curriculum*, London, Hodder & Stoughton, 1989.

Roessler, S., 'Listening comprehension in three first foreign languages: A study of beginners in two secondary schools', unpublished M.Litt. thesis, University of Oxford, 1989.

Rouve, S., 'Spanish – at last?', in Phillips, D. (ed.), *Which Language? Diversification and the National Curriculum*, London, Hodder & Stoughton, 1989.

Schools Council Modern Languages Committee, *The Second Foreign Language in Secondary Schools: A question of survival* (Series: Occasional Bulletins from the Subject Committees), London, Schools Council, 1982.

Scottish Education Department National Steering Committee for Modern Languages, *Alternatives to French as a First Foreign Language in Secondary Schools*, Edinburgh, HMSO, 1971.

Sidwell, D. and Capoore P., *Deutsch Heute 1*, Walton-on-Thames, Thomas Nelson, 1983.

—— *Deutsch Heute 2*, Walton-on-Thames, Thomas Nelson, 1984.

Smith, P.M., *Einfach toll! 1*, Cheltenham, Stanley Thornes, 1985.

—— *Einfach toll! 2*, Cheltenham, Stanley Thornes, 1986.

Stern, H.H., *Fundamental Concepts of Language Teaching*, Oxford, Oxford University Press, 1983.

Stott, D.H., *Language Teaching in the New Education*, London, University of London Press, 1946.

Thompson, M.C., 'Report on the ATG questionnaire on the position of German in schools', *Treffpunkt*, Vol. 4, No. 1, 1971.

Trace, A.S., *What Ivan Knows that Johnny Doesn't*, New York, Random House, 1961.

Tumber, M., 'Diversification: A co-ordinator's account', *German Teaching*, Vol. 2, No. 3, 1989.

Turner, F., 'Community languages: The struggle for survival', in Phillips, D. (ed.), *Which Language? Diversification and the National Curriculum*, London, Hodder & Stoughton, 1989.

University Grants Committee, *Report on Russian and Russian Studies in British Universities*, London, 1979.

Welsh Education Office, *Modern Languages other than French in Secondary Schools*, Welsh Education Survey No. 2, Cardiff, HMSO, 1973.

Westgate, D., 'French – first among equals', in Phillips, D. (ed.), *Which Language? Diversification and the National Curriculum*, London, Hodder & Stoughton, 1989.

Wood, O. and Land, V., *Verbal Test EF* (Test 128), Windsor, NFER-Nelson, 1971.

—— *Verbal Test EF Manual of Instructions* (Test 128A), Windsor, NFER-Nelson, 1971.

Woodhouse, J.R., 'OXPROD: *Il progetto Oxford per la diversificazione delle lingue straniere*', in Baldelli, I. and Da Rif, B.M. (eds), *Lingua e Letteratura Italiana nel Mondo Oggi II*, Firenze, Leo S. Olschki, 1991.

Wragg, T., 'Foreign policies', *Times Educational Supplement*, 18 March 1988.

Wyn Jones, G., 'Welsh within the National Curriculum', in Phillips, D. (ed.), *Which Language? Diversification and the National Curriculum*, London, Hodder & Stoughton, 1989.

Index